DEDICATION

This book is dedicated to the deeds and exploits, to the sacrifices and achievements of the generation of Australians who proudly served in the RAAF's Anson, Hudson and Sunderland Squadrons.

ANSON, HUDSON AND SUNDERLAND

IN AUSTRALIAN SERVICE

by Stewart Wilson

ACKNOWLEDGEMENTS

With this, the ninth book in our *Australian Air Power* series, it's time once again to thank those who have helped in the difficult task of producing two of these books every year.

After what has been a long running and successful series, listing those who have assisted may seem to be just a little glib, but rest assured, without them there would not be any books, and their help is appreciated just as much now as it was for the first book of the series.

As before, there are regular helpers, and some whose area of expertise covers the subjects presented here: Bob Piper and David Wilson from RAAF Historical, Mike Kerr, Ken Hutchison, Mark Stanley, Keith Western, Bob Livingstone, John Allen and Harry Margulies for their artwork, Robert Wiseman, Keith Hall and Eric Allen.

And also the professional and dedicated team at Aerospace Publications, especially publishers Jim and Margaret Thorn plus the long suffering production manager Maria Davey, whose common sense balances the author's whims, vagaries and creative highs and lows.

STEWART WILSON
Sydney, 1992

Published by Aerospace Publications Pty Ltd (ACN: 001 570 458), PO Box 3105, Weston Creek, ACT 2611, publishers of monthly Australian Aviation magazine.
Production Manager: Maria Davey

ISBN 1 875671 02 1

CONTENTS

FRONT COVER: Anson Mk I N4960 of No 5 SFTS, Uranquinty NSW, 1945; Hudson Mk III A16-236 *Foo* of No 2 Sqn, Hughes NT, 1943; Sunderland Mk III DD843/2E of No 461 Sqn, England, 1944. (Artwork Z Margulies) *(Drawings not to scale)*

INTRODUCTION

The ninth of our *Australian Air Power* series looks at three aircraft which although perhaps lacking the 'glamour' of some other types, were nevertheless of great importance to the Allied effort in World War II.

The Avro Anson, or "Faithful Annie" as it was affectionately known, has a special place in the history of the Royal Australian Air Force as more of them – 1,028 – were operated by the service than any other type.

Originally developed for Britain's Royal Air Force as a general reconnaissance type, the Anson was considered an advanced aeroplane when introduced to RAF service in the mid 1930s and was the first RAF operational type to feature both a monoplane configuration and retractable undercarriage.

The Anson entered RAAF service in late 1936 and in the prewar years served as a general reconnaissance type. It quickly became obsolete but gained a new lease of life as a trainer during World War II when it was used in large numbers by the British and Commonwealth air forces as part of the Empire Air Training Scheme. All but the first 48 RAAF Ansons retained British serial numbers, but the type played a vital role in Australia's war effort and in civil aviation in the postwar years.

A fine example of a civilian transport turned into a warplane, the Lockheed Hudson was one of several American designs which got its military start due to Britain's urgent needs in the late 1930s. Australia was an early customer, taking delivery of the first of 247 examples in 1940.

For the RAAF, the versatile Hudson provided the service's main offensive force in the very early days of the war against Japan, and Australian Hudson squadrons were involved in early battles against the Japanese in Singapore, Malaya and New Guinea. It was the crews of three RAAF Hudsons which first sighted the Japanese invasion force approaching Singapore. Hudsons were used for offensive operations in the New Guinea area and numerous other roles including transport, air-sea rescue, maritime patrol and ambulance.

One RAAF squadron operated the Hudson in the Mediterranean theatre of operations under RAF control, flying maritime patrol and anti shipping strikes against the German war machine. In many ways one of aviation's 'quiet achievers', the Hudson was nevertheless a vital part of Australia's war effort.

Britain's 'Flying Porcupine' and best known flying boat, the Sunderland, played a major part in the RAAF's achievements during World War II, but in Europe rather than the much closer to home war against Japan.

Only a handful of Sunderlands served with the RAAF at home, but nearly 150 of them appeared on the strength of two Australian squadrons based in Britain during the course of the war, in the process playing a major and innovative role in the battle to keep Britain's sea lanes open for the vital convoys carrying food, equipment and arms.

Between them, the two RAAF Sunderland squadrons in Britain accounted for or shared in the destruction of 12 U-boats and damaged several more as well as attacking enemy shipping and carrying out countless rescues of Allied sailors and airmen. Their story is an interesting one of which few in Australia are fully aware.

We hope you find something of interest in the stories of three largely 'unsung heroes' of the RAAF during World War II.

Classic portrait of the RAAF's first Anson, A4-1. Note the early style windscreen and the lack of a gun in the Armstrong Whitworth dorsal turret. (via David Wilson)

AVRO
ANSON

AVRO ANSON

The Avro Anson acquired several nicknames during its long career, notably "Aggie" and "Faithful Annie", the latter affectionately recalling an aircraft which proved to be a reliable, versatile and dependable machine in both war and peace.

As a light transport, trainer and armed coastal patrol aircraft, the twin engined Anson served with the Royal Air Force for no fewer than 32 years from 1936 and was that service's first aircraft combining the then advanced features of retractable undercarriage and a monoplane configuration.

In terms of numbers produced, the Anson was its manufacturer's most important aircraft, 8,113 of them coming from two production lines in Britain between 1935 and 1949 and a further 2,883 from licence production in Canada during World War II. The total of 10,996 even eclipsed the company's first classic, the Type 504 trainer, by a few hundred.

For Australia, too, the Anson was a significant aircraft, and with a total of 1,028 examples delivered from late 1936 it was the Royal Australian Air Force's most numerically important type, rivalled only by the Tiger Moth (861), Kittyhawk (848) and Wirraway (755).

As had been the case with the RAF, the RAAF initially acquired Ansons for general and coastal reconnaissance duties, although by the time war broke out in September 1939 the Avro aircraft was already considered obsolete. But with the war came the establishment of the Empire Air Training Scheme and the need for a twin engined aircraft for aircrew training, and the Anson was used in large numbers throughout the conflict in that role.

Postwar, Ansons were used by fledgling airlines all over the world. Australia was no exception with some 18 civilian operators flying former military examples, among them some illustrious names such as Adastra Airways, Airlines (WA), Butler Air Transport, East West Airlines and Brain & Brown Air Freighters. For many, the Anson was as important for their postwar re-equipment as was the larger Douglas DC-3.

Civilian Beginnings

Under the guidance of famed chief designer Roy Chadwick and general manager Roy Dobson, the pioneer aircraft company established by Alliot Verdon Roe grew during the 1920s and 1930s. Building on the success of the 504 and its derivatives, training and sporting types such as the Avian, Tutor and Cadet were produced in reasonable quantities, although other larger military and civil types were also built.

In 1928, Avro obtained a licence to manufacture the Fokker F.VIIb/3m eight passenger three engined transport, the type made famous by Charles Kingford Smith's *Southern Cross*. Called the Avro Type 618 Ten by the British manufacturer ('ten' for the the number of passengers and crew which could be carried), 14 examples were built of which half were sold in Australia. Five were delivered to Kingsford Smith's and Charles Ulm's Australian National Airways (as *Southern Cloud, Southern Star, Southern Sky, Southern Moon* and *Southern Sun*) and a further two went to the Queensland Air Navigation Co.

Roy Chadwick designed several variations of the Ten including the scaled down Type 619 Five and Six, and the larger Type 642 Eighteen, which incorporated the Ten's one piece wooden Fokker wing in slightly extended span form in combination with an entirely new fuselage. Only two 'Eighteens' were built, one with two engines and another with four.

What would later be known as the Anson had its origins in May 1933 when Imperial Airways approached Avro with a requirement for a fast aircraft capable of carrying four passengers. Part of the requirement was that the aircraft should incorporate some advanced features, including retractable undercarriage and a monoplane configuration.

Under the company designation Type 652, Roy Chadwick and his staff came up with a design for a clean, twin engined, low wing monoplane powered by two 270hp Armstrong Siddeley Cheetah V seven cylinder radial engines. The design utilised the Fokker wing in combination with a fuselage based around a welded steel tube frame with wooden formers and fabric covering. The engines were mounted on streamlined nacelles which housed the retractable undercarriage, the wheels of which slightly protruded when the undercarriage was up.

The prototype Avro Type 652A Anson, K4771, first flown in March 1935.

A well known photograph of Anson I K6285 of No 321 Squadron RAF, complete with camouflage and DF loop. The inverted triangle on the fin indicates a Dutch crew.

Maximum takeoff weight of the new design was 7,400lb (3,356kg) and performance figures included a top speed of 195mph (314km/h) and a range of 790 miles (1,271km).

The 652 recorded its maiden flight from Avro's Woodford (Manchester) facility on 7 January 1935, followed soon after by the second example. Both were delivered to Imperial Airways in March 1935, with whom they served for more than two years before being sold and later impressed into RAF service.

One further 652 was built, the 652 Mk.II in 1936. This one-off was supplied to the Egyptian government, which used it to evaluate its suitability as a transport/light bomber. With more power, higher weights and more extensive cabin glazing, this aircraft bore a closer resemblance to the Type 652A Anson, deliveries of which were already underway by the time the Mk.II was built.

Avro Type 652A Anson

In May 1934, even before the design of the first Avro Type 652 had been finalised, the British Air Ministry had issued a requirement for a twin engined general reconnaissance landplane for armed coastal patrol

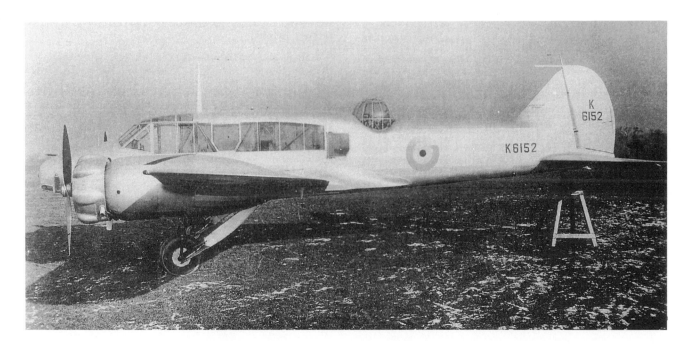

K6152, the first production Anson. The aircraft flew for the first time on the last day of 1935 and is photographed whilst being tested at the RAF's Aeroplane and Armament Experimental Establishment, Martlesham Heath in 1936.

duties. Fifteen firms submitted proposals and a short list of two was finally produced, the Avro Type 652A and the de Havilland DH.89M, a version of the Dragon Rapide biplane.

The requirement called for an aircraft with five to six hours endurance, a patrol speed of around 100 knots (185km/h), radio equipment, good visibility, a crew of two or three, the ability to carry two 100lb (45kg) bombs or flares of equivalent weight, night flying equipment and defensive armament.

Of interest is the fact that previously, the RAF's coastal reconnaissance requirements had been met by seaplanes, but for reasons of cost a landplane was now to be purchased, provided it could meet the requirements demanded of it.

Both Avro and de Havilland were awarded a contract to produce a single prototype of their designs and the two aircraft would fly comparative trials after initial testing had been carried out.

The 652A was given the RAF serial number K4771 and its first flight was made on 24 March 1935, just two weeks after the two Imperial Airways 652s had been handed over and only six months after the Air Ministry contract had been let. The pilot on the first flight was S A (Bill) Thorn.

Compared with its civilian predecessors, the Type 652A featured 335hp Cheetah IX engines (290hp Cheetah VIs were initially fitted to the prototype), a maximum weight of 7,663lb (3,476kg), square instead of oval windows, 'helmeted' rather than smooth engine cowlings, a manually operated mid-upper gun turret capable of carrying a single 0.303in Lewis machine gun plus provision for a single Vickers machine gun mounted on the port side of the nose and a modest 360lb (163kg) bomb load. Main dimensions and construction remained as for the 652.

The cockpit of an early Anson I fitted with single controls. (via Neil Mackenzie)

Testing and Orders

The official testing of K4771 was carried out at the Aeroplane and Armament Experimental Establishment (A&AEE), Martlesham Heath, during May 1935 and revealed the need for several minor changes, although the basic soundness of the design was also established. Of particular concern was a lack of longitudinal stability which made the aircraft need constant retrimming and tiring to fly for the lengthy periods involved in coastal reconnaissance. To help solve this, larger horizontal tail surfaces were fitted along with a mass balanced rather than horn balanced rudder and resulting increase in fin area.

Comparison trials against the de Havilland DH.89M were conducted by the Coast Defence Development Flight at Gosport during May and it soon became clear that the Avro 652A was far superior to its biplane competitor, and the latter quickly dropped out of contention. As the Dominie, the DH.89 nevertheless went on to serve the RAF as a navigation and wireless operator trainer in substantial numbers.

The successful use of the 652A in a Fleet Exercise in the North Sea during these trials proved the worth of the basic design and three months later, in August 1935, an Air Staff Requirement and Air Ministry Specification (No 18/35) were drawn up around

RAF Anson I K6309 of 61 Squadron RAF, again with no gun in the dorsal turret. (via Neil Mackenzie)

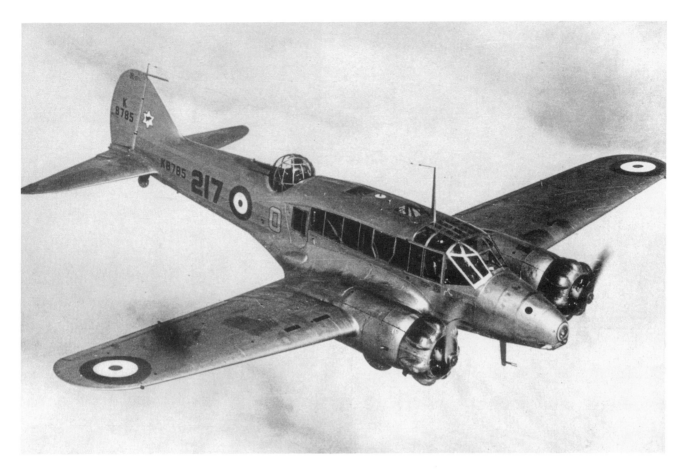

RAF Anson I K8785 of No 217 Squadron RAF. Before World War II, it was common for the squadron number to be displayed on the aircraft.

the Avro Type 652A and issued, along with an order for 174 aircraft. At the same time the name 'Anson' was given to the aircraft, after a famous English Admiral who sailed around the world in the 1740s, inflicting great damage on Spanish shipping while he was at it.

Production Ansons would feature numerous detail changes over the prototype, in addition to those aerodynamic modifications mentioned above. More powerful Cheetah IX engines would be fitted (and mounted three inches further forward), continuous cabin glazing replaced the previous individual windows and refinements were made to the aircraft's handling generally.

An undercarriage warning horn which sounded when the engines were throttled back and the wheels still retracted was considered necessary for this, the first RAF operational aircraft to feature retractable landing gear. Of course, anyone who flew an Anson will recall what was probably the aircraft's least fondly remembered feature – the manually operated undercarriage retraction and extension mechanism which required some 160 (according to the pilot's notes) torturous turns of a crank handle located next to the pilot's seat. In operations, the pilots often found it necessary to delegate this task to the navigator or wireless operator!

The first production Anson I (K6152) recorded its maiden flight from Avro's Woodford facility on 31 December 1935 with test pilot Geoffrey Tyson at the controls. Further testing of early production aircraft resulted in modified ailerons and windscreen, the latter to help the aircraft's water shedding qualities in rain and to reduce leaks. The Anson's windscreen was further modified on later Mark Is, the original raked design replaced with a more upright unit.

Into Service

The Avro Anson entered service with the Royal Air Force in March 1936. No 48 (General Reconnaissance) Squadron at Manston was the first unit equipped with the type and was joined by five other Coastal Command and four RAF Auxiliary squadrons by the time war broke out in September 1939. By then, 1,295 Ansons had been ordered for the RAF and exports had been made to Australia, Egypt, Estonia, Finland, Greece, Turkey and Ireland.

Australia was the first export customer for the Anson, 12 being diverted to the RAAF from the initial production batch in 1936 and by April 1939 a total of 88 were in RAAF service with many more to follow after war broke out. At one stage, licence production of the Anson in Australia was discussed but not followed through.

The Anson I for general reconnaissnce duties was powered by two 355hp Armstrong Siddeley Cheetah IX seven cylinder radial engines and normally carried a crew of three comprising pilot, navigator/bomb aimer and wireless operator/air gunner, the latter operating the single Lewis 0.303in machine mounted in a manually operated Armstrong Whitworth dorsal turret. The single fixed nose mounted Vickers 0.303in machine gun was operated by the pilot while the small centre section bomb bays normally accommodated two 100lb (45kg) and eight 20lb (9kg) bombs.

The Anson's fuselage was a rectangular welded steel tube structure with rigid bracing and fabric covering over wooden fairings, while the wing was of single piece cantilever design consisting of two box spars of spruce and plywood construction with plywood and spruce ribs and plywood covering. The tailplane was of similar construction to the wing and the fin and elevators were of fabric covered welded steel tubing.

Some later Anson Is were fitted with 395hp Cheetah XIX engines, all up weight was normally 7,955lb (3,608kg) and the fuel capacity of 140imp gal (636 litres) gave the Anson an endurance of more than six hours when patrolling at about 110 knots.

Although considered an advanced aeroplane when first delivered, such was the pace of development in the late 1930s that by the end of 1939 the Anson was already regarded as obsolete for Coastal Command duties and was in the process of being replaced by aircraft such as the Lockheed Hudson. Despite this, the Anson was

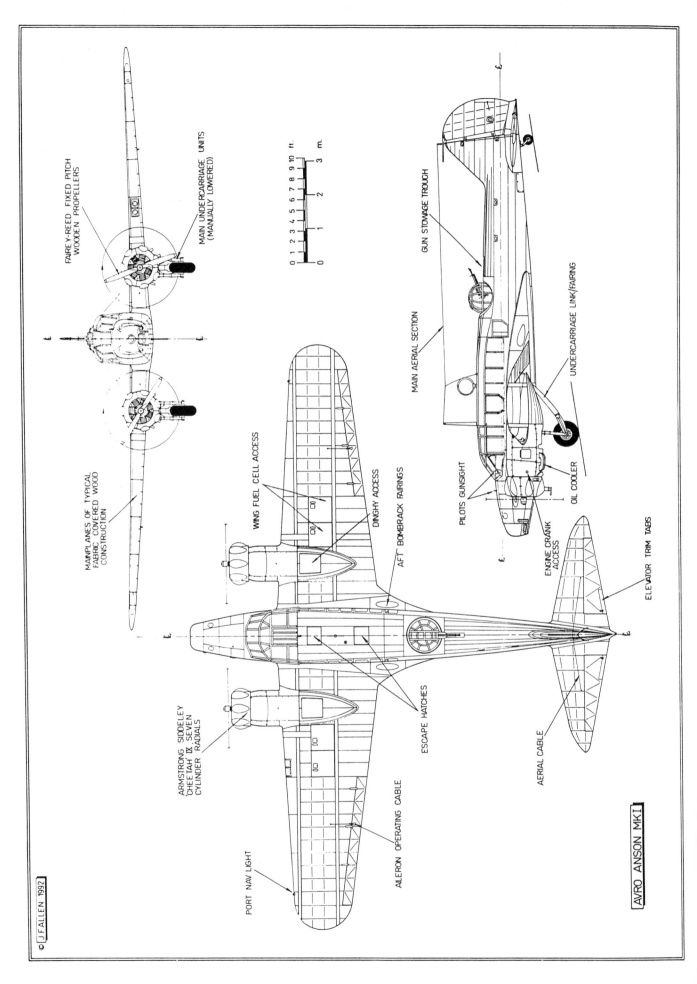

FAIREY-REED FIXED PITCH
WOODEN PROPELLERS

MAIN UNDERCARRIAGE UNITS
(MANUALLY LOWERED)

MAINPLANES OF TYPICAL
FABRIC COVERED WOOD
CONSTRUCTION

GUN STOWAGE TROUGH

MAIN AERIAL SECTION

UNDERCARRIAGE LINK/FAIRING

PILOTS GUNSIGHT

OIL COOLER

ENGINE CRANK
ACCESS

ELEVATOR TRIM TABS

WING FUEL CELL ACCESS

DINGHY ACCESS

AFT BOMBRACK FAIRINGS

ARMSTRONG SIDDELEY
CHEETAH IX SEVEN
CYLINDER RADIALS

ESCAPE HATCHES

AERIAL CABLE

ALERON OPERATING CABLE

PORT NAV LIGHT

© J F ALLEN 1992

AVRO ANSON MKI

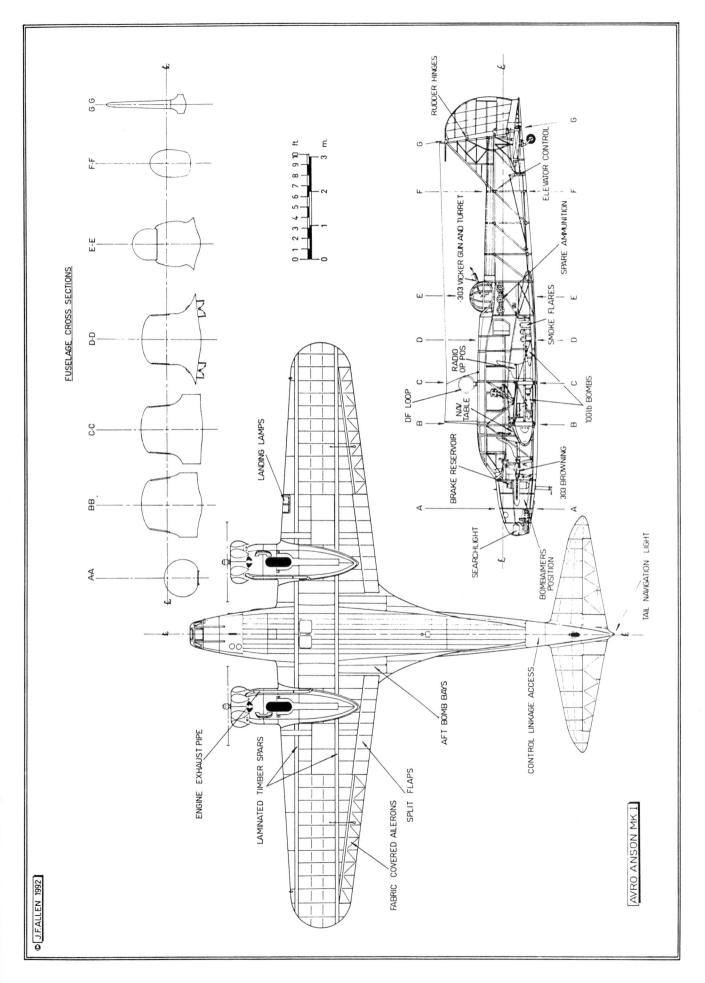

FUSELAGE CROSS SECTIONS

G-G F-F E-E D-D C-C B-B A-A

0 1 2 3 4 5 6 7 8 9 10 ft.

0   1   2   3 m.

RUDDER HINGES

G

G

ELEVATOR CONTROL

F

F

·303 VICKER GUN AND TURRET

SPARE AMMUNITION

E

E

SMOKE FLARES

D

D

RADIO OP POS

100lb BOMBS

DF LOOP

C

C

NAV TABLE

B

B

BRAKE RESERVOIR

303 BROWNING

A

A

SEARCHLIGHT

BOMBAIMERS POSITION

TAIL NAVIGATION LIGHT

LANDING LAMPS

ENGINE EXHAUST PIPE

LAMINATED TIMBER SPARS

FABRIC COVERED AILERONS

SPLIT FLAPS

AFT BOMB BAYS

CONTROL LINKAGE ACCESS

AVRO ANSON MK I

J.F.ALLEN 1992

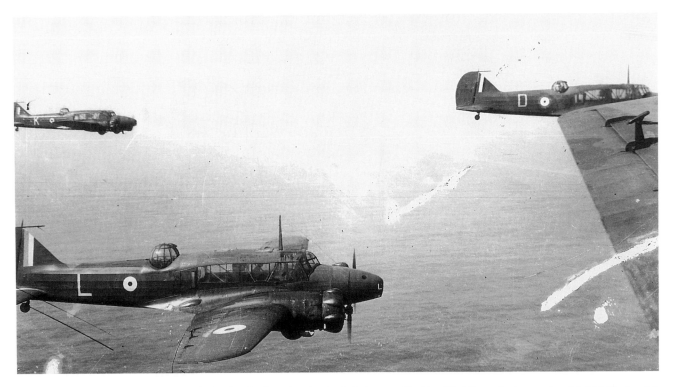

Anson Is from a wartime production batch showing the less sharply raked windscreen fitted to all but the earliest examples. (via Neil Mackenzie)

not finally replaced in RAF operational squadrons until 1941 and in the meantime saw a reasonable amount of action as it bore the brunt of coastal reconnaissance duties in the early stages of the war.

An Anson of No 206 Squadron recorded the RAF's first attack on a German U-Boat on the third day of World War II (September 5) when K6187 dropped two bombs on a submarine but without success. Two months later another Anson from the same squadron hit a surfaced U-Boat on the conning tower with its two 100-pounders but the submarine dived and escaped. If nothing else, the incident proved that heavier bombs than the Anson was capable of carrying were needed to inflict other than very minor damage on the U-Boats.

Another first involving a Coastal Command Anson was a less fortunate one. On 5 September 1939 a 269 Squadron aircraft was shot down into the North Sea by a German seaplane. The German aircraft alighted to pick up the Anson's pilot, and Plt Off L H Edwards (a New Zealander) therefore became the first 'British' officer prisoner of war of World War II.

The Anson also achieved some success as a 'fighter' of all things, accounting for a handful of Messerschmitt Bf109s and a couple of other aircraft during 1940. In one incident, in June 1940, Ansons of No 500 Squadron were attacked by nine Bf109s over the Straits of Dover. Unfortunately for two of the German pilots, No 500's Ansons had been locally modified to carry an extra window mounted 0.303in machine on each side of the cabin. These were used in combination with skilful flying by the skipper of one of the Ansons, resulting in two downed Messerschmitts and a third sent on its way with damage.

Trainer Ansons

The Anson's obsolescence in front line roles did not mean the end of its career in the air forces of Britain and the Commonwealth countries. Far from it, because it was as a trainer that the Anson thrived and was built in very large numbers.

A trainer Anson had been discussed as early as 1935 and although the general reconnaissance Anson Is were fitted with single controls only, provision had been made for the installation of easily removable dual controls. Even in the late 1930s and early days of the war, numerous Ansons had found their way into training units and had been used for communications duties.

It was the British Commonwealth Air Training Plan (or Empire Air Training Scheme) which ensured the Anson remained in large scale production during the war years. The need for large numbers of aircrew of all skills required a massive training programme encompassing several countries and thousands of aircraft of different types.

When 'The Plan' was launched the Anson was selected as its standard navigator, wireless operator and air gunner trainer and the type was also used for pilot multi-engine training. To fill these roles Mk.I Anson trainers were supplied to Britain, Australia, Canada (with several marks built there), New Zealand, South Africa and Southern Rhodesia.

Apart from the Canadian built examples, the Ansons built to fill these roles were Mk.Is, differences between the true trainers and general reconnaissance versions including the fitting of wing flaps and a mod-

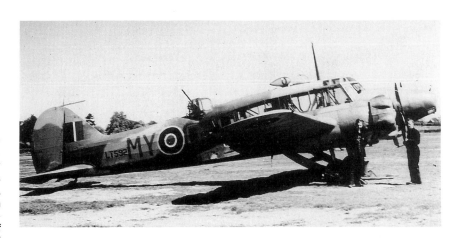

Later production Anson I LT592 of No 278 Squadron RAF with a Bristol dorsal turret fitted in place of the standard Armstrong Whitworth unit. (via Neil Mackenzie)

An RAF Anson I modified for navigation training. (via Mike Kerr)

ified windscreen design. Guns were not normally installed, although those used for the training of gunners were often later fitted with a Bristol electro-hydraulically operated dorsal turret of the type normally installed in the Bristol Blenheim. Many former operational Anson Is also found their way into the training system, some with the original Armstrong Whitworth turret still installed and some with it removed.

AVRO ANSON GR.I

Powerplants: Two Armstrong Siddeley Cheetah IX seven cylinder air cooled and supercharged radial engines each rated at 340hp for takeoff and 355hp at 7,000 feet; Fairey two bladed fixed pitch metal propellers; fuel capacity 140imp gal (636 l) in four wing tanks, provision for a 40imp gal (182 l) ferry tank in cabin.

Dimensions: Wing span 56ft 6in (17.22m); length 42ft 3in (12.88m); height 13ft 1in (3.99m); wing area 463sq ft (43.0sq m).

Weights: Empty 5,512lb (2,500kg); normal loaded 7,955lb (3,608kg); maximum 8,500lb (3,856kg).

Armament: One fixed Vickers 0.303in machine gun in nose, one Lewis 0.303in machine gun with 400 rounds mounted in Armstrong Whitworth manually operated dorsal turret; normal bomb load 360lb (163kg) comprising two 100lb (45kg) and eight 20lb (9kg) bombs.

Performance: Maximum speed 170mph (273km/h) at sea level, 188mph (302km/h) at 7,000 feet; cruising speed 159mph (256km/h) at 6,000 feet; initial climb 750ft (228m)/min; time to 10,000 feet 11.6min; service ceiling 19,500ft (5,944m); range with 200lb (95kg) bomb load 670 miles (1,078km) at 159mph; maximum range 820 miles at 125mph.

To cope with the extra numbers of Ansons required by 'The Plan', a shadow factory was built at Yeadon, near Leeds, and of the 6,742 Anson Is ultimately manufactured, 2,807 rolled out of this factory.

Until 1941, all Ansons were referred to as simply 'Mk.Is', but in that year the RAF introduced role prefixes in aircraft designations, the general reconnaissance Ansons becoming GR Mk.Is and the trainers T Mk.Is (GR.I and T.I in their abbreviated forms).

Canadian Ansons

Outside Britain, the largest user of the Anson was Canada, which received 1,528 British built Anson Is, some 223 of which were shipped without engines. Of the latter, many were fitted with American engines in place of the standard Cheetahs, thus creating new mark numbers.

The Anson III was the first to be re-engined, with 330hp Jacobs R-914 radials. This variant first flew in November 1940 and at first was not needed due to a plentiful supply of Cheetahs, but when this engine did begin to become scarce, many other Anson airframes were fitted with 'Shaky Jakes'.

The Anson IV was another conversion of the basic Mk.I airframe, this time with 300hp Wright R-975 Whirlwind engines. Like the Mk.II conversions, the Mk.IV featured smooth rather than helmeted engine cowlings. The prototype conversion was performed in Britain and flew in 1941. More conversions of Mk.I and Mk.III variants were performed in Canada as supplies of the Cheetah and then the Jacobs engine began to diminish.

The versatility of the Anson is illustrated by this South African Air Force example on floats. The aircraft is attached to No 35 Squadron, whose Sunderlands can also be seen. (via Mike Kerr)

Of the 2,882 Ansons manufactured in Canada, 1,049 were Mk.Vs (above and below) unique with their moulded plywood fuselages and 450hp Pratt & Whitney R-985 Wasp engines.

Despite the high rate of production of the Anson I in Britain, it quickly became obvious that Canada's needs for the aircraft could only be met by local manufacture of the type. Arrangements were made during 1940 for a Canadian production programme to be established, a programme which eventually saw 2,882 Ansons come off local assembly lines. The manufacturing effort was co-ordinated by Federal Aircraft Ltd and several other companies were involved, including Canadian Car & Foundry, de Havilland Canada, Ottawa Car & Aircraft, MacDonald Brothers and National Steel Car Corporation.

The first Canadian manufactured Anson variant was the Mk.II, which was similar to the British Mk.I but with Jacobs engines, fewer cabin windows and – lo and behold – hydraulically operated retractable undercarriage! No more 160 turns of the handle! The first Mk.II flew in August 1941 and 1,832 were built between then and May 1943 including 50 for the United States Army Air Force under the designation AT-20 and more than 400 which crossed the Atlantic to serve with the RAF.

The Anson V had less in common with previous models and was a peculiarly Canadian variant. Intended as a navigation trainer, it featured a completely new moulded plywood fuselage (an attempt to save strategic materials) with three circular windows per side and a pair of 450hp Pratt & Whitney R-985 Wasp Junior nine cylinder radials. With the extra power provided by the Wasps, the Mk.V was the fastest and best climbing of all the Ansons with a top speed of 202mph (325km/h), an initial climb rate of 1,300ft (396m)/min and a service ceiling of more than 21,000 feet (6,400m).

R9816, the prototype Anson IV with Wright Whirlwind engines, converted from a Mk.I.

A Canadian built Anson II, structurally similar to the British Mk.I but with Jacobs engines, revised cabin glazing and hydraulically retractable undercarriage. This example belongs to the RCAF's No 4 Bombing and Gunnery School. (via Neil Mackenzie)

and flaps. Power was provided by two 395hp Cheetah XIXs driving fixed pitch propellers, maximum weight was 9,700lb (4,400kg) and 91 were delivered from July 1944.

The Anson XII was a close relative with 420hp Cheetah XVs, constant-speed propellers behind larger spinners and a further increase in maximum weight to 10,500lb (4,763kg). All future Ansons would feature Cheetah engines of similar rating (although different Mark numbers), constant-speed propellers and maximum weights of around the same figure. The Anson XI and XII were used for various transport duties ranging from casualty evacuation to VIP and 254 of the latter were built from October 1944.

Anson Mark numbers XIII to XVII were allocated to various wartime trainer projects which never materialised, while future models were all postwar variants, some of which

The Anson V first flew in February 1943 and production amounted to 1,049 aircraft. A one-off variant flown in 1943 was the Mk.VI, intended as a gunnery trainer complete with Bristol dorsal turret. The installation proved unsatisfactory and plans to manufacture 500 examples were cancelled.

Mark numbers VII, VIII and IX were also allocated to Canadian Ansons but not used.

Later British Ansons

Although the British built Anson I and the Canadian variants accounted for the vast majority – about 90 per cent – of total Anson production, substantial numbers of later variants were nevertheless manufactured for both military and civil use as transports and trainers. This allowed production to continue postwar, finally ending in May 1952 with the delivery of the 10,996th example after a production run which lasted 17 years. Normal accommodation in the transport Ansons was two on the flight deck and six passengers in the cabin.

The Anson X was the first purely transport variant developed. Converted from Mk.Is on the production line, 103 were built from 1944 including Series 1 aircraft with Cheetah IX engines and Series 2s with Cheetah XIXs, both housed in smooth cowlings. Compared with the Mk.I, the Mk.X featured a strengthened cabin floor, an increased maximum weight of 9,450lb (4,286kg), a door on the starboard side for the loading of stretchers and – for the first time on a British Anson – hydraulically operated undercarriage.

The Anson X was extensively used by the RAF in Europe after D-Day and achieved recognition for the role it played carrying supplies to the troops at Normandy and then to rough airstrips in France and the Low Countries as the Allies advanced.

The Anson XI introduced the first major modifications to British Ansons by way of the raised cabin roofline which would characterise future variants, a reduced amount of cabin glazing and the now standard hydraulically operated undercarriage

The later Ansons were distinguishable by their raised cabin rooflines, five oval windows per side and smooth engine cowlings. These shots are of Anson C.19s, of which VL337 (lower) is a metal winged Series 2 aircraft which remained in RAF service until 1968.

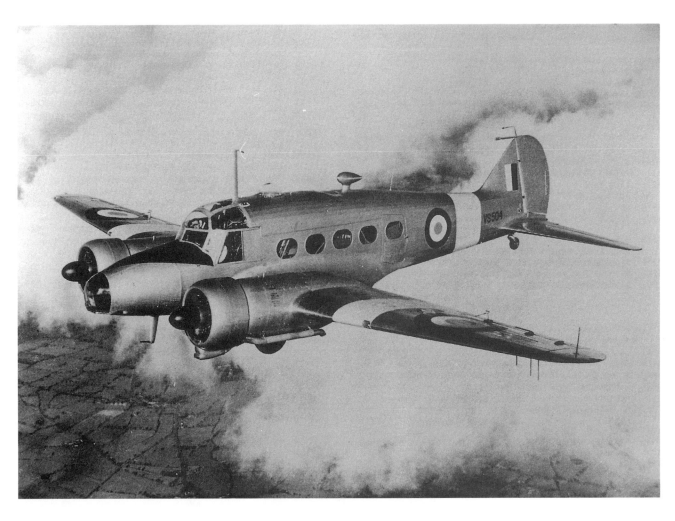

Anson T.20 VS504, one of 60 built for Rhodesia.

Production of the Anson T.21 navigation trainer for the RAF amounted to 252 aircraft from 1948. WJ509 was from the last batch of 28 Ansons to leave the production line between November 1951 and May 1952.(via Mike Kerr)

adopted Arabic rather than Roman numerals in their designations, standard practice for British military aircraft in the late 1940s and beyond.

The first of these was the Anson XIX Series 1, the first of which flew in early 1945. Distinguished from previous Ansons by its five smaller oval shaped cabin windows per side and a modified door, the XIX was powered by 420hp Cheetah XV engines. Civil versions were known as the Avro Nineteen and 140 were built, mainly for the RAF as C Mk.XIX (later C.19) for communications duties and a few for civilian operators. Sales of these later Ansons to civil operators were restricted by the large numbers of surplus Anson Is which became available after hostilities ended. More than 100 found there way onto the British civil register after 1945 and no fewer than 140 appeared on the Australian register.

The Anson XIX Series 2 followed in 1946, this version finally dispensing with the familiar wooden wing and replacing it with a fabric covered unit of metal construction and of slightly greater span. The tailplane was similarly constructed and 185 Series 2s were built. Many Anson XIX Series 1s were subsequently modified to Series 2 standards.

Three more trainer Ansons completed the mainstream family, all similar to the XIX Series 2 but built for specific tasks. The Anson T.20 was a bombing and navigation trainer (60 built) for the Southern Rhodesian Air Force fitted with a transparent nose and capacity for sixteen 8.5lb (4kg) practice bombs; the T.21 was a navigation trainer for the RAF (252 built) first flown in May 1948 and the T.22 – flown the following month – was a radio trainer for air signallers. Thirty-four were built for the RAF. Some of these latter Marks were subsequently used for communications duties and as a result received a 'C' designation prefix. The last Anson built was a T.21 (WJ561) delivered to the RAF in May 1952.

The final Anson variant to fly was the numerically out of sequence Mk.18 ten seater, 13 production examples of which (plus the prototype, converted from a Mk.XIX Series 2) were delivered to the Royal Afghan Air Force in 1948. A further 12 were built for the Indian Director General of Aviation in 1949 as the Anson 18C and used as civil radio and navigation trainers.

The Royal Air Force retired its last Anson in June 1968 after 32 years' service, although civil operations had ended some years earlier. Former military Anson Is were in many ways the small airliner/air taxi/charter/general purpose equivalent of the Douglas DC-3 after the war in many countries of the world, helping establish air services to places which didn't justify larger aircraft.

The early Ansons' wooden wing was its nemesis as far as the civilian aviation authorities were concerned and as early as 1950 the British Air Registration Board (ARB) decided that no more certificates of airworthiness would be granted to the aircraft. Although extensions were given, by the mid 1950s the Anson I had all but disappeared from British skies.

In Australia, civil Ansons were permitted to fly until midnight on 30 June 1962, ending a 26 year association, the military aspects of which are discussed in the following chapters.

ANSONS FOR THE RAAF

The mid to late 1930s was a period during which many of the world's 'free' nations became alarmed at activities which were occurring in other parts of the world, activities which had the potential to threaten world peace. Most observers considered Germany and Japan were the largest part of that threat.

Both countries were building their armed forces substantially (in Germany's case in direct contravention of the admittedly ill-advised Treaty of Versailles) and both were or would be engaging in aggressive military action, Germany in the Spanish Civil War and through more insidious excursions in Europe, and Japan in Manchuria. Additionally, Fascist Italy had entered into a pact with Nazi Germany and chose to exercise its muscle by invading Ethiopia.

Australia did not ignore the rumblings which were going on in Europe and Asia and by 1934 its still only eight years old air force began to reap the benefits of the general realisation that stronger defence forces were becoming a necessity.

The Royal Australian Air Force had been struggling just to survive over the previous few years. Its existence as a separate entity had come under threat on several occasions, mainly from senior Navy and Army officers who wanted to establish their own services' air arms and opposed an independent air force. The motives, of course, were not so much for the good of the nation but for the good of their own particular branch of the services.

By 1928 the RAAF was in a fairly uninspiring state. Equipped with mainly obsolete aircraft with little or no combat capability, its personnel were generally poorly trained and it was incapable of even adequately supporting the Navy and Army in a time of war.

In that year, Air Chief Marshall Sir John Salmond (RAF) was invited to visit Australia to report on the state of the RAAF and to make recommendations as to its future. Salmond's recommendations revolved around a general expansion of the RAAF over a nine year period, but his report was quickly shelved because there was no perceived threat to Australia at that stage and money was tight. Some of Salmond's comments dealt with emphasising the importance of Darwin to Australia's defence planning, comments that would later be fully borne out.

It was during the years after the release of the Salmond Report that the RAAF came under the greatest threat, but in 1934 the report was dusted off and re-examined under the new circumstances which prevailed. Many of its points were adopted for the 'new' RAAF, born in 1935, and although the various general purpose and training types which entered service over the next few years were of little defensive use to the nation when Japan entered the war in 1941 and Australia found itself under direct threat (there were no modern fighters), they at least indicated a changed attitude towards the RAAF and its position.

By 1938 the RAAF had eight front line squadrons, and further expansion plans saw the planned figure increase. Supporting this was the building of new airfields and the establishment of the necessary infrastructure.

Ansons Ordered

The immediate benefit for the RAAF of the events of 1934-35 was the placing of orders for more modern types of aircraft – Hawker Demon two seat fighter-bombers, Supermarine Seagull V (Walrus) amphibians and Avro Ansons.

The second half of the 1930s brought with it further uncertainty about world security and saw further orders and expansion of RAAF strength and the Australian aircraft industry generally. Before war was declared on Germany in September 1939, Short Sunderland flying boats, Lockheed Hudson reconnaissance bombers and other minor types had been ordered for the RAAF while the privately owned Commonwealth Aircraft Corporation (CAC) had been established and was building Wirraway general purpose trainers.

Of equal importance was the fact that by then it had been decided to manufacture the Bristol Beaufort bomber in Australia, thus, in conjunction with CAC's efforts, laying the foundations for a major aircraft manufacturing effort which would be of immeasurable assistance to Australia's war effort and beyond. The decision to build Beauforts in Australia was one of necessity as much as design, as Britain was having trouble supplying aircraft to other nations because it, too, was in the middle of rapid expansion and struggling to meet its own needs in the face of seemingly inevitable war with Germany.

The first expansion of the RAAF was mooted by the Australian government in December 1934 and was based on a three year programme. By July 1935 it was stated by the RAAF Chief of Air Staff (Richard Williams) that the purchase of a new type of twin engined general purpose aircraft for coastal reconnaissance was being considered.

In October 1935, Williams announced the Avro Anson had been selected to fill the role, noting it would help fill the reconnais-

Three of No 21 Squadron's newly acquired Ansons on parade with Bristol Bulldogs and Hawker Demons in 1937. A4-1, in the foreground, first flew in Australia on 2 December 1936 and was handed over to 21 Squadron a week later. (RAAF)

Anson A4-1 shortly after delivery. This aircraft survived the war and was struck off charge in 1947. (via Bob Livingstone)

those of the initial order for 48 aircraft carrying the serials A4-1 to A4-48. All were Mk.I aircraft diverted from production batches originally intended for the RAF. A4-1/K6212 was the 62nd Avro Type 652A Anson.

Not all of these Ansons were fitted with gun turrets on their arrival, many acquiring this appendage as late as 1941. Of the original 48, seven were fitted with dual controls – A4-1, -4, -5, -34, -35, -36 and -37.

Deliveries took place over the next 22 months. The first four aircraft arrived in Australia before the end of 1936 followed by 34 in 1937 and the final 10 in the second half of 1938.

There were considerable gaps between the three batches which comprised the first 48 aircraft. A4-1 to A4-12 were delivered between November 1936 and January 1937, A4-13 to A4-38 arrived between August and November 1937 and A4-39 to A4-48 didn't come to Australia until August and September 1938.

By then, five RAAF squadrons were operating Ansons, three of them Citizen Air Force units which had been established as part of the expansion programme. The first to take the Anson onto strength was No 21 at Laverton which received A4-1 only one week after its first flight in Australia. No 22 Squadron at Richmond NSW was the next to receive this "modern fighting machine" (as it was somewhat optimistically portrayed), in February 1937 and No 23 Squadron at Pearce WA (after an initial period at Laverton) in July 1937.

Two 'regular' RAAF squadrons also had Ansons on strength before the end of 1937, No 4 at Richmond NSW receiving its first in

sance and protection of shipping 'gaps', and all at a price considerably less than that of suitable flying boats. Williams pointed out that for the price of four flying boats, the RAAF could have 12 Ansons. He indicated 33 Ansons would be required.

On 11 November 1935 an order was placed for 33 Ansons and spare parts at a cost of £236,000 ($472,000). In addition, it was decided that ten additional standard Ansons and five equipped with dual controls would be required to fill the RAAF's operational needs. The orders included provision for the manufacture of the Anson in Australia at a later date. At this stage the first production Anson for the Royal Air

Force was still seven weeks away from recording its first flight.

Early Deliveries

The RAAF had to wait a year until its first Anson arrived, shipped to Melbourne from Liverpool on board the SS *Orari* and arriving on 19 November 1936. The aircraft (RAF serial K6212) was then transported to the RAAF's No 1 Aircraft Depot at Laverton where it was reassembled and test flown by Wing Commander A W Murphy on 2 December.

The RAAF allocated the serial prefix A4 to the Anson, with the first aircraft A4-1 and

Anson A4-9 in flight. This Anson's first posting was to No 21 Squadron in April 1937. Note the turret with no gun installed. (via Bob Livingstone)

Two views of Ansons from No 22 Squadron based at Richmond NSW but photographed here taking off from and flying over Mascot in 1938. Note the Hawker Demons on the ground in the upper shot. The bands around the fuselage are blue. (via Mike Kerr)

July and No 2 its first in November. In January 1939 Nos 4 and 23 Squadrons were renamed numbers 6 and 25, respectively, their bases remaining as before. A 'new' No 23 Squadron was established at Archerfield Qld in February 1939, also equipped with Ansons.

Three other squadrons were equipped with Ansons during the course of 1939 and before war was declared; No 12 at Laverton and then Darwin NT, No 14 (Pearce WA), both in February, and No 1 at Darwin in

August. By the time war broke out, the RAAF therefore had nine squadrons with Ansons on strength, some of them with other types as well.

More Orders

The problem with the supply of some British aircraft as mentioned above resulted in the RAAF's acquisition of a further 40 Ansons in 1938 and 1939. In November 1936 the Australian Minister for Defence (Sir Archdale Parkhill) announced an order for

Bristol Blenheims to equip two RAAF squadrons. Deliveries of the required 40 aircraft were expected to begin in the first half of 1937.

The Blenheims were intended to replace the yet to be delivered Avro Ansons with these squadrons, but early in 1937 it became obvious that they would not be delivered within the planned timescale due to the problems of supply from Britain. By 1938 – when there was still no sign of the Blenheims arriving – the possibility of local

Anson A4-7 of No 21 Squadron in 1938. In that year, A4-7 collided with A4-1 on takeoff, putting both out of action for some months. (via Bob Livingstone)

manufacture was considered and after further discussion it was recommended the new Bristol Beaufort (the first example of which was still to fly) be manufactured in Australia.

Eventually, this option was taken up and the first Australian built Beaufort flew from the government owned Department of Aircraft Production factory at Fishermen's Bend, Melbourne, in August 1941. Thus was established the early stages of an immense Australian industrial effort which reaped great benefits. It was perhaps fortuitous that those Blenheims were not available when required.

The lack of Blenheims in 1937/38 meant the RAAF had to order more readily available types to fill the gap. An initial 50 examples of the capable Lockheed Hudson was ordered in November 1938 with deliveries beginning in January 1940 (247 were eventually taken on charge) but before that, and out of necessity as much as anything, more Ansons were obtained as an interim measure.

It's worth noting that by 1938 the Anson's suitability as an effective weapon of defence was already being questioned – 'they will neither go anywhere very quickly nor carry a big load' and its engine out performance was questionable.

Even the British had come to similar conclusions and in June 1938 had themselves ordered Hudsons, largely to replace the already obsolescent Anson. But the 'buy British at any cost' view still had strong influence in Australia, and there was considerable furore when the Commonwealth Aircraft Corporation decided to build the North American NA-16 under licence (as the Wirraway) as its first product.

Nevertheless, there were those who thought "the primary consideration should be the defence of Australia and if we can buy aircraft which fulfil our requirements from Great Britain, we should do so. If we cannot buy them, we must still keep the primary objective in view, regardless of from where we can buy our machines. It would be better to buy six Lockheed Fourteen [Hudsons] with speed, range, big payload and consequent striking power rather than a large number of Ansons costing the same amount ..."

Hudsons were ordered (the first military aircraft purchased from the USA by Australia), but 40 more Ansons were first acquired to fill the gap and to ensure the RAAF's expansion plans were met. These were not purchased but leased. In July 1938 (by which time 38 of the original order for 48 Ansons had been delivered, the remainder arrived over the next two months), it was proposed that additional Ansons be obtained from the British Air Ministry on a charter basis and paid for at a rate of £10 ($20) per flying hour.

The result was the delivery of 40 extra Ansons to the RAAF between November 1938 and April 1939. As these aircraft were still owned by Britain, they were not allocated RAAF serial numbers in the A4 sequence, but retained their Royal Air Force serials instead. All were Mk.I aircraft and the first batch arrived in Melbourne on board the SS *Taranaki*.

Ansons for the Empire

By far the greatest proportion of the 1,028 Ansons which eventually saw service with the RAAF were the 937 Mk.Is delivered to Australia between 1940 and 1944 under

the auspices of the Empire Air Training Scheme. This organisational triumph for the training of Commonwealth aircrews will be discussed in more detail in a later chapter; suffice to say at the moment that the scheme was approved in October 1939 with Canada, Australia and New Zealand the main participants in descending order of input.

Australia's contribution was set at the establishment of ten Elementary Flying Training Schools (EFTS), eight Service Flying Training Schools (SFTS), four Air Observer Schools (AOS), four Bombing and Gunnery Schools (BAGS), four Wireless Air Gunner Schools (WAGS), one Radio Operator School, two Air Navigation Schools and three Initial Ground Training Schools, all of which were planned to be in place by April 1942.

For Australia, the standard aircraft types to be used were the Tiger Moth and Wirraway for basic and advanced pilot training, respectively, the Anson for multi-engine, advanced, observer and navigation training and the Fairey Battle for weapons training. There were variations on this – 391 Airspeed Oxfords arrived from Britain, for example – but that was the basic line up.

The Tiger Moths and Wirraways were manufactured in Australia and it was agreed that a total of 1,160 aircraft would be paid for and/or supplied by Britain, including 233 Wirraways, 336 Battles, 486 elementary training aircraft (Tiger Moths) and 591 Ansons. The latter figure was increased to 765 in April 1940, but – as noted above – the final number of Ansons which arrived on behalf of the EATS was 937.

Although most of these Ansons spent time with various training units, many of

Low over the trees in the standard prewar silver finish, A4-31 served with No 4 Squadron (later retitled No 6) at Richmond from August 1938. It had two mid-air collisions with other Ansons during its life, the second one (with A4-6) in February 1942 destroying both aircraft. (RAAF Historical)

Surrounded by its Hawker Demon 'mates', Anson A4-34 of No 2 Squadron is photographed at Laverton in 1938. (via Bob Livingstone)

them also flew with operational squadrons, flights and miscellaneous units. Additionally, the surviving Ansons delivered before the war also moved between units.

The Ansons delivered to Australia during the war years were all Mk.I trainers which differed externally from the earlier aircraft by virtue of their less sharply raked windscreens. All retained Royal Air Force serials. Some were fitted with turrets, others were not, and others had turrets fitted locally.

Some had air-surface vessel (ASV) radar installed, not only for training purposes but also because even late in the war, some Ansons were still being used for coastal patrol duties. The ASV installation caused one or two problems, as discussed in an RAAF Headquarters Southern Area memo dated February 1944: "If ASV equipment is carried the maximum permissable all up weight of 8,800lb is exceeded if depth charges to a total weight of 500lb are carried unless steps can be taken to reduce weight elsewhere. Eastern Area have [sic] instructed their [sic] Ansons to remove the front gun and ammunition and this represents a saving of 56.5lb.

"A further saving of 160lb can be effected by removing the self sealing material from the fuel tanks. This has already been approved for all training Ansons but RAAF Headquarters is unwilling to approve it for operational Ansons apparently on the grounds that all operational aeroplanes should be fitted with self sealing tanks.

"It is considered, however, that the advantage of carrying an extra depth charge would far outweigh any advantage to be gained from having self sealing tanks in this theatre of operations.

"As the Ansons have (with front gun removed) no defensive armament, their tactics would be to keep out of gun fire range of submarines, and it is considered that the advantage to be derived from self sealing tanks is therefore negligible. It is therefore requested that you approve the principle of removing the self sealing material from the tanks of Anson G/R squadrons for the purpose of enabling the second depth charge to be carried.

"It is also desired to raise with you the question of the fitment of ASV equipment to Anson aeroplanes. The position does not appear to be entirely satisfactory for several reasons.

"The ASV equipment has to be operated by the WAG (wireless-air gunner) who has to maintain a listening watch on the W/T equipment at the same time. It is considered that this will involve considerable strain on the WAG and it is thought that the result will be that the ASV equipment can only be used for short periods at a time.

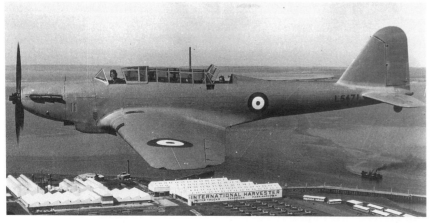

The four aircraft most associated with Australia's contribution to the Empire Air Training Scheme, the (top to bottom) Tiger Moth, Wirraway, Anson and Battle.

A prewar shot of Anson A4-31 in formation with several flights of de Havilland Tiger Moths. The Anson's undercarriage is down because even it was too fast for the Tigers! (Bob Piper)

Doubts about the supply of sufficient Ansons for the EATS in 1940 resulted in the importation of 391 Airspeed Oxfords.

"It is realised that ... the ASV equipment is only to be turned on when the visibility falls below three miles but this would of course apply to the entire time during a night flight ...

"If the ASV equipment was removed the result would be that extra fuel to the weight of about 150lb could be added, thus increasing the capacity by about 20 gallons and giving an extra three-quarters of an hour range. Additional range is of considerable importance in this area where many of the ships being escorted have to be picked up and escorted at a considerable distance from the nearest aerodrome.

"Even a small increase in range has considerable effect on the number of details required for a dawn to dark cover. It is therefore recommended that the question of fitting ASV equipment to the Anson aeroplane be reconsidered".

If nothing else, the above emphasises the limitations of the Anson in its design role, as it had been quickly overtaken by larger, faster, longer ranging and more capacious

RAAF ANSONS SUMMARY OF DELIVERIES			
Mark	Qty	Delivery	Remarks
I	12	11/36-01/37	A4-1 to A4-12
I	26	08/37-11/37	A4-13 to A4-38
I	10	08/38-09/38	A4-39 to A4-48
I	17	11/38-01/39	RAF serials
I	23	03/39-04/39	RAF serials
I	937	05/40-05/44	RAF serials
XII	1	01/45	RAF NL153
XIX	2	11/47	RAF VM374/375

Ansons A4-34 and A4-27 pose for the camera prewar. A4-27 only survived until May 1938 when it crashed on the Green Hills bombing range near Liverpool NSW. (via Ted Bouquet/Bob Livingstone)

With the coming of war in September 1939 the RAAF's Ansons began to acquire more subdued colour schemes, in the case of these No 1 (top) and No 2 Squadron aircraft, overall foliage green. (via Neil Mackenzie)

aircraft capable of happily accommodating the ever increasing equipment fit needed for maritime reconnaissance duties. The Anson was obsolescent as an operational aircraft even before World War II had begun; by the later stages of the war it was certainly obsolete.

But as a trainer, 'Faithful Annie' was far from finished. The first batch of wartime deliveries arrived at No 1 Aircraft Depot on 23 May 1940 and comprised four aircraft: R3334, R3337, R3339 and R3342. The delivery flow picked up from there, annual totals reaching 92 in 1940, 277 in 1941, 242 in 1942, 189 in 1943 and 137 in 1944. The final Anson I batch was handed over almost exactly four years later, on 29 May 1944.

Local Production

It was noted earlier that the original Anson purchase contract contained provision for local manufacture of the type. This option was considered later on and involved more than a little political and industrial intrigue. Of course the Anson was never built in Australia, but the events leading to this situation are of interest. It should be noted that early plans revolved around all of the EATS Ansons arriving in Australia *sans* wings, which would be locally manufactured and installed. It was quickly realised that this would not be possible.

Events began in December 1936 with the incorporation of a company called Airplane Construction Development Pty Ltd, headed by the managing director of Greater Union Theatres, Stuart Doyle. The company's intention was to establish a factory in Sydney to manufacture aircraft, and over the next four years various plans were implemented for the manufacture of several British types including the Miles Magister basic

trainer and Airspeed Envoy and Consul twin engined light transport/trainer, or Oxford in its military form. Additionally, the company announced it had been awarded the Australian marketing rights of certain Italian types.

None of these plans came to fruition, nor did further ambitions to build the Armstrong Siddeley Cheetah engine, as used in the Oxford and Anson. In 1938 the company (now known as Aircraft Development) announced it had secured Australian manufacturing rights for the Cheetah and the following year a partnership between it and the respected firm Clyde Engineering for the manufacture of unspecified aircraft and engines was also announced.

In December 1939 Clyde Engineering and the Australian government discussed plans pertaining to the Anson, namely the assembly and delivery of the aircraft, the manufacture of wings and the maintenance of airframes and engines.

One month later, in January 1940, the whole grand plan promoted by Aircraft Development ground to a halt as it was discovered the company had no arrangements with Avro or Armstrong Siddeley whatsoever for the Australian production of Ansons or its engines! In early May the agreement between Aircraft Development and Clyde Engineering was terminated.

In the meantime, there was much 'to-ing and fro-ing' over the Anson (or parts of them) local manufacture issue. Someone remembered the licence production provision in the original contract, but it was discovered the Australian government had not signed the appropriate document; in February 1940 Clyde was advised it would be given a contract to produce 200 sets of Anson wings; later in the same month the subject of Anson wing manufacture was officially suspended; one day later it was reopened with the Clyde plan submitted again to the War Cabinet; in March Avro was formally approached about the manufacture of wings in Australia; in the same month the idea was dropped again.

But the saga continued: in May 1940 (just after the Clyde/Aircraft Development agreement had been terminated) it was reported that Clyde would probably receive a contract to manufacture up to 300 wing sets for Ansons as well as Cheetah engine spares and other work; in June investigations into the manufacture of 800 Ansons over a three year period was investigated; and in August government approval for Australian Anson production was given and Sydney's Bankstown Aerodrome nominated as a possible site for the factory.

All this activity was due to doubts about Britain being able to supply sufficient Ansons to meet the needs of the EATS. But local production plans created their own

RAAF ANSONS ANNUAL DELIVERIES	
1936	3
1937	35
1938	24
1939	26
1940	92
1941	277
1942	242
1943	189
1944	137
1945	1
1946	nil
1947	2
TOTAL	**1028**

Front on view of an early RAAF Anson clearly shows the 'helmeted' cowlings around the Armstrong Siddeley Cheetah seven cylinder radial engine. (via Neil Mackenzie)

problem, particularly those pertaining to the supply of engines, resulting in alternatives to the Cheetah being examined including American Wright Whirlwind and Jacobs powerplants, but even these were in doubtful supply. Canadian built Ansons used either 330hp Jacobs L-6 or 450hp Pratt & Whitney Wasp Junior engines.

The engine supply problem was the penultimate nail in Anson Australian manufacture plans; the final one was the October 1940 announcement that Airspeed Oxfords were being obtained to complement the Anson in the various training roles it fulfilled and to help overcome any shortfall. The first of 391 Oxfords arrived in Australia even before the announcement of their acquisition had been made.

In early April 1941 the issue was finally closed when the Aircraft Production Commission announced: "We are unlikely to undertake production of the Anson complete in Australia". The wording ("unlikely" still left the door slightly ajar, but it was never opened and no Ansons were built in Australia.

The Final Trio

After delivery of the EATS Ansons was completed in 1944, just three more of the type appeared in the RAAF's hands, two of them postwar. All three retained RAF serials and the aircraft were the only RAAF Ansons which were not Mk.Is.

The first to arrive was Anson XII NL153, in January 1945. This was a VIP aircraft which was operated by the Governor General's Flight at Canberra alongside an Avro York and a Percival Proctor. NL153 was disposed of in 1953 and served with civilian operators until 1955 when it was damaged as a result of a groundloop and withdrawn.

The final two RAAF Ansons were metal winged Mk.XIXs, VM374 and VM375. They were delivered in November 1947 and used at the Woomera SA rocket range as communications aircraft and by No 34 Squadron. VM374 crash landed near Port Lincoln SA in December 1954 after an engine fire, while VM375 went into storage in October 1955, ending just under 19 years of RAAF Anson flying.

VM375 was sold in 1957 and survived until 1961 in the hands of various civilian owners. In March 1961 the Anson crash landed after engine failure and was damaged beyond repair. Parts of this aircraft survive today in Australia's only airworthy Anson.

NL153, the single Anson XII delivered to the RAAF in 1945 for service with the Governor General's Flight. HRH The Duke of Gloucestor received a small fright in this aircraft at Canberra in March 1945 when the undercarriage collapsed whilst taxying. (via Bob Livingstone)

Restored Anson VH-ASM (ex W2068) at Sydney Airport (top) in 1987 in original East West Airlines livery and W2599 (bottom) in trainer yellow languishing at Bankstown in 1964. (Bob Livingstone/Eric Allen)

Still airworthy in 1992, Anson VH-BAF (ex MH120) flies on Anson MK.XIX metal wings. It is photographed at Bankstown in 1966 (top) and at Essendon (bottom) a decade later. (Eric Allen)

ANSONS SERVING AUSTRALIA

21 Squadron RAAF

The first RAAF squadron to receive Ansons was No 21 (City of Melbourne) at Laverton, A4-1 arriving in December 1936, just one week after it had been test flown after arrival in Australia.

The squadron had been formed the previous April under the command of Sqdn Ldr J H Summers and its initial equipment comprised a mixture of Hawker Demons (four), Westland Wapitis (two) and DH Gipsy Moths (three).

With the arrival of Ansons, the fleet remained mixed as the squadron undertook patrol and reconnaissance work, mercy flights, bush fire patrols, mock attacks on airfields and buildings, Army and searchlight battery co-operation flights and combined operations with the Navy operating from airfields on the Victorian coast and the islands near Tasmania.

December 1937 saw a significant survey flight take place, one intended to discover suitable emergency landing fields in the central Gippsland area of Victoria. The chosen areas went on to become permanent RAAF stations – Bairnsdale (the site of No 1 Operational Training Unit during the

A trio of No 6 Squadron Ansons in formation, sometime in the second half of 1939. The official caption to this photograph lists the date as August 1940, but by then none of these Ansons were with 6 Squadron! (via Neil Mackenzie)

Anson A4-8 of No 22 Squadron near its base at Richmond NSW in 1937. It crashed near this spot in October 1938. (Ted Bouquet)

Commanding officer's 'inspection of flying equipment' at No 14 Squadron, Pearce WA during 1939. The squadron's first two COs – Sqdn Ldr Lachal and Flt Lt Pearce – were also the first two to command No 10 Squadron and its Sunderlands in Britain. (RAAF Historical)

war), East Sale and West Sale, where the Bombing and Gunnery School was located.

When war was declared in September 1939, No 21 Squadron was commanded by Sqdn Ldr D A Connelly, who was replaced by Wng Cdr F N Wright the following month. At that stage the squadron operated Ansons and Wirraways and it recorded its first operational mission of the war in December 1939 when four Ansons (three operating from Laverton and the other from Mount Gambier SA) assisted in the escorting of a convoy around the south-east tip of Australia.

Subsequently, the Ansons were used on anti submarine patrols and the Wirraways for general duties, while in February 1940 the squadron took on a dual training/operational role. This was a temporary expedient, as in August 1940 No 21 Squadron moved to Singapore, initially equipped with Wirraways but shortly afterwards with Brewster Buffalos, whereupon it was renamed No 21 (Fighter) Squadron. Activities with Ansons had ceased three months earlier.

22 Squadron RAAF

No 22 Squadron had a three year acquaintance with the Anson, receiving its first aircraft (A4-3) in February 1937. The 'City of Sydney' squadron was formed at Richmond NSW in April 1936 under the command of Sqdn Ldr D E L Wilson, and like the other Citizen Air Force units which flew Ansons (Nos 21, 23 and 25) it operated a mixed fleet of aircraft in its early days, including Demons and Gipsy Moths.

The Ansons added a maritime capability to the squadron and before the war engaged in exercises with the Navy as well as searches, passenger flights and other miscellaneous activities. At the outbreak of war, No 22 Squadron had four Ansons and eight Demons on strength, a reduction in numbers compared with a few months earlier. These remaining Ansons were used mainly on coastal patrol and search duties until withdrawn in May 1940.

The squadron was a participant in April 1939 exercises involving eight RAAF squadrons, warships and merchant shipping over an area stretching from Port Stevens on the New South Wales central coast to Cape Otway in Victoria. Other Ansons were supplied by Nos 2, 6 and 21 Squadrons along with Demons and Seagull Vs from other squadrons.

The exercises were held over three days and involved covering large stretches of water, apparently with satisfactory results. Soon, some of these aircraft and squadrons would be patrolling for real enemy shipping and submarines, as well as helping protect the many troopships departing Australia for North Africa and the Mediterranean.

No 22 Squadron went on to become the only RAAF unit to fly Douglas Boston light bombers, and one of its members, Flt Lt Bill Newton, was posthumously awarded the RAAF's only Victoria Cross of the Pacific war.

22 Squadron Ansons formate over Sydney in 1938. (via Mike Kerr)

Italy entered the war on 10 June, and the *Romolo* had left Brisbane five days earlier. The order to shadow the ship was issued as it was certain Italy would declare war on Britain and its Allies within a few days. A joint RAAF/RAN effort followed as *Romolo* headed north but it was abandoned by its crew on 12 June and set on fire near the Solomon Islands. No 23 Squadron contributed to the first stage of the operation.

An interesting series of sorties in August 1939 saw the squadron sent out to search for what was described as an 'enemy' submarine (a few weeks before war was declared!) near Palm Island off the north Queensland coast, with no result.

The squadron converted to Lockheed Hudsons later in the same year.

4 and 6 Squadrons RAAF

No 4 Squadron was another which underwent a change of name in early 1939. Originally formed in 1916, it was disbanded as a unit of the Australian Flying Corps in 1919 and reappeared in May 1937 at Richmond NSW as a general reconnaissance squadron initially equipped with Hawker Demons and from July 1937 with Ansons. A4-5 was the first Anson taken on strength.

Like the other squadrons operating Ansons at the time, a large part of 4 Squadron's activities were based around naval co-operation, but other tasks (such as transporting VIPs) provided some variety.

An interesting part of the squadron's history was recorded in September 1937 when it was called upon to join in the search for the missing Dr Clyde Fenton, a pioneer flying doctor and pilot who was lost in the Northern Territory. Fenton had departed Newcastle Waters in a de Havilland Moth but had been forced down. He was found alive a week later. The 4 Squadron Anson allocated to the search was A4-5 flown by Flt Sgt Whetters.

No 4 Squadron was renamed No 6 on the first day of 1939, still based at Richmond and still equipped with Ansons, while No 4 Squadron's name reappeared in 1940 as an army co-operation squadron flying Wirraways.

23 and 25 Squadrons RAAF

There were two squadrons which operated Ansons titled No 23, the first being formed at Richmond NSW in May 1937 and remaining there until March 1938 when it moved to Pearce WA. In January 1939 the squadron was renamed No 25. A 'new' No 23 Squadron was formed at Richmond NSW the following month and moved to Archerfield, Brisbane, in August.

The original No 23 Squadron received its first Anson (A4-4) in July 1937, that and subsequent Ansons joining the squadron's original Hawker Demons. From Laverton it conducted mainly training flights but the move to Western Australia saw the squadron's activities expand to include Army and Navy co-operation, meteorological and photographic flights.

The change of title to No 25 Squadron made little difference to the unit's day to day activities but the outbreak of war saw it become fully operational and employed on convoy protection duties and anti submarine patrols in the Fremantle and Rottnest Island areas. The squadron operated Ansons as a main operational type only until April 1940, although postwar it did fly a single example between 1949 and 1951 on training and communications duties.

The reincarnated No 23 Squadron indulged in many Navy co-operation exercises whilst it was based at Richmond (including a number at night involving shadowing and illuminating) and the move to Queensland saw more of the same, including contributing to the shadowing of the Italian ship *Romolo* in June 1940.

A prewar 22 Squadron lineup at Richmond with Ansons in the front rank and Demons behind.

Miscellaneous 1930s RAAF Ansons: (top) 23 Squadron's Ansons and Demons at Laverton in 1939; (centre) 1 Squadron Ansons with N4873 in the foreground, possibly photographed within days of the declaration of war in September 1939; (bottom) formation of 4 or 6 Squadron aircraft. The squadron was named No 4 when Ansons were first taken on strength in July 1937 and retitled No 6 in January 1939. (via Bob Livingstone/Neil Mackenzie)

No 6 Squadron's origins could also be traced back to World War I, and like its predecessor had lain dormant during the inter war years. Main activities continued as before with naval co-operation exercises predominant, the Ansons operating over large areas of the New South Wales coast. In early 1940 the squadron's Ansons conducted numerous patrols and searches at sea to protect the ships carrying the 2nd AIF to North Africa. By April 1940 Lockheed Hudsons had largely replaced the Ansons and the squadron moved on to active service in Australia and overseas.

2 Squadron RAAF

No 2 Squadron operated Ansons from its Laverton base for a period of nearly three years from November 1937 until August 1940 when they were replaced by Lockheed Hudsons.

After an 18 year hiatus, No 2 Squadron was reformed at Laverton in May 1937 as a general reconnaissance unit initially equipped with two Hawker Demons. Like the other GR squadrons of the time its fleet was mixed and by 1938 included Ansons, Demons, Bristol Bulldogs and later Wirraways.

The squadron's first Anson was A4-33, freshly delivered from the United Kingdom and the lead example of 21 Ansons which would eventually serve with the squadron. Of the prewar units, 2 Squadron operated more Ansons than any other.

Prewar activities were typical including navigation, reconnaissance, naval co-operation exercises and making appearances at air shows to 'show the flag' in the face of increasing international uneasiness. One particular sea exercise in August 1939 involved a search off Port Phillip for the overdue German passenger-cargo vessel *Strassfurt*. According to the squadron historian: "The search revealed nothing apart from the very limited range of Anson aircraft", a telling comment.

At the time of the declaration of war on Germany, No 2 Squadron was commanded by Wng Cdr A M Charlesworth, who was succeeded by Sqdn Ldr F W Thomas during the following month. Ten Ansons were on strength at the time and the prime activity was seaward patrols for enemy raiders and convoy protection, including that which carried the 2nd AIF to the Middle East in January 1940. The squadron's main base remained Laverton during this period with detachments flying from other airfields including Cressy in Tasmania.

The searches for enemy raiders were a vitally important part of the early stages of the war and all Anson squadrons were involved in this. The importance of shipping between the east coast capital cities and Adelaide in particular should not be underestimated, especially when taking into account the lack of standard gauge railways between the states.

As it happened, several ships were lost or damaged to enemy guns and mines around the Australian coast in the second half of

1940, most of them on the eastern sea-board or around Bass Strait. But by then the Ansons had generally been replaced by Hudsons in the squadrons.

12 and 13 Squadrons RAAF

Formed at Laverton in February 1939, No 12 (General Reconnaissance) Squadron was intended to be based at Darwin as the strategic importance of Australia's most northern city had been recognised by the politicians and senior RAAF officers who formed policy.

The squadron's first commanding officer was Sqdn Ldr C Eaton AFC, an airman who had made a name for himself in 1929 when he organised the air and ground search for the Westland Widgeon *Kookaburra* which had gone missing in the Northern Territory whilst itself searching for Charles Kingsford Smith's *Southern Cross*. Smithy and his crew were found safe, but the Widgeon's two crew members, Keith Anderson and Bob Hitchcock, perished. This was the incident known as the 'Coffee Royal Affair', and for his efforts Eaton was awarded the Air Force Cross.

No 12 Squadron's initial equipment comprised four Demons and four Ansons and the unit remained at Laverton until July 1939

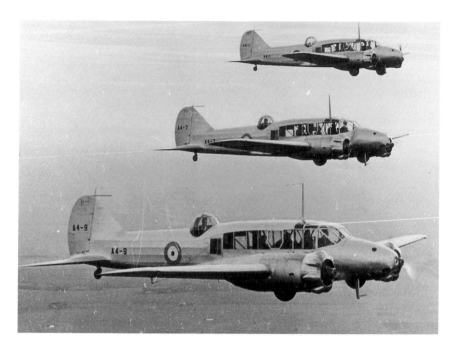

A4-1, -7 and -9 in formation in 1937. (via Bob Livingstone)

Three Ansons from No 14 Squadron flew around Australia in a navigation exercise during November 1939. Here, A4-4, N4868 and N4916 are being refuelled at Derby WA (top) and at another aerodrome en route. (via Neil Mackenzie)

when it began the move to Darwin, its advance party becoming the first RAAF airmen to be permanently stationed in the Northern Territory. Coinciding with the move (which took two months to complete) was the replacement of the squadron's Demons with Wirraways.

The squadron flew its first patrol from Darwin on 31 August and continued operating Ansons until June 1940 when the two squadron flights using them and the attached personnel were used to form a new squadron, No 13, at Darwin. No 12 Squadron therefore became a Wirraway unit and later in the war flew Vultee Vengeances and B-24 Liberators on operations to the north of Australia.

No 13 Squadron took eight of 12 Squadron's Ansons when it was formed in June 1940, but almost immediately they were replaced by Hudsons which were more suitable for the relatively long range patrols demanded of them.

14 Squadron RAAF

Joining No 25 Squadron at Pearce WA, No 14 Squadron was formed in February 1939 and was unusual among the prewar general reconnaissance squadrons in that it did not operate a mixed fleet of aircraft. Instead, it accepted six Ansons as its initial equipment and flew a total of 12 of them over the next 16 months before they were replaced by Hudsons.

The squadron's first commanding officer was Flt Lt C W Pearce and it was subsequently led by Sqdn Ldr L V Lachal, Flt Lt B R Walker and Sqdn Ldr R F M Dalton during the time Ansons were operated.

Before war was declared in September 1939, No 14 Squadron flew Army co-oper-

Anson A4-3 at Cloncurry on 27 September 1937! At that time the aircraft was in the service of No 22 Squadron. It later served with No 25 Squadron and spent its wartime years with various flying training units including 1 and 4 SFTS. (via Bob Livingstone)

While WAAAF mechanics and a driver tinker with motor vehicles, Anson DJ417 stands in the background minus its dorsal turret. Delivered in 1942, DJ417 served with training units and No 66 Squadron.

ation exercises and training flights, including many night cross country navigational exercises. One long range navigational exercise in November 1939 took three Ansons around Australia. With the coming of hostilities in Europe the emphasis switched to seaward reconnaissance patrols along a large stretch of the West Australian coastline. Wyndham and Derby were used as temporary bases, as was Albany, and many patrols were conducted in conjunction with No 25 Squadron.

By May 1940 the Ansons had been replaced by Hudsons, although in the same month the squadron lost its first aircraft when Anson A4-4 crashed near Eildon Weir Vic whilst *en route* to Camden NSW from Point Cook in Victoria. All aboard died but the wreckage and bodies were not found until January 1941.

1 Squadron RAAF

The last RAAF squadron to operate Ansons in the prewar period was No 1, the Australian Flying Corps' first squadron and one which can trace its origins back to 1915. The squadron had been based at Laverton during the 1930s, equipped with Westland Wapitis, Bristol Bulldogs and Hawker Demons and received its first Anson (A4-35) just ten days before the declaration of war. The commanding officer at the time was Sqdn Ldr P G Heffernan, followed by Flt Lt I J Lightfoot in December 1939 and Sqdn Ldr A G Carr in March 1940.

No 1 Squadron operated Ansons only until April/May 1940 when Hudsons replaced them and the squadron was sent to Singapore. In the meantime, the Ansons flew numerous sea patrols, the first of them off Port Phillip where they joined No 2 Squadron in the search for the German ship *Strassfurt*. Other convoy protection and reconnaissance patrols kept the squadron busy until it converted to Hudsons and moved overseas.

Wellesley Escort

In January 1938 the Royal Air Force established a Long Range Development Unit with the intention of undertaking a flight from Britain to either Singapore or Australia. After some modification to the plan, three modified Vickers Wellesley single engined bombers departed Ismailia, Egypt, in early November 1938 in an attempt to fly non stop the 7,158 miles (11,519km) to Darwin.

Two of the aircraft made it (one had to land in Timor due to a lack of fuel before continuing) and the flight took a bit over 48 hours to complete. A new distance record was established which stood for eight years.

After completion of the record flight, the Wellesleys undertook an around Australia publicity tour escorted by RAAF Ansons A4-23, -28, -30 and -45, drawn from Nos 21 and 22 Squadrons.

Ansons of No 6 Squadron, some of them displaying the early 'F' squadron code. Note the mixture of silver and green colour schemes.

There were a couple of postscripts to the adventure, one of them the forced landing performed by one of the Wellesleys near Windsor NSW when its Bristol Pegasus engine failed shortly after takeoff from nearby Richmond air base. The aircraft was dismantled and shipped back to England while the other aircraft continued the tour.

Further misfortune befell one of them, which suffered a broken oil line over Western Australia and was forced down. Difficult to extricate from its 'middle of nowhere' position, the Wellesley was offered for tender, purchased locally and ended its days as an instructional airframe at Melbourne's Engineering School. The remaining Wellesley abandoned the tour and was shipped back to England!

Accidents

The early days of Anson service with the RAAF did see some controversy, particularly with regard accidents, not just with the Avro aircraft but with RAAF types generally.

The Hawker Demon was the main 'villain' of the RAAF safety controversies of the late 1930s, although the Anson was also implicated in a campaign which if nothing else underlined a lack of knowledge of things aeronautical by politicians, the press and the public. Unfortunately, nothing much has changed six decades later!

Not that the RAAF, its pilots, ground crews and policies were completely blameless of course, a lack of de-icing equipment and blind flying equipment contributing to several accidents. Unfortunately, pilot 'foolhardiness' and the bending of rules was also a major player.

The first Anson lost was 22 Squadron's A4-27 in May 1937. The aircraft was exercising over the Green Hills bombing range near Liverpool NSW when it banked steeply and apparently stalled, crashing and killing all three on board.

Then followed a series of accidents involving Ansons, some of them resulting in the loss of aircraft and aircrew, others resulting in damage. These are listed in the table below and apply only to accidents in the period 1937-39 and exclude several very minor incidents:

RAAF ANSON ACCIDENTS 1937-39

Date	Serial	Remarks
05/37	A4-27	crashed Green Hills Bombing Range NSW
11/37	A4-10	landed wheels up Inverell NSW, RTS
01/38	A4-19	landed wheels up Richmond NSW, RTS
04/38	A4-1	landed wheels up Richmond NSW, RTS
04/38	A4-2	forced landing Box Hill NSW (oil shortage), RTS
05/38	A4-27	stalled and crashed Green Hills Bombing Range NSW
05/38	A4-26	hit fence during night landing Laverton Vic, RTS
06/38	A4-22	landed wheels up Canberra ACT, RTS
07/38	A4-8	landed wheels up Richmond NSW, RTS
07/38	A4-33	skidded on landing Laverton Vic, RTS
07/38	A4-33	hit object on landing Laverton Vic, RTS
08/38	A4-29	crashed into hill in fog Arthur's Seat, Dramona Vic
08/38	A4-36	forced landing due ice Whitfield Vic, RTS
08/38	A4-1/7	collided on t/o King Island, both RTS
09/38	A4-35	hit tree night landing heavy rain Pt Cook Vic, RTS
09/38	A4-15	forced landing into ditch King Island, burned
09/38	A4-37	hit by A4-42 on ground Laverton Vic, both RTS
09/38	A4-37	undershot landing Laverton Vic, RTS
10/38	A4-8	broke up during 'power dive' Windsor NSW
11/38	A4-32	collided with Demon A1-49, RTS
11/38	N1332	hit fence on landing Laverton Vic, RTS
12/38	A4-19	landed wheels up Richmond NSW, RTS
12/38	A4-6	landed wheels up Richmond NSW, RTS
12/38	A4-36	hit towed target, RTS
01/39	A4-36	landed wheels up Richmond NSW, RTS
02/39	A4-18	taxied into Seagull A2-1 Richmond NSW, RTS
02/39	A4-31	engine failure forced landing Richmond NSW, RTS
02/39	A4-33	hit flares during night landing Laverton Vic, RTS
02/39	N1336	forced landing during Laverton-Pearce flight, RTS
04/39	A4-32	engines stopped and crashed Riverstone NSW
05/39	A4-11	descended through thick fog into Port Phillip Bay Vic
05/39	A4-17	hit hangar on landing Laverton Vic, RTS
09/39	A4-28	taxied into sandbag Richmond NSW, RTS
09/39	N1333	port undercarriage collapsed Laverton Vic, RTS
09/39	N4955	hit fence on landing Richmond NSW, RTS
10/39	A4-48	overshot and hit fence Laverton Vic, RTS
11/39	A4-31	mid air collision with A4-19, both RTS
11/39	A4-30	ground collision Richmond NSW, RTS
12/39	A4-17	crashed on landing Pate River Tas
12/39	N4887	crashed after night t/o Richmond NSW

Notes: RTS = returned to service (after repairs if required); t/o = takeoff.
The above is not a list of every incident involving Ansons during the period stated but of those which resulted in write-offs or damage of some kind. The number of wheels up landings is undoubtedly due to inexperience with retractable undercarriages, while several aircraft appear more than once.

Operational Ansons: AW665 of 71 Squadron at Lowood in 1943 (left) and Ansons of 67 Squadron at Laverton in 1945 (right). Note the Beaufighter, Beaufort and Wirraway in the background. (via Neil Mackenzie)

67 Squadron flew its Ansons from Laverton and other Victorian airfields between 1943 and 1945 on anti submarine and shipping protection patrols. In the upper shot the squadron's Ansons share the ramp with Mosquito FB.40 A52-43. (via Neil Mackenzie)

Some accidents created particular interest, including that involving A4-8 in October 1938 when the aircraft appeared to power dive, resulting in a wing detaching and parts of the aircraft being scattered over a wide area of McGrath's Hill, near Windsor NSW.

The pilot – who was killed – was a Cadet who had only 82 hours total flying time of which 37 were solo. The Coroner's inquest into the crash found the Ansons were not being properly inspected before height tests, that A4-8 was 'not in good order' and that too much was expected of the inexperienced pilot. The RAAF denied the Coroner's comments but training methods were reviewed nevertheless.

A sidelight to the crash was allegations of gagging the press by the RAAF's refusal to publish evidence relating to alleged defects in Ansons, while a later accident in the same area (A4-32 in April 1939) saw a news photographer clash with members of the guard when he tried to photograph the scene. This incident resulted in a meeting between the Australian Journalists Association, the Australian Newspapers Conference and the Prime Minister.

The lack of blind flying instruments in about 30 Ansons resulted in their being grounded in May 1939 pending installation of the equipment. This followed the crash of A4-11 in the same month, the aircraft having descended through fog – the pilot intending to get his bearings – and crashing into Port Phillip Bay.

A4-11 had no blind flying instrumentation, while the accompanying A4-45 was so equipped and survived the poor visibility. The 40 Ansons leased from Britain and delivered in 1938-39 were already fitted with blind flying instrumentation.

Wartime Squadrons

By the end of 1940 the Anson was all but finished as a regular squadron aircraft, replaced by types such as the Lockheed Hudson. The training of Empire Air Training Scheme airmen became its primary role for the remainder of the war, although many examples flew with operational squadrons and other units.

In most cases, the squadrons which operated Ansons during the war years used them as 'hacks' in conjunction with their regular aircraft or in the case of transport squadrons, supplementing larger aircraft or replacing earlier types pending new arrivals. Three RAAF transport squadrons operated Ansons, No 33 (at Port Moresby) 1942-43, No 34 (Darwin) in 1942 and No 35 (Pearce) 1942-43.

Communications Flights (renamed Communications Units in October 1943 and in some cases Local Air Support Units) used reasonable numbers of Ansons including No 1 CU at Laverton and Essendon Vic (which operated 29 Ansons between 1940 and 1946, No 2 (Mascot and Wagga Wagga NSW), No 3 (Mascot), No 4 (Archerfield Qld), No 5 (Garbutt Qld), No 6 (Darwin, Batchelor and Manbullo NT), No 7 (based at Pearce WA with numerous detachments

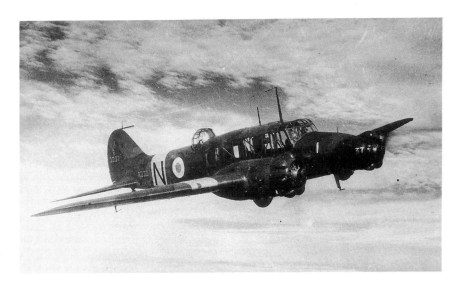

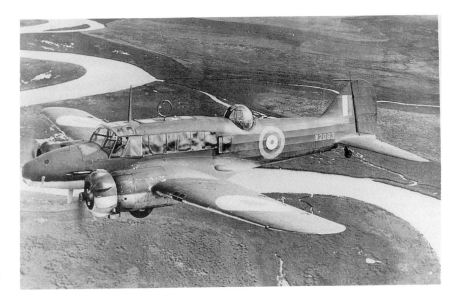

EATS Ansons (from top): R3337 of 1 Air Navigation School; W2083 of the General Reconnaissance School and R3543 of 1 Air Observers School. (via Bob Livingstone)

around the state), No 8 (New Guinea), No 9 (New Guinea, Morotai and Labuan), No 10 (Cairns Qld and Morotai), No 11 (Morotai with a detachment to Manila in 1945) and No 12 in New Guinea after the war.

The Communications Units played a largely unsung but vital role in the war effort, conducting many and varied flights with activities ranging from carrying personnel and stores to delivering mail. In many cases they provided a lifeline for the operational squadrons, particularly those operating near the front line. Most CUs had replaced their Ansons with more capable types by 1945.

Coastal Patrols

Although well and truly obsolete in its original maritime reconnaissance role by the time Japan entered the war in December 1941, that act provided the Anson with another chance to engage in some active service, albeit relatively briefly.

Japan presented a serious threat to shipping around Australia, especially on the eastboard with the result that in 1942 some training units were ordered to establish the necessary infrastructure to form reserve squadrons capable of patrolling these waterways. Fears of Japanese raiders were not entirely without foundation, as events proved.

In 1943 alone, 21 Australian, American, British, Norwegian and Yugoslavian ships were sunk in the area of coastline between the New South Wales/Victoria border in the south and off Bundaberg in Queensland. The tonnage lost in that year was more than 109,000, most of them torpedoed, and most off the coast of New South Wales.

Four squadrons were raised to help the situation, all of them equipped with Ansons. The Anson's poor range and small offensive load was always recognised as a major drawback, but there was nothing else available. Some were equipped with ASV radar, but as noted in the previous chapter, its incompatibility with the Anson (due to its effect on useful load and crew efficiency) resulted in requests to remove it.

The four squadrons were Nos 66 based at Bundaberg Qld, No 67 (Laverton Vic), No 71 (flights at Amberley and Bundaberg Qld plus at Coffs Harbour NSW) and No 73 at Nowra NSW.

No 66 Squadron was formed at Bundaberg in May 1943 as a separate unit based on No 8 Service Flying Training School as a lodger unit. The squadron replaced No 71 which had been formed the previous December drawing personnel from 8 SFTS but had moved to Lowood Qld as a separate unit.

No 67 Squadron was formed at Laverton in January 1943 equipped with 14 Ansons. It operated from Laverton, Mallacoota, Yanakie and Bairnsdale during its period of operations, and like the other squadrons

carried out numerous seaward patrols looking for enemy shipping and submarines as well as participating in naval co-operation exercises and searches for missing or overdue vessels and aircraft.

No 73 Squadron was formed at Cootamundra NSW in July 1942, drawing personnel from No 1 Air Observers School. Nowra NSW became the squadron's main base in September 1942, but detachments also operated from Moruya, Camden, Richmond and Coffs Harbour during its period of operation, the latter in July and August 1943 when No 71 Squadron's detachment temporarily moved out.

For the most part, the squadrons' patrols were without incident and involved countless hours of vigilance with little to show for it. But there were several incidents which livened things up and indicated an extensive Japanese presence off the east coast of Australia.

In February 1943 No 67 Squadron made several possible sightings of submarines but could not attack, while in April the 4,782 ton Yugoslav ship MV *Recina* was torpedoed and sunk off the NSW/Victoria border. An escorting vessel dropped depth charges but no enemy was sighted. In the same month, two of the squadron's Ansons dropped their bombs on a possible enemy submarine just 20 miles (32km) east of Wilson's Promontory, and a search insti-

Wide open spaces at No 4 Service Flying Training School, Geraldton WA, with Ansons on the flight line and undergoing maintenance. W2085 in the foreground was delivered in April 1941. (via Neil Mackenzie)

gated on reports of a submarine, survivors and wreckage, found some of the latter.

The squadron was declared non operational on 17 August 1945 – two days after the Japanese capitulated – and was disbanded the following November.

No 66 Squadron was established with a strength of 18 Ansons plus the assistance of a flight of Beauforts from No 32 Squadron. The squadron began operational flying in July 1943, the first sortie being flown on the 26th of that month by the Commanding Officer, Sqdn Ldr R F Wiley and his crew in Anson DG868.

No 66 Squadron survived only until January 1944 when it was disbanded and its personnel posted to 8 SFTS and 71 Squadron. During its brief period of patrol work, the squadron did not once sight any enemy shipping or submarines.

Nos 71 and 73 Squadrons were both disbanded in August 1944 after their periods of patrolling, and again the enemy sightings were a rare event. However, in March 1943 No 71 Squadron Anson AW516 dropped what is recorded as being the first 250lb (550kg) bomb against an enemy submarine, while later in the same month Anson DG907 was fired upon by a submarine, without success.

Aircrew for the Empire

The philosophical basis of the Empire Air Training Scheme was to provide aircrew for the Royal Air Force, drawing from the Commonwealth nations. The result was a remarkable scheme intended to provide 50,000 aircrew each year, 11,000 of them from Australia. Canada, New Zealand, Australia and Rhodesia took the lion's share of the responsibility, with the first three also providing the bulk of personnel. Thus was established a complicated but successful system which achieved its stated aims.

There was some discussion as to each country's involvement along the way, but these were overcome for the greater good, particularly considering the scheme was established in October 1939 and was up and running in Australia by April 1940 when the first intake of pilot trainees was inducted. Simultaneously, Canada's first intake began training.

As noted previously, Australia's contribution was set at ten Elementary Flying Training Schools (EFTS), eight Service Flying Training Schools (SFTS), four Air Observer Schools (AOS), four Bombing and Gunnery Schools (BAGS), four Wireless Air Gunner Schools (WAGS), one Radio Operator School, two Air Navigation Schools and three Initial Ground Training Schools. These establishments were scheduled to be in place by April 1942, and in addition to these, numerous schools for the training of ground crews were also set up.

The standard aircraft types to be used in Australia were the Tiger Moth, Wirraway, Anson and Fairey Battle, although others were also used, notably a large quantity of Airspeed Oxfords.

Occupational Hazards 1 (top to bottom): R3521 of 6 SFTS after ground looping at Mallala SA in December 1942; R3558 and N4977 of 4 SFTS Geraldton after the former landed on the taxying latter in December 1941; R3530 of 6 SFTS after its undercarriage failed on landing at Mallala in February 1945. (R J Wiseman/RAAF Historical)

After training, the airmen were posted to the Royal Air Force but usually served with squadrons reflecting their nationality of origin. This idea came about due to concerns that national identities would be lost if overseas airmen who had passed through the EATS were simply posted to normal RAF squadrons. The fear was that the idea of the EATS simply supplying 'cannon fodder' for the British might develop.

Early on, these squadrons contained more British servicemen (including commanding officers, usually) than Australians, Canadians, or New Zealanders, but the numbers increased as the war progressed. Airmen serving with the EATS squadrons wore their own nation's uniforms, and the squadrons' national identities soon developed.

Squadrons formed around EATS personnel were given distinctive numbers (450 to 467 in the case of the RAAF) and operated as part of the Royal Air Force flying that service's aircraft.

The Australian EATS syllabus is presented in abbreviated form below. Of note is the fact that numbers of Australian pilots, observers and gunners began their training in Australia and completed it in Canada. In the case of these pilots, *ab initio* and elementary flying training was performed at home, and by March 1941 there were nearly 1,200 Australian trainees in Canada, nearly half of them pilots. Other trainees learned their skills in Southern Rhodesia – mainly pilots but also gunners and observers.

EATS AUSTRALIAN CURRICULUM

Pilots

Initial Training School	14 weeks
Elementary Flying Training School	12 weeks
Service Flying Training School	22 weeks
(Intermediate Squadron 12 weeks)	
(Advanced Squadron 10 weeks)	
Bombing and Gunnery School	2 weeks
TOTAL	50 weeks

Air Observers

Initial Training School	12 weeks
Air Observers School	12 weeks
Bombing and Gunnery School	8 weeks
Air Navigation School	4 weeks
TOTAL	36 weeks

Air Gunners

Initial Training School	8 weeks
Wireless Air Gunners School	24 weeks
Bombing and Gunnery School	4 weeks
TOTAL	36 weeks

On the completion of these courses, trainees would be sent to an embarkation depot to await sailing instructions or posting to an Operational Training Unit in Australia.

Ansons Everywhere

In the thick of all this massive training activity was the humble Avro Anson, now performing a role for which it was well suited and which extended its usefulness considerably after it had quickly become obsolete in its original operational role.

Occupational Hazards 2 (top to bottom): DJ213 of the General Reconnaissance School after crash landing in fog near Rosedale Vic in February 1945; W2111 of 1 Communications Unit had its undercarriage collapse whilst taxying at Tocumwal NSW in July 1945; N1336 of the General Reconnaissance School suffered an engine failure in March 1945 and was unable to maintain height. It came down in a metre of water just off Raymond Island, near Paynesville Vic. (RAAF Historical)

Apart from the squadrons, flights and other flying units with which it served, the Anson appeared on the books of numerous training establishments during the war and operated from no fewer than 54 bases in all States and Territories.

The table below lists them, their base (or bases) and the period of service during which Ansons were on strength.

RAAF TRAINING UNITS WITH ANSONS					
Unit	**Base/s**	**Period**	**Unit**	**Base/s**	**Period**
Armament School	Point Cook Vic	1940-42	Central Gunnery School	Williamtown NSW	1942
	Hamilton Vic	1942-43		Mildura Vic	1942-43
	Nhill Vic	1943-44		Cressy Tas	1943-45
Air Armament School	Nhill Vic	1944	General Reconnaissance School	Point Cook Vic	1940
Air Armament and Gas School	Nhill Vic	1944-48		Laverton Vic	1940-43
	East Sale Vic	1946		Bairnsdale Vic	1943-46
Advanced Flying & Refresher Unit	Deniliquin NSW	1944-46	2 Operational Training Unit	Port Pirie SA	1942
1 Air Gunnery School	West Sale Vic	1943-45		Mildura Vic	1942-46
1 Air Navigation School	Parkes NSW	1940-43	7 Operational Training Unit	Tocumwal NSW	1944-46
2 Air Navigation School	Mt Gambier SA	1941	8 Operational Training Unit	Narromine NSW	1944
	Nhill Vic	1941-44		Parkes NSW	1944-46
1 Air Observers School	Cootamundra NSW	1940-43	Radar School	Richmond NSW	1941-45
	Evans Head NSW	1943-45	School of Army Cooperation	Canberra ACT	1942-46
2 Air Observers School	Mt Gambier SA	1941-46	School of Air Navigation	East Sale Vic	1946-50
3 Air Observers School	Port Pirie SA	1943-46	1 Service Flying Training School	Point Cook Vic	1940-44
1 Air School	Laverton Vic	1940	2 Service Flying Training School	Wagga Wagga NSW	1940-42
	Point Cook Vic	1940	3 Service Flying Training School	Amberley Qld	1940-42
1 Bombing and Gunnery School	Evans Head NSW	1940-43	4 Service Flying Training School	Geraldton WA	1941-45
2 Bombing and Gunnery School	Port Pirie SA	1941-43	5 Service Flying Training School	Uranquinty NSW	1941-46
3 Bombing and Gunnery School	West Sale Vic	1942-43	6 Service Flying Training School	Mallala SA	1941-45
Central Flying School	Point Cook Vic	1940	7 Service Flying Training School	Deniliquin NSW	1941-44
	Camden NSW	1940-42	8 Service Flying Training School	Bundaberg Qld	1941-45
	Tamworth NSW	1942-44	School of Photography	Canberra ACT	1944-46
	Parkes NSW	1944		Point Cook Vic	1942-45
	Point Cook Vic	1944-47	Signals School	Ballarat Vic	1940-46
	East Sale Vic	1947-	1 Wireless Air Gunners School	Parkes NSW	1941-44
Central Gunnery School	East sale Vic	1942	2 Wireless Air Gunners School	Maryborough Qld	1941-44
			3 Wireless Air Gunners School		

The Ansons of the Communications Units and Local Air Service Units provided a valuable service at home and overseas, delivering everything from mail and people to vital supplies. This aircraft (possibly from 9 CU) is operating over Bougainville at dot feet – which is slightly lower than dot metres! (via Neil Mackenzie)

Top to bottom: Anson W2124 of 4 SFTS Geraldton WA; W1941 of 6 Communications Unit at Port Keats Mission NT in October 1945; W2181 of 6 CU on the beach at Peron Island NT with the legend 'Fenton's Flying Freighters' on the nose. (via R J Wiseman)

Piggy Back Ansons

The intensity of the flying training being performed in Australia and other parts of the world during the war years resulted in a very large number of accidents. Many resulted in tragedy, others in injury, others in the cost of machinery rather than human – and still others seem almost comical.

One of the latter is possibly Australia's best known flying accident – two Ansons stuck together, one on top of the other and both being brought safely to earth, with one crew member suffering minor back injuries when he bailed out of the lower aircraft.

The fun started on the morning of 29 September 1940 when two Ansons attached to No 2 Service Flying Training School at Wagga Wagga NSW departed on a cross country training flight. Whilst cruising at 1,000 feet near the small town of Brocklesbury in the Riverina district, the two Ansons (each with two crew on board) lost sight of each other and N4876 (flown by trainee LAC Leonard Fuller with observer Ian Sinclair) descended on to L9162 (LACs Jack Hewson and Hugh Fraser) from the starboard rear quarter.

Somehow, the Ansons became locked together and continued flying despite the fact that the impact had crushed the starboard 'greenhouse' of the lower aircraft and the two port engines had come together with horrible grinding noises. The upper Anson was being kept in place by virtue of its adversary's turret jutting into the port wing root and the lower aircraft's fin and rudder was neatly supporting N4876's port tailplane.

That no-one was seriously injured or killed there and then was a miracle, what with propellers flailing about and shattered perspex flying around; that all survived and the aircraft brought safely back to earth was even more miraculous.

The occupants of the lower Anson bailed out, although Hewson was impeded by the crushed cabin and suffered minor injuries. The top Anson was quickly reduced to a single crew member when Fraser was ordered out by Fuller, who had assessed the situation and decided a reasonably controlled forced landing was not impossible.

With power still available from his Anson's starboard engine and ailerons, elevators and rudder providing just enough authority to keep the two Ansons more or less under control, Fuller began an eight kilometre glide which ended on a property belonging to a Mr T Murphy, some seven kilometres south-west of Brocklesbury. Fuller was uninjured.

Amazingly, N4876 suffered relatively little damage and after repairs flew on with the RAAF. L9162 didn't fly again, but continued to serve its country as an instructional airframe. Leonard Fuller went on to serve with the RAAF in Europe and won the Distinguished Flying Medal. He was killed in 1944 in a most inappropriate manner considering his exploits in the air – whilst riding a bicycle in Sale, Victoria, he was hit by a bus ...

Two views of the most famous Anson incident of them all, the 'piggy back' landing of N4876 and L9162 near Brocklesbury in September 1940. (via Neil Mackenzie)

Anson MG973 of the Survey Flight displays its modified side fuselage glazing. This was one of the RAAF's last Ansons, delivered in March 1944. (via Mike Kerr)

Confessions of An Anson Captain

The following piece was provided by a former RAAF pilot who one day discovered he was going to convert to the Anson. This he was told, and two weeks later his log book contained the necessary endorsement proclaiming to the world: 'Aircraft Captain – certified by me this 2nd day of August 1945 to be qualified for appointment as a Captain of an Avro Anson aeroplane – Group Captain Commanding Air Gunnery School West Sale' ...

"July 18 had dawned, as usual bitterly cold at the Air Gunnery School, West Sale, with a heavy frost on the ground and clear blue skies. The pilots of B Flight, 20 years old veterans with about 400 hours in their log books flew Fairey Battles towing drogues or Wirraways doing curves of pur-

suit on Avro Ansons fitted with camera guns in the turret. We never knew what, if anything, the trainee gunners hit.

"I had had a 6am takeoff that day in a Fairey Battle towing a drogue for three hours over Bass Strait. Sundry Beauforts from the OTU at East Sale had come and taken pot shots at the drogue whilst I fervently hoped half a mile of wire was enough and that the almost customary glycol leak from the Merlin didn't happen.

"After landing I joined my colleagues in our snug flight hut. The pot bellied stove was doing its stuff whilst we honed our skills on a game of '500'. Have you noticed how ex pilots are very good card and snooker players?

"We were actually paid to do all this; the princely sum of 18 shillings and ninepence

($1.87) per day changed hands – maybe we should have been doing the paying as peace, quiet and snug serenity reigned.

"Suddenly, the peace was shattered as the door swung open and in strode Squadron Leader Baldwin, the Chief Flying Instructor. He pointed three times. 'You, you and you', he barked. Despite hiding behind the chimney of the stove I got in the way of a pointing finger and was thus 'volunteered'.

"The CFI's instructions were simple: 'Report at once to A Flight, you are doing a conversion course on Ansons', he advised, if that's the right word.

"My log book shows on that day one hour dual on Anson LT736, 'familiarity on type' and two hours dual on LT714, 'stalls, steep turns, single engined flying, turns, approach and landing'. It doesn't mention anything about the seemingly thousands of handle turns required to get the undercarriage up, or the non existent ability to climb with one engine out ...

"The weather then closed in so exactly one week later I soloed on the Anson. Trustingly, the powers-that-be made me a Captain, with paperwork to prove it.

"First and foremost, 'Annie' was faithful and forgiving, I suppose the direct result of a wing loading of under 21lb/sq ft at maximum weight. Flying the aeroplane was so uneventful memories are few, but no-one who flew Ansons will ever forget manually winding up the undercarriage -it was hard work. If one's intended flight was short – say about 20 minutes – one simply left the wheels down. Slug-like progress became even more sluggy but at $1.87 *per diem*, who cared?

Communications Unit Ansons on Bougainville Island in December 1944. (via Neil Mackenzie)

VH-ASM (ex W2068), the Anson which flew East West Airlines' inaugural service from Tamworth NSW to Sydney on 23 June 1947. The aircraft was restored for static display between 1972 and 1987. It illustrates a typical postwar civil conversion, with smooth engine cowlings, airliner style windows (there were numerous variations on this) and reshaped nose.

The first Anson sold by the Commonwealth Disposals Commission in 1946 was W2145, which after conversion to civilian specifications became VH-AQV 'Nemesis' of the NSW Police. (George Canacott)

Line up of East West Airlines Ansons at Tamworth in the late 1940s with VH-ASM and VH-AYI (ex DJ322) prominent.

"Another memory was the little game the other two former single engined pilots and myself sometimes played. The object was simple – to be stopped (undamaged, hopefully) as close as possible to the perimeter fence after landing – that is at the touchdown end of the landing run!

"This involved putting 'Annie' into the 'precautionary attitude' – a high angle of attack, lots of power (power, Anson?), about 45-50mph on the clock and brakes on, which made it interesting. About 30 feet up over the fence, an extra squirt of 'power' to reduce the rate of descent and crunch! The Anson stopped in a very short distance indeed!

"And we were paid! I'm still smiling".

Navigator's Nightmare

In contrast with the relaxed pilot in the reminiscences above, this piece was written in 1945 by a new navigator – Flt Sgt G A Wright – and published by the RAAF Directorate of Public Relations in the book *Victory Roll* Under the heading 'Trainee Navigator', the words capture the anguish expressed by many a navigator – tyro or veteran – when horrible doubts that he's got his sums right begin to encroach. The scene could be inside any Anson or Oxford at any Air Navigation School ...

"Briefing is over and it is almost dark. You lug your equipment over the tarmac. It is

VH-AGA (ex VH-AVT/R9883) served with Adastra Aerial Surveys for more than a decade until 1959. It survives at the Camden Museum of Aviation.

Three Australian civvie Ansons (top to bottom): VH-AKI (ex DJ165) was exported to Britain in March 1947; the Air Express Co obtained short nose Anson VH-BBI (DG727) in 1953 after it had first served with Bega Freight Services, Western Airways and East West Airlines; by contrast, the Petroleum Drilling Corporation's VH-BKU (W2084) had a lengthened nose. (via Mike Kerr)

cumbersome and weighs you down. Your instruments slide from under your arm and clatter to the ground. You grope about in the half light, cursing.

"The stale smell of petrol reaches you as you near the aircraft. The engines are ticking over. The pilot is early tonight. The WAG [Wireless Air Gunner] is jumbling with his set as you clamber inside. It is almost dark now. You make your way to the table. Something sharp strikes your shin. You curse and chafe at the pain.

"The table light is not working properly. It flickers off and on irritatingly. The pilot wants the first course. You hand it to him and he sets it hurriedly on the compass. You wonder if he has set it correctly.

"Soon the long flare path faces you. The WAG is still tinkering with his infernal set. The engines suddenly spring to life; the brakes are off and you surge forward. Blobs of green light from the instruments blink at you in the darkness of the aircraft.

"Out on the port beyond the red light at the wingtip you can see other lights circling the 'drome. There is a crackle on the intercom. The pilot informs you that you have reached the operational height. He is setting course over the 'drome. You jot the details in your log. The point of your pencil snaps. You curse and snatch another.

"The lights of the 'drome are far behind. Below you lies empty blackness. A helpless feeling numbs your body. The heavens are dotted with stars. You're in a flurry. You can't distinguish one from another, yet you knew them all on the ground last night.

"You feel worried. If only you could see the ground. You sit down and grope for your dividers. You rescue them as they are disappearing down a crack. You note with dismay that your stock of well sharpened pencils has diminished. They've rolled off the table into the dark confines of the floor – lost forever.

"So and so town should be coming up soon, you estimate. You clamber up and peep through the window over the pilot's shoulder. He's just sitting there muffled up in his flying suit watching his instruments. Ahead on the horizon appears a dual glare. Yes, there's the town. Yes, of course it is, you tell yourself hopefully. The flame of confidence within you kindles. Yes, you're dead on track. It is not so bad after all, this night flying – perhaps ...

"Time passes by. Pieces of paper, books, broken stubs of pencil begin to clutter up your table. The intercom crackles. The pilot asks what time we'll arrive at town B. You jumble among the rubbish on your table and grab your 'mike'. 'Twenty-two fifty', you tell him. You glance at your watch. It is 2249. You inform the pilot we should be there, almost.

"There's a stunned silence. 'What?' echoes over the 'phones. Your heart edges its way up into your mouth. There's no town to be seen – nothing but darkness. A cold feeling comes over your heart. Visions of bailing out flash past. You catch a glimpse of the wireless operator. He is sound asleep over his table. Something inside you says, 'Poor chap! He doesn't know he is lost'.

Anson VH-AZX (ex LT737) at Bankstown (top) in 1964, two years after all Ansons were grounded in Australia. Avro Nineteen VH-RCC (bottom) was built postwar as a civil Anson and briefly operated in Australia between 1962 and 1964. (Eric Allen/Robert Wiseman)

"The pilot says presently: 'There's a town out to starboard. I think that is the one we're after'. You breathe easier, praying that it is. The Great Navigator lends you a hand. It is the town.

"Hours slip by. You see the welcome flare path rushing up to meet you. You're home. You got back anyway ..."

Anson Disposals

The Anson's career with the RAAF effectively ended shortly after hostilities ceased in 1945. By the end of the year few units still operated 'Faithful Annie' as no longer needed training organisations closed their doors. Some flew on for a few years, and there were the two Mk.XIXs which arrived in

1947 for use at the Woomera Rocket Range and remained in service until 1954/55, but by 1946 large numbers of Ansons were parked at locations in all states, awaiting disposal.

Unlike combat types, former military Ansons had a potential market for sale to civilian purchasers and after a survey was conducted for the retention of 80 good aircraft for postwar RAAF use, more than 600 others were offered for disposal through the newly formed Commonwealth Disposals Commission for as little as £250 ($500) each or £150 ($300) each for purchases of ten or more at a time. More than 180 were quickly sold under these circumstances in 1946, most of them ferried to civil aerodromes for conversion to civil specifications or resale.

Remaining Ansons passed to the Department of Aircraft Production for disposal on an 'as is, where is' basis. As these aircraft were not considered to be airworthy, they usually had their wings hacked off to ensure no attempt was made to fly them away. As was the case with many aircraft types, farmers were predominant among the buyers, using the fuselages for sheds and the various components for other useful purposes. Cheetah engines were also disposed of with prices starting at around £25 ($50 each) and reducing with quantity.

Private enterprise quickly entered the scene with the formation of the Aircraft Disposals Co (ADC) which bought 42 Ansons in 1946-47 of which 37 were eventually placed on the Australian civil register. ADC

The only airworthy Anson in Australia in 1992 was Terry Brain's VH-BAF (MH120), a hybrid combining an Anson I fuselage with the metal wings of the former RAAF Anson XIX VM375. These photographs were taken in the late 1960s at Parafield SA. (R J Wiseman)

Not a former RAAF Anson but a British one, VH-RCC (ex G-AHXK) was a civilian Avro Nineteen which was brought to Australia for Nicholas Air Charter in 1962. It ended its days on Parafield's fire dump. (via Bob Livingstone)

converted the aircraft to a more suitable civil specification by installing eight passenger seats, long range fuel tanks, baggage lockers, electric starters, propeller spinners, smooth engine cowlings, radio, new paint and reworking the original side glazing to produce airliner type individual windows.

ADC's customers included Guinea Air Traders, New England Airways, Consolidated Press, the Vacuum Oil Co and Thiess Brothers plus other companies associated with ADC and even overseas customers.

Early customers for Ansons sold by the Commonwealth Disposals Commission included the NSW Police Department (W2145/VH-AQV) in May 1946 and W2260/VH-AXC for the Royal Flying Doctor Service.

It is not the intention of this book to cover postwar Anson civil operations in detail, but to mention some of the operators who flew the aircraft in the late 1940s and 1950s gives some indication of its importance in the development of Australian civil aviation in those years – Adastra Airways, Airlines WA, Brain & Brown Airfreighters, Butler Air Transport, East West Airlines, Flinders Island Airways, Guinea Air Traders, MacRobertson Miller Aviation, New England Airways, Woods Airways and Papuan Air Transport, to name a few. Other operators of interest include Joh (later Sir Joh) Bjelke-Petersen, the former Queensland premier who used an Anson for agricultural work and the CSIRO (rainmaking experiments).

Some 150 Ansons eventually carried Australian civil registration markings.

The Anson I's glued wooden wing and tailplane construction brought its use to an end in July 1962. A series of accidents involving other types of similar construction forced the Australian Department of Civil Aviation to introduce restrictions on Anson I

operations in July 1961 and from January 1962 overwater flights and the carrying of passengers was banned. Then it was announced that from 1 July 1962 Anson Is would have their Certificates of Airworthiness cancelled, on safety grounds revolving around the Anson's glued wing joints and its poor single engine performance.

To commemorate the occasion, three Ansons belonging to Brain and Brown Airfreighters and Flinders Island Airways flew over Melbourne in formation: VH-FIA/AW965, VH-FIC/AW658, VH-BSF/W1954). VH-BEL/W2121 was the last to fly, its C of A extended to 4 September 1962 in order to complete a survey contract in Western Australia.

In 1992, several Ansons were in various stages of restoration in Australia and just one is airworthy, Brain and Brown's modified Mk.I VH-BAF (ex VH-BLP/MH120). This

Anson's specification came about in 1962 in an attempt to sidestep the grounding order by mating a metal wing from the former RAAF Mk.XIX VM375 to the fuselage, along with Cheetah XV engines and hydraulically operated flaps and undercarriage.

The company had plans to convert other Ansons to the same specification but a market did not exist for them and the idea foundered. Despite this, VH-BAF earned its keep for another ten years and since then has been flown by its owner, Terry Brain, as a private aircraft, appearing at air shows from time to time.

At the time of writing, this aircraft was for sale. Hopefully it will remain not only airworthy but also in Australia as a reminder of an extremely important aircraft in the RAAF's history, and the most numerous of the many types the RAAF has operated over the years.

The end of the road – Syd Marshall's Ansons grounded at Bankstown in 1962. (Peter Gillies)

RAAF AVRO ANSONS

Abbreviations: u/c – undercarriage; soc – struck off charge; t/o – takeoff; GG – Governor General; cvtd – converted.

FIRST ORDER
All Anson Mk.I

RAAF No	RAF No	Deliv	Disposal/Remarks
A4-1	K6212	11/36	soc 08/47
A4-2	K6213	12/36	scrapped 11/45
A4-3	K6214	12/36	scrapped 10/44
A4-4	K6214	01/37	crashed near Eildon Weir Vic 05/40
A4-5	K6215	01/37	crashed Glenbrook NSW 01/41
A4-6	K6217	01/37	crashed Mallala SA 02/42, collision with A4-31
A4-7	K6218	01/37	soc 07/47
A4-8	K6219	01/37	crashed McGrath's Hill NSW 10/38
A4-9	K6220	01/37	cvtd instructional airframe 02/45
A4-10	K6221	01/37	soc 10/47
A4-11	K6222	01/37	crashed into Hobson's Bay Vic 05/39
A4-12	K6223	01/37	scrapped 11/44
A4-13	K8792	08/37	soc 02/47
A4-14	K8793	08/37	soc 05/47
A4-15	K8794	08/37	forced landing into ditch King Island 09/38
A4-16	K8795	08/37	soc 02/47
A4-17	K8796	08/37	instructional airframe 06/40 after accident
A4-18	K8797	08/37	soc 05/47
A4-19	K8798	09/37	soc 02/47
A4-20	K8799	09/37	crashed near Ballina NSW 05/44
A4-21	K8800	09/37	instructional airframe 09/44
A4-22	K8801	09/37	soc 05/48
A4-23	K8802	09/37	soc 07/47
A4-24	K8803	09/37	soc 02/47
A4-25	K8804	09/37	soc 10/47
A4-26	K8805	09/37	soc 08/47
A4-27	K8806	10/37	crashed Green Hills bomb range Liverpool NSW 05/38
A4-28	K8807	10/37	scrapped 04/46
A4-29	K8808	10/37	crashed in fog Arthur's Seat Vic 08/38
A4-30	K8809	10/37	sold 07/46, became VH-BFJ
A4-31	K8810	10/37	collided with A4-6 and crashed Mallala SA 02/42
A4-32	K8811	10/37	crashed Riverstone NSW 04/39
A4-33	K8812	10/37	scrapped 01/45
A4-34	K8840	10/37	instructional airframe 08/44
A4-35	K8841	10/37	crashed near West Maitland NSW 01/40
A4-36	K8842	11/37	instructional airframe 08/44
A4-37	K8843	11/37	soc 08/47
A4-38	K8844	11/37	soc 02/47
A4-39	L7913	08/38	scrapped 11/45
A4-40	L7914	08/38	soc 02/47
A4-41	L7915	08/38	soc 02/47
A4-42	L7916	08/38	scrapped 02/46
A4-43	L7917	08/38	scrapped 10/44
A4-44	L7918	08/38	sold 11/46, became VH-BFK
A4-45	L7919	08/38	crashed on t/o near Townsville Qld 06/44
A4-46	L7920	08/38	hit on ground by landing N4936 Mt Gambier SA 05/42
A4-47	L7921	09/38	soc 02/47
A4-48	L7922	09/38	instructional airframe 02/45

SECOND ORDER
All Anson Mk.I, retained RAF serials

Serial	Deliv	Disposal/Remarks
L9161	12/38	scrapped 07/45
L9162	12/38	piggy back landing with N4876 Brocklesbury NSW 09/40, became instructional airframe
L9163	12/38	landing accident Point Cook Vic 04/40
N1330	11/38	soc 05/47
N1331	11/38	scrapped 07/44
N1332	11/38	instructional airframe 01/45
N1333	12/38	soc 02/47

Serial	Deliv	Disposal/Remarks
N1334	12/38	soc 07/47
N1335	12/38	crashed near Young NSW 06/43
N1336	12/38	forced landing Lake King Vic 03/45
N4868	12/38	landing accident 09/44
N4870	12/38	soc 02/47
N4873	12/38	sold 12/46, became VH-BFL
N4876	12/38	soc 10/47
N4879	01/39	scrapped 02/46
N4883	01/39	soc 02/48
N4887	01/39	crashed near Richmond NSW 12/39
N4891	03/39	soc 02/47
N4895	01/39	soc 02/47
N4899	03/39	scrapped 11/43
N4904	02/39	sold 02/47, became VH-BBN
N4908	05/39	soc 02/48
N4912	02/39	soc 05/47
N4916	03/39	soc 02/47
N4918	02/39	soc 05/47
N4920	03/39	crashed near Morwell Vic 02/45
N4921	03/39	soc 02/48
N4926	03/39	scrapped 09/43
N4931	03/39	scrapped 07/44
N4936	03/39	sold 07/46, became VH-ARK
N4941	03/39	soc 02/47
N4946	03/39	storm damage Benalla Vic 02/46, scrapped
N4955	04/39	soc 05/47
N4960	04/39	soc 08/47
N4965	04/39	soc 08/47
N4970	04/39	wheels up landing Plank Point SA 06/43
N4977	04/39	soc 03/47
N4984	04/39	soc 07/47
N4996	04/39	crashed on approach Kojarena WA 07/43
N5003	04/39	scrapped 11/43

EATS ANSONS – SUMMARY OF SERIAL NUMBERS
All Anson Mk.I, retained RAF serials

K8713

N5122 N9616 N9775 N9902 N9953 N9954 N9981

R3334 R3337 R3339 R3342 R3378 R3453 R3455 R3456 R3457 R3474 R3475 R3512 R3516 R3518 R3520 R3521 R3524 R3525 R3528 R3529 R3530 R3531 R3532 R3537 R3539 R3540 R3541 R3542 R3543 R3544 R3545 R3548 R3549 R3550 R3551 R3552 R3553 R3554 R3556 R3557 R3558 R3559 R3560 R3561 R3581 R3582 R3583 R9743 R9883 R9884 R9885 R9886 R9887 R9888 R9894 R9896 R9897 R9898 R9899 R9928 R9935 R9936

W1521 W1522 W1529 W1530 W1531 W1532 W1533 W1534 W1535 W1537 W1538 W1539 W1540 W1544 W1545 W1546 W1547 W1559 W1560 W1580 W1584 W1585 W1587 W1588 W1589 W1599 W1601 W1604 W1605 W1608 W1609 W1655 W1657 W1658 W1663 W1664 W1717 W1718 W1719 W1720 W1756 W1757 W1938 W1939 W1940 W1941 W1943 W1945 W1948 W1949 W1950 W1952 W1953 W1954 W1955 W1958 W1959 W1960 W1961 W1964 W1965 W1966 W1970 W1971 W1990 W1991 W1994 W1995 W2000 W2001 W2015 W2020 W2022 W2023 W2037 W2038 W2039 W2040 W2041 W2042 W2043 W2044 W2045 W2046 W2047 W2048 W2050 W2051 W2052 W2053 W2054 W2058 W2062 W2065 W2067 W2068 W2070 W2072 W2078 W2080 W2083 W2084 W2088 W2091 W2092 W2093 W2094 W2095 W2096 W2097 W2098 W2099 W2109 W2110 W2111 W2112 W2114 W2116 W2117 W2121 W2124 W2129 W2131 W2132 W2133 W2135 W2141 W2145 W2146 W2148 W2149 W2150 W2151 W2152 W2153 W2156 W2157 W2158 W2164 W2165 W2172 W2181 W2188 W2211 W2221 W2231 W2239 W2240 W2244 W2253 W2254 W2255 W2256 W2257 W2260 W2261 W2262 W2265 W2267 W2270 W2271 W2273 W2274 W2275 W2276 W2277 W2278 W2364 W2365 W2366 W2367 W2368 W2369 W2370 W2372 W2373 W2374 W2375 W2376 W2377 W2378 W2434 W2435 W2443 W2448 W2451 W2472 W2473 W2481 W2483 W2486 W2488 W2493 W2494 W2495 W2501 W2508 W2510 W2522 W2524 W2529 W2530 W2540 W2542 W2556 W2557 W2558 W2563 W2564 W2565 W2568 W2569 W2570 W2574 W2575 W2579 W2582 W2586 W2589 W2591 W2598 W2599 W2616 W2618 W2619 W2620 W2638 W2639 W2655 W2657 W2659 W2660

AW451 AW483 AW484 AW485 AW486 AW518 AW519 AW593 AW618 AW658
AW659 AW660 AW661 AW664 AW665 AW666 AW667 AW668 AW669 AW674
AW675 AW676 AW677 AW678 AW679 AW680 AW681 AW682 AW683 AW751
AW796 AW797 AW798 AW799 AW800 AW801 AW845 AW846 AW847 AW848
AW849 AW864 AW865 AW866 AW867 AW868 AW872 AW873 AW874 AW875
AW877 AW878 AW879 AW880 AW902 AW903 AW904 AW905 AW906 AW907
AW908 AW913 AW914 AW915 AW917 AW918 AW941 AW963 AW965 AW967

AX113 AX117 AX120 AX121 AX123 AX124 AX126 AX127 AX147 AX148 AX220
AX223 AX224 AX225 AX236 AX237 AX238 AX240 AX241 AX249 AX250 AX251
AX252 AX261 AX262 AX263 AX264 AX265 AX266 AX267 AX280 AX281 AX282
AX285 AX286 AX289 AX299 AX302 AX303 AX305 AX344 AX350 AX354 AX355
AX416 AX417 AX420 AX421 AX424 AX425 AX438 AX439 AX441 AX442 AX443
AX466 AX467 AX468 AX470 AX471 AX505 AX506 AX509 AX510 AX576 AX577
AX613 AX614 AX616 AX617 AX618 AX619 AX630 AX632 AX633 AX634 AX642
AX643 AX655 AX656

DG696 DG697 DG698 DG725 DG726 DG727 DG728 DG729 DG730 DG731
DG732 DG733 DG734 DG735 DG750 DG751 DG753 DG768 DG824 DG826
DG827 DG837 DG838 DG842 DG843 DG860 DG865 DG866 DG867 DG868
DG869 DG870 DG871 DG876 DG880 DG895 DG896 DG900 DG901 DG907
DG908 DG911 DG912 DG913 DG914 DG919 DG925 DG927 DG933 DG934
DG935 DG936 DG940 DG941

DJ113 DJ115 DJ118 DJ121 DJ138 DJ141 DJ162 DJ164 DJ165 DJ166 DJ171
DJ172 DJ173 DJ175 DJ176 DJ177 DJ188 DJ213 DJ214 DJ215 DJ223 DJ224
DJ225 DJ226 DJ227 DJ228 DJ231 DJ232 DJ233 DJ234 DJ235 DJ236 DJ237
DJ245 DJ246 DJ287 DJ288 DJ290 DJ291 DJ320 DJ321 DJ322 DJ323 DJ324
DJ325 DJ326 DJ327 DJ330 DJ336 DJ339 DJ340 DJ349 DJ350 DJ351 DJ352
DJ353 DJ354 DJ355 DJ386 DJ387 DJ416 DJ417 DJ430 DJ431 DJ437 DJ445
DJ446 DJ447 DJ448 DJ459 DJ460 DJ474 DJ475 DJ476 DJ497 DJ498 DJ503
DJ504 DJ505 DJ506 DJ507 DJ508 DJ514 DJ515 DJ516 DJ549

EF839 EF858 EF917 EF918 EF919 EF920 EF921 EF922 EF932 EF924 EF954
EF955 EF960 EF961 EF962 EF977 EF989

EG127 EG128 EG236 EG319 EG367 EG392 EG415 EG417 EG418 EG421
EG422 EG425 EG426 EG430 EG446 EG465 EG466 EG473 EG474 EG487
EG489 EG494 EG503 EG504 EG530 EG531 EG533 EG534 EG535 EG552
EG556 EG591 EG701 EG702

LT132 LT134 LT159 LT178 LT181 LT187 LT195 LT196 LT198 LT200 LT202
LT254 LT293 LT294 LT296 LT428 LT445 LT577 LT587 LT708 LT710 LT711
LT712 LT714 LT715 LT726 LT732 LT733 LT734 LT735 LT736 LT737 LT773
LT779 LT780 LT781 LT782 LT783 LT784 LT792 LT793 LT929 LT930 LT931
LT932 LT956 LT996 LT997 LT998 LT999

LV122 LV123 LV128 LV129 LV130 LV131 LV154 LV155 LV156 LV157 LV203
LV204 LV205 LV206 LV207 LV210 LV211 LV212 LV262 LV263 LV264 LV265
LV281 LV284 LV285 LV286 LV287 LV288 LV289 LV293 LV294 LV295 LV296
LV321

MG120 MG122 MG123 MG124 MG125 MG128 MG129 MG130 MG141 MG142
MG143 MG161 MG162 MG163 MG165 MG165 MG166 MG168 MG169 MG172
MG173 MG174 MG177 MG178 MG179 MG180 MG187 MG188 MG189 MG190
MG191 MG193 MG194 MG195 MG196 MG197 MG214 MG215 MG216 MG217
MG222 MG223 MG224 MG225 MG226 MG229 MG230 MG231 MG232 MG233
MG255 MG256 MG270 MG271 MG272 MG273 MG274 MG275 MG279 MG280
MG281 MG304 MG306 MG307 MG308 MG309 MG310 MG342 MG343 MG344
MG345 MG346 MG349 MG381 MG388 MG389 MG390 MG391 MG392 MG422
MG423 MG436 MG447 MG448 MG449 MG450 MG452 MG453 MG454 MG456
MG457 MG520 MG521 MG522 MG526 MG527 MG528 MG530 MG531 MG654
MG655 MG656 MG686 MG722 MG723 MG724 MG727 MG728 MG729 MG732
MG733 MG734 MG735 MG757 MG770 MG773 MG774 MG775 MG778 MG779
MG780 MG795 MG796 MG800 MG805 MG813 MG836 MG838 MG841 MG842
MG843 MG845 MG846 MG847 MG849 MG850 MG851 MG853 MG867 MG868
MG869 MG871 MG872 MG873 MG888 MG889 MG897 MG898 MG900 MG917
MG919 MG921 MG922 MG923 MG925 MG926 MG927 MG971 MG973 MG974
MG975 MG977 MG978 MG979 MG982 MG983 MG987 MG988 MG989 MG992
MG993

MH114 MH115 MH116 MH120 MH121 MH122 MH126 MH127 MH128 MH131
MH132 MH135 MH149 MH150 MH151 MH177 MH178 MH179 MH180 MH218
MH219 MH220 MH222 MH223 MH224 MH226 MH227
NK153

Others

NL153 (Mk.XII) del 01/45 for GG's Flight; sold 02/53, became VH-PDC
VM374 (Mk.XIX) del 11/47; u/c up crash landing Port Lincoln SA 12/54
VM375 (Mk.XIX) del 11/47; sold 03/57, became VH-BIX

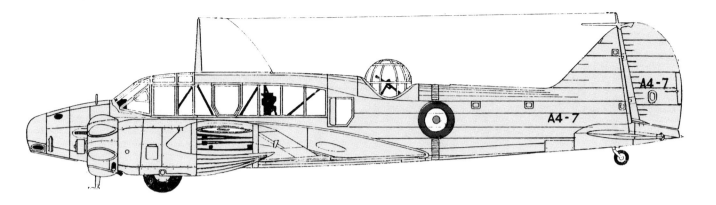

Anson MkI A4-7 of No 21 Sqn, 1939
Silver overall with medium blue fuselage bands and black serials.

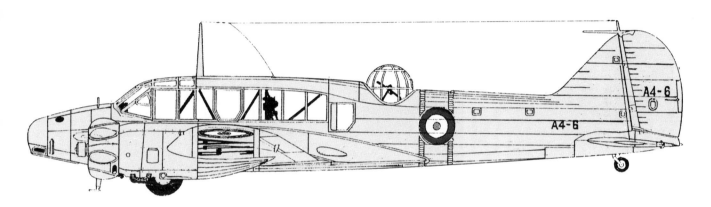

Anson MkI A4-6 of No 22 Sqn, 1939
Silver overall with medium blue fuselage band and black serials.

Anson MkI A4-31/F of No 6 Sqn, 1940
Dark green and dark earth and night (black) undersurface. Light grey code and serial.

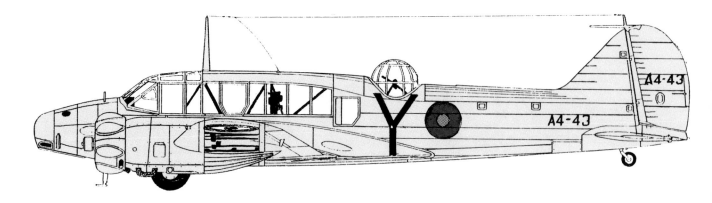

Anson MkI A4-43/Y of No 1 Communication Flight, 1941
Silver overall with black code and serial.

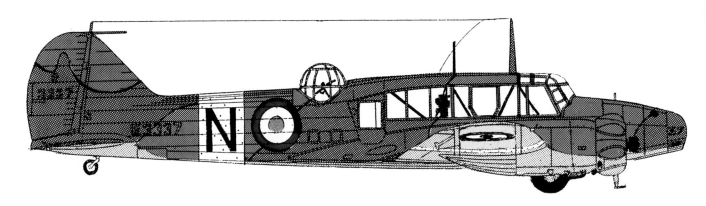

Anson MkI R3337/N of No 13 Sqn, 1941
Dark green and dark earth upper surface with sky blue undersurface. Yellow band around fuselage and wings. Black code and light grey serial. White 37 on nose.

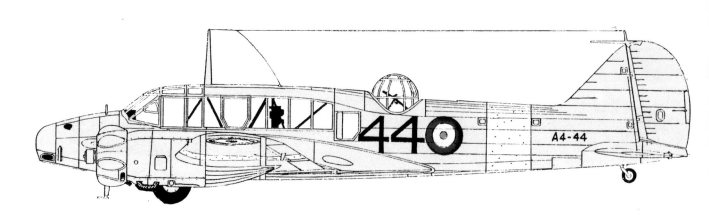

Anson MkI A4-44, 1941
Silver overall with yellow fuselage and wing bands. Black 44 and serial.

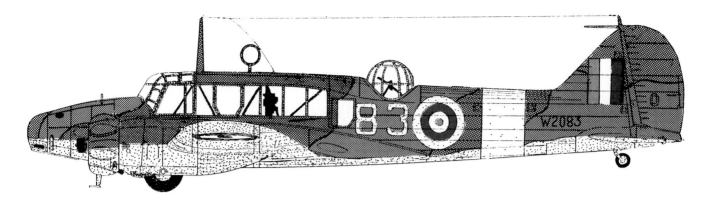

Anson MkI W2083 of No 3 EFTS, 1942
Dark green and dark earth upper surface with light grey undersurface. Yellow 83 and bands around fuselage and wings. Black serial.

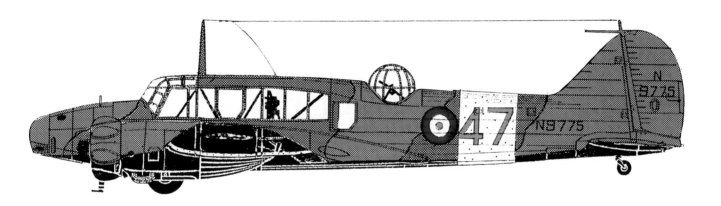

Anson MkI N9775/47
Dark green and dark earth upper surface with night undersurface. Yellow bands around fuselage and wings with red 47 and black serial. No roundels on upperwing surfaces.

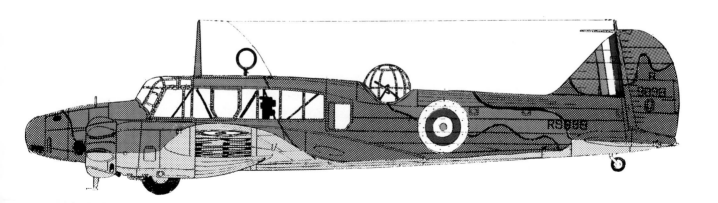

Anson MkI R9898
Dark green and dark earth upper surface with sky blue undersurface. Black serial.

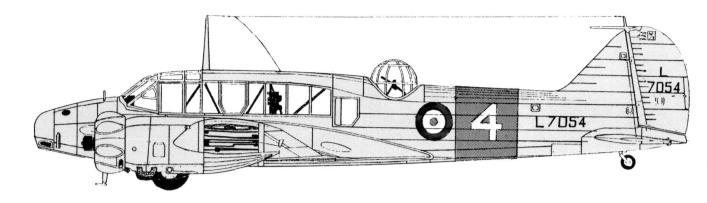

Anson MkI L7054
Silver overall with red fuselage band and white 47. Black serials.

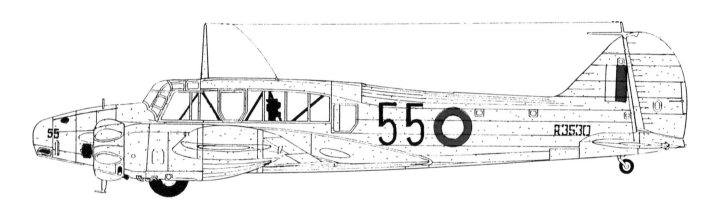

Anson MkI R3530/55 of No 6 SFTS, 1945
Yellow overall with black 55 and serial. White fin tip.

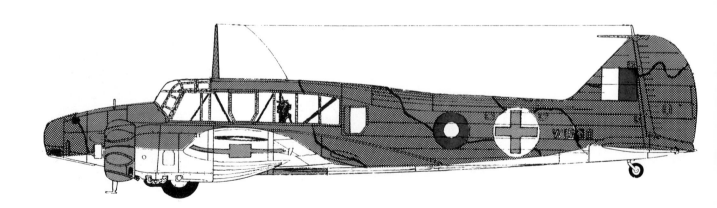

Anson MkI W1530 of No 2 AAU, 1945
Dark green and dark earth upper surface with white undersurface, under wings and fuselage and light grey serial. Red cross on white disc. Red lower half of engine cowling. Red cross under wings.

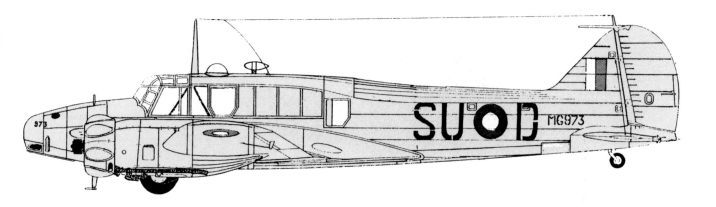

Anson MkI M6973/SU-D of Survey Flight, 1946
Silver overall with black codes and serial.

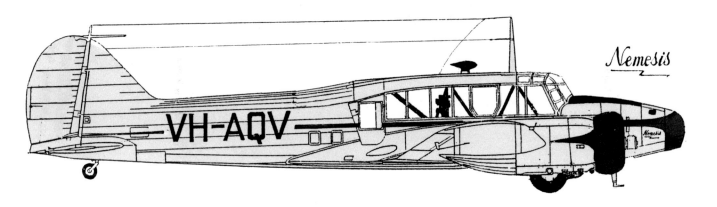

Anson MkI VH-AQV (ex-RAAF W1245) of NSW Police Aviation Section, 1945
Silver overall with black codes, anti-glare panel on nose and bullet fairing on top of fuselage. Dark blue fuselage flash and engine cowling. Name appears in dark blue on right side only.

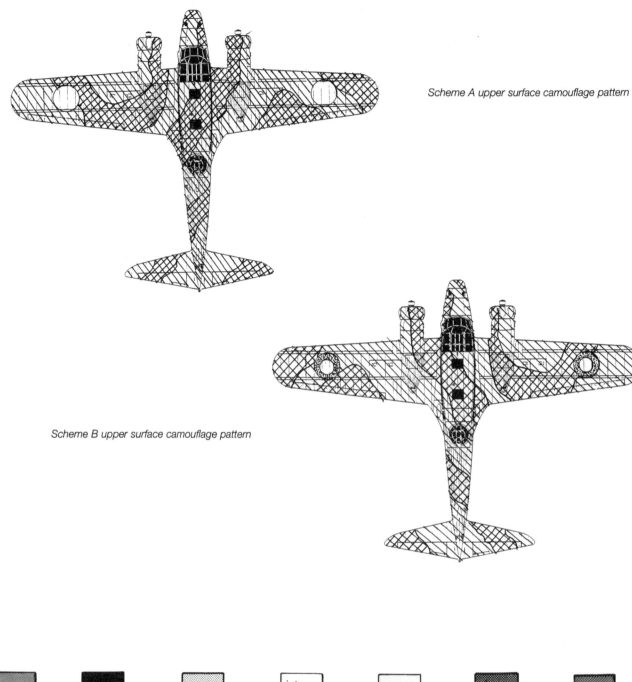

Scheme A upper surface camouflage pattern

Scheme B upper surface camouflage pattern

*Dark
Earth*

*Dark
Green*

Silver

Yellow

Sky Blue

*Insignia
Blue*

*Insignia
Red*

LOCKHEED
HUDSON

A formation of RAAF Hudson Is (equivalent to the RAAF's Mk.IV) from No 23 Squadron shortly after delivery in 1940. The RAAF received a total of 247 Hudsons, the early batches of which were diverted from British orders.

LOCKHEED HUDSON

There are several American aircraft manufacturers who owe a substantial proportion of their wartime and postwar prosperity to the unsettling events in Europe during the 1930s – the rise of Nazi Germany and the realisation by the British in the latter part of the decade that war was almost inevitable.

It was against this background that Britain's need to re-arm – and quickly – was established. It became obvious that local resources would not be able to provide the number and variety of aircraft required, resulting in 1938 in the establishment of the British Purchasing Commission (BPC) whose role it was to acquire foreign aircraft for the Royal Air Force and Royal Navy, principally from the United States of America.

Orders placed by the BPC were directly responsible for the beginnings of many development programmes in the USA, and it was in British service that most of these aircraft began their operational careers.

Among them are several famous types, including the Liberator, Wildcat, Mustang and the Lockheed Hudson. In British hands, the 'general reconnaissance' Hudson became the first American aircraft to see action in World War II.

The Hudson was one of those largely unsung types of aircraft which served the Allies faithfully and well during the war on most fronts and with little fanfare. The air forces of Britain, Canada, the United States, New Zealand, the Nertherlands, China, Brazil and of course Australia operated the type in a variety of roles ranging from the original maritime patrol through to trainer, transport, bomber and numerous other general roles.

Derived from the Lockheed Model 14 Super Electra 12 passenger transport, the Model 14L/214/414 Hudson first flew in December 1938 and by the time production ended in mid 1943, a total of 2,941 examples had been built, most of which served

with the Royal Air Force and Commonwealth countries.

The Royal Australian Air Force received 247 Hudsons between January 1940 and May 1942 in several versions. These served with 12 squadrons in the Australia/South West Pacific areas and further British aircraft served with No 459 (RAAF) Squadron in the Mediterranean theatre of operations.

The Lockheed Twins

The evolution of the Hudson began in the early 1930s when the Lockheed company realised it needed a modern replacement for its successful Vega and Orion single engined commercial aircraft. At the time, the Great Depression was well established and with new commercial orders thin on the ground and military orders from the isolationist US government equally difficult to come by, American aircraft manufacturers generally were finding the going tough. New, 'sellable' products were essential for

A Wright Cyclone powered Hudson I from the first production batch, built for the RAF in 1939. Britain's 1938 order for 250 Hudsons was by far the largest Lockheed had received to that point. (Lockheed)

the survival of any manufacturer, and it was with this in mind that Lockheed began development of the first of a series of all metal, retractable undercarriage twin engined light transport aircraft distinguished by their low wing, twin tail design.

The first of them was the L.10 Electra, a 10 passenger aircraft powered by either Pratt & Whitney or Wright radial engines of 400-450 horsepower and capable of the then high cruising speed of up to 195mph (314km/h).

The L.10 first flew in February 1934 (after the larger Douglas DC-1/2 and Boeing 247) and entered service with Northwest Airlines in August of the same year. The design was successful, with 148 being manufactured over the next seven years. Of these, the vast majority went into commercial service in the USA and elsewhere, flying with airlines such as Pan Ameri.a Cubana, Braniff, Lan-Chile and Trans Canada. Two Australian operators, Ansett and Guinea Airways, also bought Electras. A handful was operated by the US military.

Of interest is the fact that while American manufacturers like Douglas, Lockheed and Boeing were building and selling modern metal monoplane airliners from the mid and late 1930s, the ish – with one or two

Lockheed's twin tail predecessors to the Hudson, the ten passenger L.10 Electra (top) of 1934 and the six passenger L.12 'Electra Junior' (bottom) of 1936. Both were of all metal construction with retractable undercarriage and offered high performance for their day. (Lockheed/Stewart Wilson)

exceptions – were still making wooden fixed undercarriage biplanes such as the de Havilland Dragon Rapide and DH.86.

The L.10 Electra was followed in 1936 by a similar but smaller aircraft intended for feeder line use, the six passenger L.12, still named Electra. Being smaller and lighter than the L.10 but similarly powered, the L.12 was faster, offering a cruising speed of more than 200mph (321km/h). Production amounted to 114 aircraft, many of which were impressed into US military service as the Army Air Force's C-40 and the Navy's JO series. Australia also saw the L.12 before the war, serving with Guinea Airways and the Zinc Corporation for VIP duties and operated by the company's private airline, Associated Airlines. More L.12s flew with Associated after the war.

The next step in the Lockheed twins series was the L.14, a larger aircraft than its predecessors designed to carry 12 passengers but at much higher speeds and over longer ranges than before. Dubbed 'Super Electra' by its manufacturer, the L.14 was powered by two 750hp Pratt & Whitney Hornet or 760/820hp Wright Cyclone radial engines which enabled it to cruise at up to 240mph (386km/h) and over a maximum range (at reduced cruising speed) of some 2,000 miles (3,218km). The L.14's maximum takeoff weight of 17,500lb (7,938kg) was about 75% greater than that of the L.10 and twice that of the L.12.

Although sharing a similar configuration to the smaller aircraft (including the now characteristic Lockheed twin tails), the L.14 was a substantially different aircraft with a deep fuselage section, a mid rather than low set wing and for the day innovative large Fowler flaps which markedly increased wing area when extended.

Of all metal construction, the L.14 fuselage comprised a monocoque fuselage of

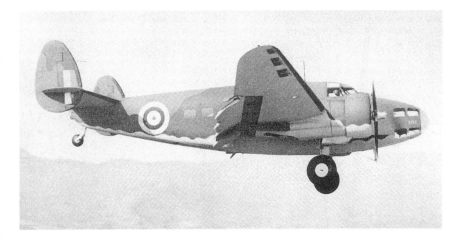

An early RAF Hudson I on short finals, displaying the distinctive and large Fowler flaps.

portly elliptical cross section with flush rivetted skinning, while the 65ft 6in (19.96m) span wing was of cantilever single spar design with stressed skin covering and fuel tanks built into the centre section. The hydraulically operated single wheel main undercarriage retracted rearwards into the engine nacelles and the tailwheel was fixed. When retracted, the main wheels projected slightly out of the nacelles, as had been the case in the earlier aircraft.

The first Super Electra flew in July 1937, by which time some 30 had already been ordered by airlines in the USA and overseas. Northwest was again the first to put the type into service, doing so in October 1937.

A well known customer was Howard Hughes, who in 1938 flew a Super Electra around the world in 3 days 19 hours and 4 minutes, while in the same year an Air Afrique aircraft set a new Paris to Algeria record of 3 hours 55 minutes. Another notable

flight was recorded in September 1938 when an L.14 was used to fly British Prime Minister Neville Chamberlain to Munich for his historic but ill-fated meeting with Adolf Hitler. Several L.14s saw service with Australian operators before the Pacific war began.

Lockheed built 112 Super Electras, but perhaps ironically, the greatest number was built under licence in Japan by Kawasaki and Tachikawa. Powered by 900hp Mitsubishi Ha-26-II engines, the Japanese aircraft were locally designated Ki-56 and 119 of them were manufactured by Kawasaki before the end of 1941 while several hundred others were built during the war years by Tachikawa without the benefit of a licence. Japan Airways had earlier purchased American built L.14s.

L.14 was very much the Hudson's immediate predecessor, the latter being in most

The Lockheed 14, immediate predecessor of the Hudson and the aircraft on which the latter was based. This example was delivered to Guinea Airways in 1938 but crashed at Katherine NT the following year.

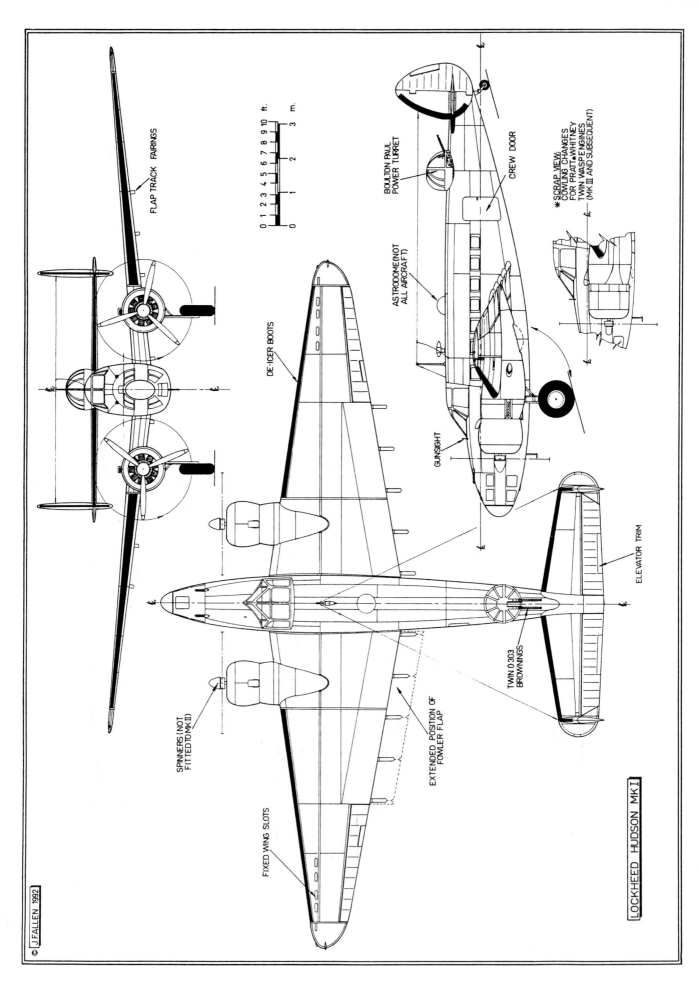

FLAP TRACK FAIRINGS

ft.
m.

DE-ICER BOOTS

BOULTON PAUL
POWER TURRET

ASTRODOME (NOT
ALL AIRCRAFT)

CREW DOOR

*SCRAP VIEW:
COWLING CHANGES
FOR PRATT & WHITNEY
TWIN WASP ENGINES
(MK III AND SUBSEQUENT)

GUNSIGHT

ELEVATOR TRIM

SPINNERS (NOT
FITTED TO MK II)

TWIN 0·303
BROWNINGS

EXTENDED POSITION OF
FOWLER FLAP

FIXED WING SLOTS

LOCKHEED HUDSON MK I

© J.FALLEN 1992

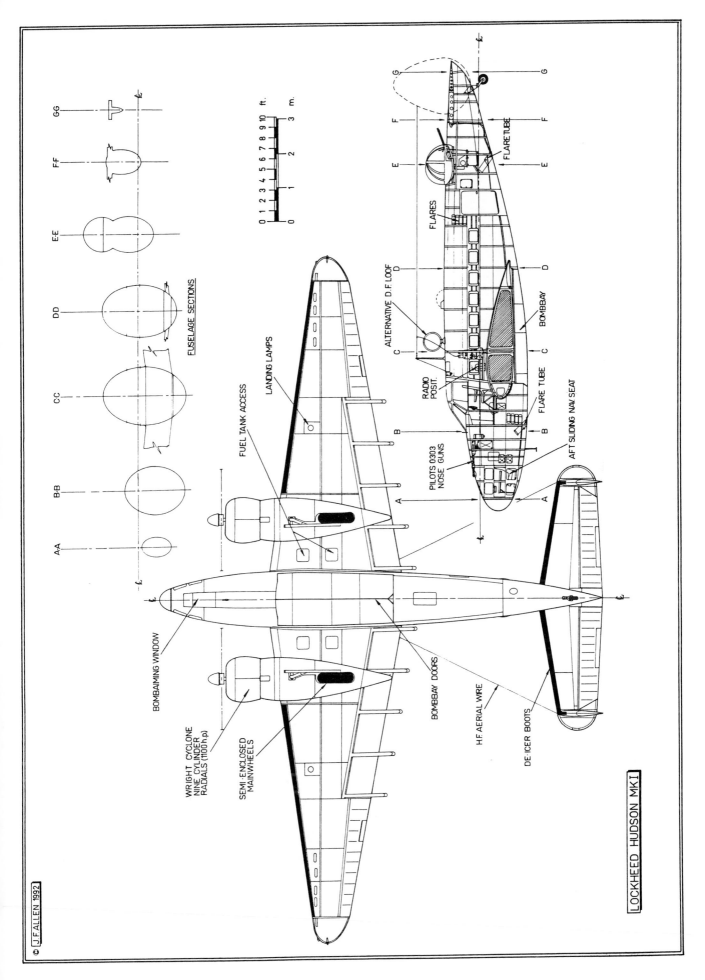

GG

FF

EE

DD

FUSELAGE SECTIONS

CC

BB

AA

ft.

m.

10
9
8
7
6
5
4
3
2
1
0

3

2

1

0

G

F

FLARE TUBE

E

FLARES

ALTERNATIVE D.F. LOOP

D

BOMBBAY

C

RADIO POSIT.

B

FLARE TUBE

AFT SLIDING NAV SEAT

A

PILOTS 0303 NOSE GUNS

LANDING LAMPS

FUEL TANK ACCESS

BOMBAIMING WINDOW

WRIGHT CYCLONE NINE CYLINDER RADIALS (1100 h.p.)

SEMI-ENCLOSED MAINWHEELS

BOMBBAY DOORS

H.F. AERIAL WIRE

DE-ICER BOOTS

LOCKHEED HUDSON MKI

© J.F.ALLEN 1992

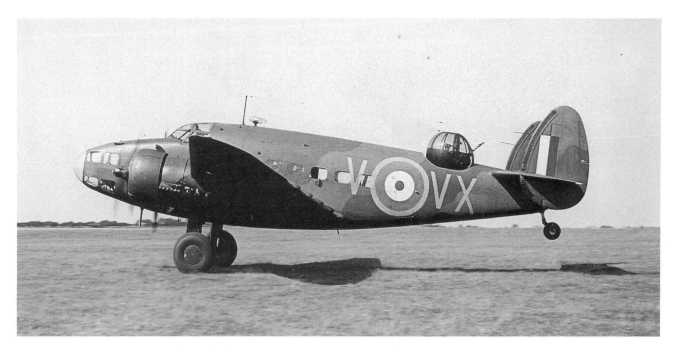

An RAF Hudson I about to leave the ground. This view shows to advantage the Hudson's portly fuselage and the dominant Boulton Paul dorsal turret. (via Neil Mackenzie)

ways simply a military version of the civil aircraft, developed with great haste at the request of the British. The result was Lockheed's first military aircraft and the ancestor of a long range of reconnaissance bombers with a predominately maritime bent.

From Super Electra to Hudson

When the British Purchasing Commission delegation visited the USA in April 1938 its immediate intention was to order training aircraft. Two types were required, a single

engined advanced type and a multi engined aircraft for navigation and pilot training. The first requirement was met by an initial order for 200 North American Harvards while the latter was eventually filled by the British Avro Anson rather than an American design.

At the time, Lockheed was not exactly flush with orders. Most contracts for its Models 10, 12 and even the quite new Model 14 had been filled and the company was looking for any work to keep its lines open. The Model 14 was considered by the

BPC as a possibility to fill the multi engined trainer requirement, while as far as the company was concerned, a bomber version of the Model 14 was the only remotely military aircraft it had to offer.

Work on the design of a bomber development of the L.14 had begun some months before the BPC's visit, so when Lockheed was told the British were coming to visit, a wooden mockup was rapidly constructed and given the company designation Model B14, the 'B' for 'bomber'.

Well worn Hudson IIIA BW450 of the Royal Canadian Air Force. The 'A' suffix to the designation meant the aircraft was supplied under the terms of Lend-Lease. (via Neil Mackenzie)

Hudsons for Britain await delivery and final assembly outside Lockheed's Burbank factory in 1939/40. Early examples were delivered directly to Britain by ship, but the USA's Neutrality Act of September 1939 meant they first had to be flown to the US/Canadian border, pulled across the border by mule and then despatched to Britain. (Lockheed)

Underside view of a Hudson I as it approaches to land. For their day, the area increasing Fowler flaps were considered innovative. (via Neil Mackenzie)

The B14 mockup created interest among the British visitors, not as a navigation trainer but as maritime reconnaissance bomber for the RAF's Coastal Command and a possible replacement for the Avro Anson.

The mockup showed a Model 14 with gun turrets in the nose and upper rear fuselage, a bomb bay capable of accommodating a load of 3,300lb (1,497kg) with the bombs stacked vertically, and a crew of four with the navigator's station located behind the bomb bay. The navigator also served as the radio operator and ventral gunner, firing an aft facing retractable machine gun in the lower fuselage.

The British were suitably impressed with the mockup and therefore what the real aircraft might offer, but suggested some changes, particularly of the interior arrangement. It was considered the navigator's position was too far away from the pilot and modifications were requested.

Lockheed responded quickly, modifying the mockup within 24 hours and presenting an interior redesign which moved the navigator forward to the nose area. This neces-

sitated the elimination of the nose turret, replacing it with two fixed guns.

Things then moved quickly, with Lockheed representatives travelling to London to finalise a purchase contract. In the meantime some further refinement of the design was undertaken including replacing the original 900hp Wright GR-1820-F62 Cyclone nine cylinder single row radial engines with a more powerful variant of the same powerplant, the 1,100hp GR-1820-G102A. In addition, a Boulton Paul two gun dorsal turret replaced the original single gun American unit, guns were standardised to the normal British 0.303in calibre and the bomb load was reduced to 1,600lb (726kg) in a redesigned and more conventional underfloor bay. The normal bomb load comprised a mix of up to four 250 pounders and/or ten 100 pounders with the latter limited to six if four of the larger bombs were carried.

The standard crew of the proposed aircraft (now called Model B14L by its manufacturer) was set at four (pilot, bombardier/navigator, radio operator, gunner) while a fifth crewmember to operate the ventral gun would be added later.

Contracts for the British purchase of 200 Lockheed Model B14Ls were signed in June 1938 and included an option to purchase a further 50 aircraft. These numbers were subsequently substantially increased, Britain eventually purchasing more than 800 aircraft and receiving a further 1,170 under the terms of Lend-Lease.

The company designation Model B14L was changed to Model 214 for what would be named 'Hudson I' by the British, and some later marks were known as Model 414s. The aircraft was named after Henry Hudson, the 17th Century English navigator credited with the discovery of the Hudson River and Hudson Bay in Canada.

A Problem of Production

One of the terms of the purchase contract was that Lockheed should deliver 200 aircraft "and as many more up to a total of 250" by December 1939, just 18 months after the contract was signed. This presented large problems to the manufacturer as it had until then been producing relatively modest quantities of aircraft and was, as noted above, short of work, capital and

Hudson V AM562 of the RAF, from the last Hudson batch to be purchased outright by Britain before Lend-Lease was introduced. This variant was powered by Pratt & Whitney Twin Wasp engines, identifiable by their longer cowlings with cowl flaps at the rear. (via Neil Mackenzie)

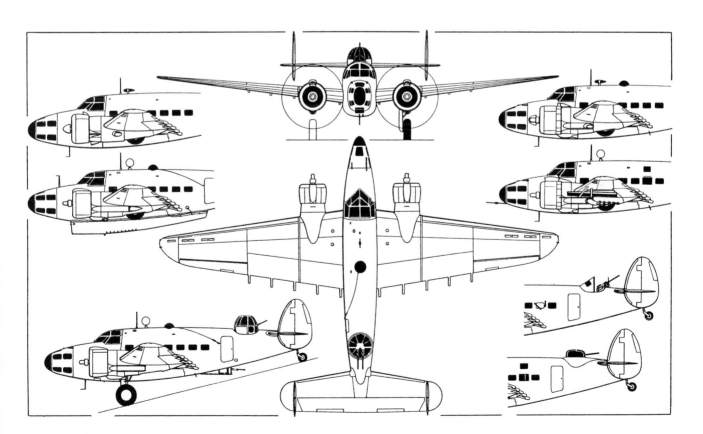

The main three view drawing depicts the Hudson IIIA; the A-29, A-29A and PBO-1 were similar. The forward fuselages (left) show the Mk.I (upper) and Mk.III with lifeboat (lower). The forward fuselages (right) show the Mk.IV (upper) and the Mk.VI in its anti shipping version. The rear fuselages (right) show the A-29 (upper) and AT-18 (lower).

Head on detail of an RAAF Hudson I showing the nose glazing and the Twin Wasp engines' cowling. (via Neil Mackenzie)

factory space when the British order – by far the largest won by Lockheed to that point – was placed.

Rapid expansion was therefore necessary, and to meet its obligations Lockheed borrowed $US1.25m, raised another $US3m through a stock issue, nearly trebled its workforce to some 7,000 during the course of 1939 and sub-contracted a healthy amount of parts assembly work to Rohr Industries due to a lack of floorspace at its own Burbank, California, factory. Despite this, the required production rate of about five Hudsons per week was going to be difficult to achieve but despite some early and minor delays Lockheed succeeded admirably and in fact delivered 250 Hudsons to the RAF nearly two months before the required date. Of those, 28 went to the Royal Canadian Air Force.

The first Hudson (RAF serial number N7205) recorded its maiden flight on 10 December 1938. Flight testing revealed no serious problems and by the end of January 1939 four aircraft had been completed and flown and deliveries were ready to begin. The first aircraft arrived in Britain by ship in February and the first examples to reach an operational unit (N7210 and N7212, the sixth and eighth aircraft) were delivered to No 224 Squadron at Thornaby, East Yorkshire, in May.

Most Hudsons delivered to Britain during 1939 were shipped across the Atlantic from New York after first having been flown across the USA from the factory. The passing of the USA's Neutrality Act in September 1939 (which banned US citizens from delivering arms to the by then fighting Europeans) created the need for alternative arrangements, and these were met by flying the Hudsons from California to a point on the US/Canadian border in North Dakota from where they were pulled across the border by mules after completion of the necessary paperwork.

The Hudsons of RAF Coastal Command were quickly into action when war with Germany was declared in September 1939, the American type providing a substantial increase in capability compared to the Ansons which it generally replaced. The addition of ASV (air-to-surface vessel) radar from early 1940 on some aircraft added to the capability.

Some actions in which RAF Hudsons were involved include the successful interception of a Dornier Do 18 flying boat over the North Sea by a 224 Squadron aircraft in early October 1939, numerous encounters with U-boats, the locating of the German prison ship *Altmark* in a Norwegian fjord in February 1940, attacking the battlecruiser *Scharnhorst* in June 1940 and again two years later when the ship, in company with the *Prinz Eugen* and *Gneisenau*, attempted to break out of Brest in the action now known as the 'Channel Dash'. In 1943, a Hudson recorded the first sinking of a U-boat using rocket projectiles, a feature

added to some RAF aircraft in that year. Four 60lb (27kg) rockets were fitted under each wing .

As the war progressed an ever growing number of roles was found for the Hudson including transport (up to 14 troops could be carried if the turret and other items of equipment were removed), meteorological reconnaissance, VIP transport and air-sea rescue, for which role an underfuselage airborne lifeboat could be carried. The Hudson's versatility ensured it remained in service throughout the war and for a time afterwards, even though production ended in 1943.

Hudson Variants

As the main customer for the Hudson throughout its production life, the Royal Air Force's variants represented the major changes to the aircraft's specification, although models peculiar to the US military were also produced. These are described below.

Production of the Hudson I reached 350 aircraft and was followed by a small number of Hudson IIs which were basically similar to the original version except for the fitting of constant-speed Hamilton Standard Hydromatic propellers in place of the original Hamilton two position units, an increase in maximum weight from 19,500lb (8,845kg) to 20,000lb (9,072kg), some structural strengthening and improvements to exterior finish.

Some good front end detail of RAAF Hudson III A16-172 with Wright Cyclone engines. On the original print the stencil 'US ARMY AIR CORPS A-29 SER 41-23608' can just be made out under the cockpit window. (via Neil Mackenzie)

An RAF Hudson VI on duty somewhere in the Middle East. Note the open cowl flaps behind the Pratt & Whitney engine. (via Neil Mackenzie)

A US Army AT-18A navigation trainer with Pratt & Whitney engines and no guns. Compared with the British and Commonwealth air forces, relatively few 'Hudsons' (the name was never adopted by the Americans) served with their country of manufacture. (Lockheed)

LOCKHEED HUDSON I and III

Powerplants: (I) Two Wright
GR-1820-G102A Cyclone nine cylinder single row air cooled radial engines with single speed mechanical supercharger each rated at 1,100hp for t/o and 900hp at 6,700ft. Three bladed Hamilton Standard two position propellers of 10ft 6in (3.20m) diameter.
(III) Two Wright GR-1820-G205A Cyclones with two speed superchargers each rated at 1,200hp for t/o and 900hp at 14,200ft. Three bladed Hamilton Standard Hydromatic constant-speed propellers of 10ft 6in (3.20m) diameter.
Fuel capacity (I/III) 536imp gal (2,437 l) in four wing centre section tanks.
Dimensions: (I/III) Wing span 65ft 6in (19.96m); length 44ft 3.75in (13.50m); height 10ft 10.5in (3.32m); wing area 551sq ft (51.18sq m); undercarriage track 15ft 4in (4.67m).
Weights: (I) Empty 12,100lb (5,488kg); max takeoff 19,500lb (8,845kg); max wing loading 35.39lb/sq ft; max power loading 8.86lb/hp.
(III) Empty 13,160lb (5,969kg); max takeoff 20,00lb (9,072kg); max wing loading 36.30lb/sq ft; max power loading 8.33lb/hp.
Armament: (I/III) Maximum bomb load 1,600lb (726kg) comprising four 250lb (113kg) and six 100lb (45kg) bombs; two fixed Browning 0.303in machine guns in upper nose with 500rpg; one optional Vickers 0.303in machine gun in retractable ventral hatch with 500 rounds; two optional Vickers 0.303in beam machine guns in rear fuselage with 500rpg; two Browning 0.303in machine guns in dorsal Boulton Paul turret with 1,000rpg.
Performance: (I) Max speed 222mph (357km/h) at 7,900ft; max cruise 191mph (307km/h) at 10,000ft; economical cruise 155mph (249km/h) at 10,000ft; time to 10,000 feet 10.0min; service ceiling 21,000ft (6,400m); range with max bomb load 925 miles (1,488km); range with max fuel 1,140 miles (1,835km) at 191mph (307km/h), 1,355 miles (2,180km) at 155mph (249km/h).
(III) Max speed 252mph (406km/h) at 15,000ft; max cruise 196mph (315km/h) at 10,000ft; economical cruise 155mph (249km/h) at 10,000ft; time to 10,000ft 8.8min; service ceiling 25,000ft (7,620m); range with max bomb load 780 miles (1,255km); range with max fuel 1,355 miles (2,180km) at 155mph.

The Hudson III represented a more substantial revision with the fitting of 1,200hp GR-1820-G205A Cyclone engines with two (instead of single) speed superchargers for improved performance at altitude, the ventral gun as a standard installation, fuselage flotation bags, additional emergency equipment including a dinghy incorporated in the jettisonable rear door and provision for the fitting of a 208imp gal (946 l) removable cabin fuel tank for ferrying.

The first 187 Hudson IIIs retained the previous standard fuel capacity of 536imp gal (2,437 l) in four wing centre section tanks but the subsequent 241 aircraft had additional wing tankage which increased the normal capacity to 856imp gal (3,891 l). These aircraft were designated the Hudson III (LR).

A different type of engine was the main difference between the Hudson III and IV, the latter carrying the company designation Model 414. The Wright Cyclones were replaced by 1,200hp Pratt & Whitney R-1830-SC3G Twin Wasp 14-cylinder two row radials fitted with single speed superchargers. Fuel capacity was as per the standard Hudson III and just 30 went to the RAF of which eight were diverted to Australia. Perhaps confusingly, the designation Hudson IV was allocated to aircraft ordered

The Lockheed Lodestar, an increased capacity development of the Model 14/Hudson initially built as a 14 passenger civil transport (top) but subsequently used by the US military (bottom) and its Allies as a general purpose transport and under various designations. (Lockheed)

One of 273 AT-18 gunnery trainers delivered to the USAAF with two 50-calibre Browning machine guns mounted in a Martin Dorsal turret. (Lockheed)

by the Royal Australian Air Force in 1939 but these aircraft were locally referred to as Mks I and II. This and other confusions will be discussed in the following chapter.

The Hudson V was also fitted with Twin Wasp engines, this time the R-1830-S3C4-G variant with two speed superchargers. Hamilton two-position propellers were also installed along with the extra fuel capacity of the Hudson III (LR) in 207 of the 409 aircraft delivered to the RAF.

The Hudson V was the final variant of the aircraft to be purchased outright by Britain – subsequent deliveries (from March 1941) coming under the arrangements put in place for Lend-Lease. Aircraft delivered under Lend-Lease acquired an 'A' suffix to their designations. The vast majority were initially Hudson IIIAs and then Hudson VAs. From late 1940 Hudsons were no longer shipped to Britain but fitted with cabin fuel tanks and flown across the Atlantic via

Gander, Newfoundland and Aldergrove in Northern Ireland.

The final variant for the RAF was the Hudson VI, a development of the Mk V with constant speed propellers and which could be converted to a troop carrier if the turret was removed. Britain received 450 examples.

Further development of the basic design during World War II resulted in the heavier and more powerful Ventura and Harpoon, the former also operated by the RAAF. (Defence PR)

American Hudsons

The name 'Hudson' was never adopted by the US military, but the aircraft received a string of designations for service with the USAAC/USAAF and US Navy and for the purposes of meeting the requirements of Lend-Lease, which dictated that aircraft being supplied to the Allies under those terms first had to be acquired by the USAAF or USN. In this case, the aircraft obviously required an American military designation.

The A-28 designation covered 52 Hudsons IVs supplied to the RAAF (see next chapter), A-28A applied to the RAF's Hudson V, the A-29 was the Hudson IIIA and the A-29A designation was given to aircraft delivered to the RAF, RAAF, RCAF, RNZAF and signified a convertible troop carrying interior. The A-29B was a photo-reconnaissance conversion of A-29 and A-29A aircraft retained by the USAAF.

The US military made little use of the Hudson compared with Britain and the Commonwealth, but several hundred aircraft served with it nevertheless. Of the A-29 production run of 616, 153 were retained by the USAAF and 20 went to the USN as PBO-1s. USAAF aircraft did not have the Boulton Paul turret fitted but an open dorsal gun position equipped with a single 50 calibre machine gun.

Versions built specifically for US requirements were the AT-18 gunnery trainer with two 'fifties' in a Martin dorsal turret while the AT-18A was a navigation trainer without guns. Both versions were usually powered by Pratt & Whitney engines and production amounted to 217 and 83, respectively.

The Lodestar

A direct development of the L.14/214/414/Hudson series was the L.18 Lodestar, initially built as a civil transport offering larger capacity (14 passengers) than the L.14 Super Electra. First flown in September 1939, the Lodestar combined the power-plants of the L.14 (P&W Hornets initially, Wright Cyclones later) with a fuselage 5ft 7in (1.71m) longer, a wing of similar span to that of the L.14 but of revised planform, and increased weights.

The design was subsequently adapted for military use and widely used by the USAAF as a general purpose transport, by the USN as a staff and command transport and also by the RAF, which had four squadrons operating in the Middle East for general and air ambulance duties. In military service the Lodestar could accommodate up to 18 passengers and the type operated under numerous designations, depending on whether the aircraft were converted or impressed civilian machines (C-56A to E, C-57B to D, C-59, C-60, C-66, C-111) or built specifically for the military (C-56, C-57, C-60A, US Navy R50). In RAF service the aircraft were designated Lodestar I (a civil model), IA and II, the latter pair equivalent to the USAAF's C-59 and C-60, respectively.

The Royal Australian Air Force acquired ten Lodestar IIs in 1943-44, using them until 1947.

The line of twin tailed Lockheed aircraft did not end with the Hudson and Lodestar. Further development was undertaken during the war, resulting in the heavier and more powerful Ventura patrol bomber (again originally developed to meet British requirements, this time for a Hudson replacement) and the Harpoon, which finally dispensed with the basic Hudson/Lodestar wing. The Ventura also saw service with the RAAF, 75 of them being delivered from 1943.

The Harpoon represented the end of the line for a remarkable series of aircraft, although for Lockheed, its wartime experience in building maritime patrol bombers for the Allies stood it in good stead for the years ahead and resulted in the Free World's two standard maritime/anti-submarine aircraft types, the Neptune and Orion.

HUDSONS FOR AUSTRALIA

The Munich crisis, the resultant realisation that modern aircraft were urgently required for the Royal Australian Air Force and doubts about the supply of aircraft from the United Kingdom were catalysts to the chain of events which saw the Lockheed Hudson general reconnaissance bomber enter service with the RAAF in early 1940.

As referred to in the Anson section of this book, there was considerable activity surrounding the choice of an Anson replacement in the second half of the 1930s, even though that aircraft had only recently entered service. The Bristol Blenheim had originally been chosen as the RAAF's new general reconnaissance bomber type, but its availability was under question. From there, the situation developed until it was finally decided to manufacture the Bristol Beaufort in Australia, the local production run eventually amounting to 700 aircraft between 1941 and 1944.

In the meantime, consideration was given to more readily available alternatives to tide the RAAF over until the Beaufort situation was resolved and aircraft became available. Among them was the Lockheed Hudson, which had first been suggested in early October 1938, still two months before the prototype had flown in the USA and five months after the type had been ordered in quantity for the RAF.

Hudsons Ordered

Things moved quickly in October 1938, helped by an increase in the RAAF budget. Initial negotiations were conducted with Lockheed's Australian agent, Brown & Dureau Ltd but the emphasis soon switched to dealings with the British Air Ministry which had already ordered the Hudson. It was considered to be in Australia's best interests if the aircraft were purchased in conjunction with that order.

These negotiations were of great historical significance, as they resulted in orders for the first American combat aircraft to serve with the RAAF.

The base price quoted to Australia was $US93,580 per aircraft, calculated on the British Air Ministry contract rate of $US84,470 plus $US5,200 for the redesign and structural alterations necessary for the airframe to accept the Pratt & Whitney Twin Wasp engines specified by the RAAF instead of the standard Wright Cyclones. The decision to install different engines was influenced by the rating of aviation fuel available in Australia and by the fact that the Commonwealth Aircraft Corporation had a licence to locally manufacture the Wasp, although no CAC built engines were in any event installed as original equipment on Australian Hudsons.

The balance of $US3,910 per aircraft was made up of the greater cost of the Twin Wasp over the Cyclone, the costs associated with a relatively small order and increases in the cost of some materials and the manufacturing process itself. Nevertheless, the price was queried by Australia, which indicated it expected a reduction in the base cost as it was considered the 50 aircraft being discussed were to be part of the British Air Ministry's order for 200 plus 50 options.

Nevertheless, authority was given to exceed the quoted base cost if necessary as it included propeller anti-icing and the necessary fittings for airframe de-icing but not the actual de-icing boots, which would add another $US1,845 to the price of each aircraft.

Other items covered by the initial proposals included the supply by Lockheed of one set of master tracings suitable for reproduction at no cost, flight and service manuals, and the provision of spares at extra cost. Australian licence production of the Hudson was specifically excluded from the earliest discussions, although the question of Lockheed setting up a factory was briefly considered and rejected.

On 2 November 1938 the Australian Prime Minister (Mr J A Lyons) announced an order for 50 Hudsons at a total cost of £1.4m ($A2.8m) or £24,000 ($A48,000) per aircraft. The order was formally approved in January 1939, accompanied by the usual "we must buy British" chorus from senior quarters. These opinions completely failed to take into account that Britain itself was buying large quantities of American aircraft and the reason the Hudson was considered in the first place – the unavailability of suitable British types – was more valid than ever.

Delivery of the first aircraft was scheduled for June 1939 with completion of the order by January 1940. The first date slipped by seven months, the second by two months.

RAAF Hudson I A16-35, or 'A-16-35' as it was painted on the aircraft. The serial numbers were styled in this manner on the first 100 aircraft to arrive in Australia. (via Neil Mackenzie)

A16-6 was the first Hudson to fly in Australia after assembly at No 2 Aircraft Depot, Richmond, taking to the air in February 1940. (via Neil Mackenzie)

Hudson IIs for the RAAF awaiting assembly at Richmond, probably in March 1940; A16-55 in the foreground. The first 100 aircraft were all delivered by the end of June.

COPY OF OUTWARDS WIRELESS MESSAGE

D. 8211, 7.37.—C. 8751.

TO: AUSTAIR:

FROM: AIR BOARD:

L.654 - 15/12 -   137, 138,139 -
7/12

AIR. Lockheed agents here quoted on 10/10/38 and confirmed
8/11/38 base price of $93,580 per aircraft. This figure stated
to be calculated on Air Ministry contract rate, now known to be
$84,470, plus $5,200 for redesign and structural alterations to
take P. & W. engines, balance accounted for by additional cost
of engines over Wright, smaller order and increased price of
materials and production but details of these items not given.
The base price of $93,580 therefore appeared reasonable but
from information your A.L. 3 - 18/11 - where base price $80,690
mentioned we expected a reduction our base price by including
our order with Ministry's extension order for 50. Reference
your questions - (A) Authority is granted exceed base price
of $93,580 provided you and Ministry satisfied that,
having regard our alterations, the price we pay compares
favourably with Hudsons supplied to Ministry. (B) Base
price included anti-ice on airscrews and installation fittings
to take deicing equipment on leading edges fins etc. but not
the actual overshoes, a price but not firm quote for which was
given on about 18/11/38 at $1,845 at Goodrich works.
(C) Understand from terms of contract we would get one set of
master tracings free and these will be suitable for reproduction
here, also flight and service manuals. Agree contract not
intended cover manufacturing rights, you to make best arrangements
possible regarding provision spare parts lists, as extra to
contract.   (D) Unless you can come to better terms no alternative
but accept terms of Air Ministry contract. (E) Agree to carry
flight test risks as mentioned in contract. (F) Would prefer
if at all possible financial adjustments being effected by Air
Ministry on our behalf, High Commissioner's Office to adjust
with Ministry. If this is not practicable advise immediately
when other best arrangements will be made through Treasury here.
(G) Agree to contractor sending pilot-mechanic and foreman-
erector to Australia, submit details of proposals. (H) Regarding
turret agree accept aircraft as supplied Air Ministry. We will
fit rear mounting locally, also Vickers V front guns. (I) 12
spare engines will be ordered against Indent 693, aircraft and
engine spares to values quoted in my 433/21/11 against Indents
694 and 695.   (J) Include provision for R.A.A.F. pilot for
testing in case availed of. (K) Reference shipping noted and
agreed to but consider that up to 14 days' free storage should
be allowed if ships' bottoms unavailable Los Angeles, make
best terms. (L) Appreciate contractor's liability ceases on
delivery f.o.b. Los Angeles, you make suitable amendments to
Ministry contract to cover. (M) Noted re Appendix A items, we
will conform to Air Ministry arrangements. We would prefer
Pioneer instruments to Kollsman if no delay or extra cost
involved.

A/Cdre(A.M.S.)

Hudson I A16-42 and Hudson IIs A16-55/73 in formation, showing the temporary fairing covered open dorsal gun position. A16-42 and -73 carry the early single letter 'F' code of No 6 Squadron at Richmond. (via Bob Livingstone)

A Question of Armament

A source of considerable discussion in the period between the ordering and delivery of the first Hudsons was that of their gun armament, the original intention being to replace the front Brownings with Vickers weapons as the latter was being produced by the Small Arms Factory at Lithgow, NSW. Also, the dorsal turret installation was subject to changes, a cypher from the Air Board to the Australian Liaison Officer in January 1939 stating that "[the] turret is not to be supplied as we will fit locally designed mountings to take Vickers type G/O [gas operated] guns. Front gun will be Vickers Mk.V fitted here but aircraft should be fitted with all necessary apparatus for pneumatic firing ..."

This message was in reply to an earlier one from the Liaison Officer to the Air Board which pointed out that an extensive redesign would be necessary to accommodate Vickers guns in the standard turret: "... complications would be caused by the change from belt fed installation to pan fed installation and stowage would have to be found for spare magazines ... solenoid firing units would also have to be redesigned and there would be doubts about ammunition chutes ..."

By April 1939 the Air Board had not finally decided what the dorsal turret specification would be: "... we may take (A) RAF [Boulton Paul] turret or some modification thereof, (B) ask contractor to design and fit rear mounting to take our gun [the Vickers], (C) design and fit local type mounting ..."

These and other indecisions were beginning to cause delays by May 1939, compounded by the fact that Lockheed's own schedules had slipped somewhat, although they were being caught up. The change of powerplant was also the source of some delays, but the dorsal guns fitting was the major cause along with smaller items such as deciding on what type of parachute (seat or lap pack) would be provided for the pilot and navigator.

The fitting of a manually controlled dorsal turret was also investigated, and although its installation involved no structural alterations, it could prevent the fitting of a powered turret later on. This idea was found

Although numerically the RAAF's first Hudson, A16-1 was officially taken on charge in February 1940, the month after the first few aircraft. (via Neil Mackenzie)

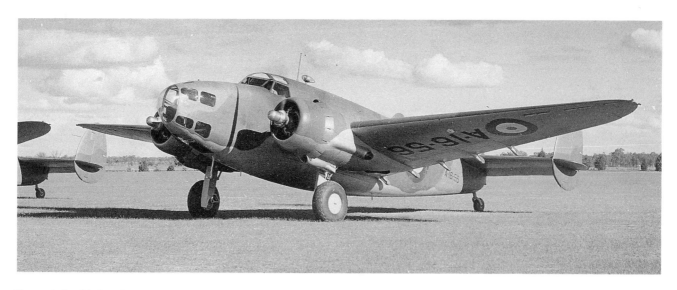

Nice portrait of Hudson II A16-56 running up its engines before takeoff from Richmond in early 1940. This aircraft was lost in action in March 1942.

to be impractical and was reported as such by Lawrence Wackett (CAC's general manager) who in April 1939 departed for the USA for courses in maintenance and overhaul in company with five other engineers.

Wackett reported in a cable to the Air Board: ''Flight trial of manually operated turret revealed serious buffeting at landing speed and no way overcoming this without major redesign. Only other possible mount-

ing limited to arc 90 degrees between fins. Consider this poor and recommend Boulton Paul turret if obtainable ...''

The issue was finally resolved in June 1939 in favour of the Boulton Paul turret, but early Australian Hudsons were delivered without dorsal turrets and some were temporarily fitted with a single gun mounting under a low fairing, others with a plain cover over the hole which would eventually be

filled by a turret and still others flew with the exposed hole!

The following RAAF Minute Paper, reproduced here in full due to its interest, summarises the situation, the options and the recommendation. It is dated 7 June 1939.

Cockpit shot of a No 2 Squadron Hudson (A16-12) in 1941 fitted with dual controls. The entrance to the nose area can be just made out behind the starboard rudder pedals. (Murray Lawson via Ken Hutchison)

SUBJECT: ARMAMENT - HUDSON AIRCRAFT

SECRETARY:

Following the conversation between the Minister
and the Chief of the Air Staff at which the probable necessity
for power operated turrets in the Lockheed Hudsons was discussed,
I am directed to inform you that the standard R.A.F. armament
for this type is, in front, two Browning guns and, in rear, a
power operated Boulton-Paul turret fitted with two Browning guns.
If this installation was followed in the Royal Australian Air
Force, it would mean the introduction of another type of gun into
the Service and another type of turret (the Beaufort turret is a
Bristol type).   When the order for the aircraft was under
consideration this was thought undesirable, particularly as a
satisfactory gun (the Vickers Mk. V) was in production in our
own factories.   For this latter reason it was then decided to
fit Vickers Mark V guns in the front position.   As for the rear
armament it was unfortunately the case that it was impracticable
to mount the Vickers Mk. V in any existing turret, whilst the
Beaufort turret which mounted the Vickers Class K gun (being
introduced to the Service as a replacement for the Lewis) was
unsuitable for installation in the Hudson.

2.   The Air Ministry was accordingly instructed to
arrange for the Vickers Mk. V to be fitted as the front gun in
our Hudsons, and the question of the rear armament was left in
abeyance whilst alternatives, which might be acceptable without
introducing the new type of gun, were examined.

3.   The main alternatives were -

(a) Design of special power operated turret suitable for
      the Hudson and which would take a gun already in the
      Service or adapted for introduction.

(b) Modification of existing designs as an alternative
      to (a).

(c) Design of a simple manually operated mounting which
      could carry the Lewis or Vickers K.

Alternatives (a) and (b) proved impracticable.   Turrets are now
most intricate and have cost the British Government huge sums in
development.   Their modification would not only be costly but
could not be completed under a very long period.   This left
alternative (c).

4.   The use of a simple manually operated free mounting
has the advantage of low cost and allows of the use of a standard
gun.   On the other hand, there is no doubt that, owing to the
high air pressure on the gun and gunner due to the high speed of
the aircraft, deflection aiming would be impossible and fire
restricted to a small arc in the immediate rear of the aircraft.
Nevertheless it was decided to investigate this alternative and
this was one of the duties to be performed by the Director of
Technical Services (Wing Commander Wackett) on his visit to the
makers' works in the United States.

/Page 2...

ARMAMENT - HUDSON AIRCRAFT

5.   The Director of Technical Services has now
investigated various alternative arrangements for a simple
manually operated mounting and has reported that, of two gun
mountings available, one revealed serious defects in flight
trials and which could not be overcome without major
alterations in design, whilst the other had such a limited arc
of fire that it could not be recommended.   After completing
his investigations he states that there appears to be no
alternative (from a technical point of view) to fitting
Boulton-Paul turrets, and recommends accordingly.

6.   In the meantime the Board has been considerably
exercised in mind as to whether anything less than a power
operated turret could be accepted for the Hudson, in view of
the fact that General Reconnaissance aircraft normally operate
alone and at distances to sea.   It would seem that the crews
of these aircraft should be given every opportunity to defend
themselves and also be given facilities with which they can
attack other aircraft.   With the speed at which the Hudson will
operate, a power turret is essential for the free guns if all
round or reasonable arcs of fire are to be obtained.   It might
even be dangerous for an aircraft to proceed on a task with such
a limited arc of fire as obtainable with a manually operated
mounting.   Turrets are provided in the Beaufort.

7.   For these reasons, and supported by the investigations of the Director of Technical Services in the United States,
the Board has reached the conclusion that the Hudsons must be
fitted with Boulton and Paul power operated turrets.

8.   It follows from this conclusion that the Browning
gun must be introduced into the Royal Australian Air Force.   This
was inevitable in any case as, for instance, the four guns in the
"Sunderland" rear turret are of this type, and it would be quite
impracticable for these turrets to take any other type.

9.   On the question of the front gun in the Hudson, on
which a decision had been made to fit Vickers Mark V, as mentioned
above, advice has been received from the contractor that, in order
to carry out the redesign work associated with the departure from
the standard R.A.F. Browning gun, deliveries of the first aircraft
would be delayed four months.   Now that the Browning gun is to
be introduced for the rear turret, there is little reason why it
should not be used in front as well.   It would, indeed, be an
advantage, as maintenance problems would be simplified, especially
in squadrons.   The Board has therefore decided to fit the standard
R.A.F. Browning gun in the front positions in lieu of the Vickers
Mark V, and thus obviate the long delay in delivery of the aircraft.
(Even after removing this cause of delay it is likely that
deliveries will be two months later than originally arranged.)

10.   With the adoption of the foregoing armament policy
regarding the Hudson, some reduction in Air Board orders on the
Munitions Supply Board for Vickers Mark V guns may be necessary.
The supply situation in this respect is being investigated and
will be discussed in due course with that Board.   It might be
mentioned that this introduction of the standard R.A.F. gun (the
Browning) into the Royal Australian Air Force foreshadows its
eventual local manufacture in lieu of the Vickers Mark V.

11.   In conformity with the above Air Board decisions,
the contractor for the Hudsons has been instructed to proceed on
the basis of fitting Boulton and Paul turrets and Browning guns

/Page 3...

3

<u>ARMAMENT - HUDSON AIRCRAFT</u>

right through, whilst the Air Ministry has been requested to allocate 50 Boulton and Paul turrets and 200 Browning guns to Australia, pending receipt of official order.

12.   The foregoing is submitted for the information of the Minister. Supplementary orders for the turrets and guns will be prepared and submitted for approval as soon as estimated prices are available.

Signature

S e c r e t a r y,
<u>AIR BOARD</u>

7th June, 1939

[stamp] THE SECRETARY
AIR BOARD
Secretary.
15 / 6 / 39.

[stamp] APPROVED
14 JUN 1939
MINISTER FOR DEFENCE

[handwritten notes]

A.M.S. ...... 22/6.

Please attach up to Hudson Equipment file.

We are awaiting a reply from A.L.O. to a Signal (P369. 5/6)

regarding the cost of B.P. Turrets and Browning

See A.L. 746. 20/6 / Guns. - Have we had reply yet.

24/6   *[initials]* 27/6

More Orders, First Deliveries

While preparations for the delivery of the RAAF's first 50 Hudsons were going ahead – preparations which included the arrival in Australia of Lockheed personnel who would supervise the assembly and testing of the Hudsons at No 2 Aircraft Depot at RAAF Richmond, west of Sydney – plans were afoot for the ordering of more aircraft.

In August 1939 the purchase of an additional 30 Hudsons was approved by the Air Board with 20 more approved the following month. These additional 50 Hudsons were ordered by the British Air Ministry on behalf of the RAAF in the same month, meaning that all 100 now on order were in effect diverted from RAF orders.

The base unit cost of this second batch was slightly more than the first – $US94,845 – a price which included installation of equipment, flight testing, disassembly and shipping to Australia. This batch of Hudsons was also Pratt & Whitney powered and differed from the original 50 mainly in having Hamilton Standard Hydromatic constant-

Rear fuselage detail of No 2 Squadron's A16-12 showing the temporary dorsal gun fitting. (Murray Lawson via Ken Hutchison)

speed propellers fitted instead of two position units. The new propellers accounted for the price increase.

Twelve of the second order were specified to be equipped with dual controls, and deliveries were scheduled to begin immediately, a target which was not met (initial deliveries of the first batch were still two months away) although delivery of all 100 aircraft was completed by June 1940, just three months late.

To differentiate between the two batches, the aircraft were designated Hudson I and Hudson II, a source of confusion as they were really equivalent to the forthcoming RAF Twin Wasp powered Hudson IV, while the designations Hudson I and II as applied by the British referred to Wright Cyclone engined aircraft! There would be further confusion over RAAF Hudsons and their powerplants, as noted below.

For service with the RAAF, the Hudson was given serial numbers in the A16 series, A16-1 to -50 covering Mk.I aircraft and A16-51 to -100 referring to Mk.IIs. The manufacturer's designation for these aircraft was Model B14S, while of interest was the way the serial numbers were painted onto the first 100 Hudsons upon arrival. Instead of the standard A16-1 (or whatever), the serials were presented as A-16-1, and so on.

The payment scheme proposed when the second 50 Hudsons were ordered involved the transfer of various sums of money to Lockheed between November 1939 and March 1940, specifically (in US dollars): November $530,000, December $1,220,000, January $530,000, February and March $760,000 each. In addition, an allowance of $US295,000 was made for the supply of 18 spare engines, airframe de-icing boots and dual conversion sets, adding about $US60,000 to the monthly payments.

There was a period of doubt that any of the Hudsons would be delivered to Australia when the USA announced its Neutrality Act two days after war broke out in September 1939 – embargoes on the delivery of aircraft awaiting assembly and/or delivery were suggested – but this was overcome and the Hudsons could be shipped as planned, albeit some months later than had been intended.

The first batch of nine Hudsons (A16-2 to A16-10) was transported to Richmond after being unloaded at Sydney docks and taken on RAAF charge on 26 January 1940. A16-1 arrived with the second batch early in February, while all of the first 50 had arrived by early March. Delivery of the second order began at the same time, and by late June 1940, the RAAF had taken possession of all 100 Hudsons.

The first to fly was A16-6 (on February 13 or 14), flown by Lockheed test pilot L D Parker with the RAAF's Sqdn Ldr H B Seekamp and Flt Sgt Connolly also on board the aircraft. A pool of instructors was drawn from civilian pilots who were licenced to fly the civil Lockheed 14 and by April

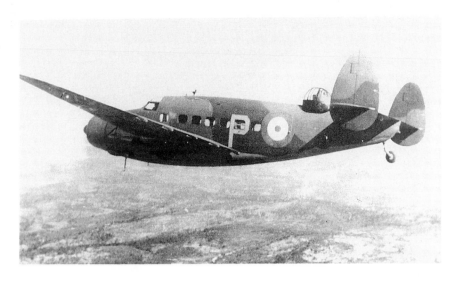

Two shots of No 14 Squadron Hudsons at Pearce WA in 1940 and displaying the early 'P' code of that squadron. (via Neil Mackenzie)

1940 crew familiarisation flights were being conducted from Laverton.

By that date, the RAAF had 79 Hudsons on strength, 63 of them at Richmond and the remainder at Laverton. An early demonstration of the Hudson's long range capabilities was made in the same month when four aircraft flew from Richmond NSW to Pearce WA, a distance of 2,120 miles (3,411km). Only one fuel stop was made, at Ceduna in South Australia, and the journey took 13 hours 15 minutes from go to whoa.

Squadron service for the Hudson began in March 1940 with the equipping of No 1 Squadron at Laverton, and by the end of 1940 the RAAF had seven additional Hudson squadrons operational – No 2 (Laverton), No 6 (Richmond), No 7 (Laverton), No 8 (Canberra), No 13 (Darwin) No 14 (Pearce) and No 23 (Archerfield), in most cases replacing Ansons.

Further Orders

By late 1940 there were some delays in the delivery of Avro Ansons to the RAAF, with some 90 aircraft arrived under the Empire Air Training Scheme schedule in addition to the 88 delivered prewar. Larger numbers had been expected by then, with the result that some of the training organisations were below aircraft strength.

Among these was the General Reconnaissance School, and to help overcome the shortfall it was suggested in December 1940 that two secondhand Lockheed 14s be purchased from the USA.

The two civilian L.14s were available ex Galveston, Texas, through the local Australian agents W R Carpenter & Co Ltd at a price of £23,500 ($47,000) each. The same aircraft could be obtained via the British Purchasing Commission at £20,312 ($40,624) each or at a package price of

Maintenance work on Hudsons of No 2 Squadron at Laverton, photographed in May 1941 from inside another Hudson. Note that the Boulton Paul dorsal turret is fitted to the aircraft. (Murray Lawson via Ken Hutchison)

£60,000 ($120,000) including freight, packing and spares.

It was therefore recommended that the aircraft be purchased for the General Reconnaissance School but in January 1941 the Australian Air Board was advised that only one of the L.14s was available, and this in combination with an increase in the delivery tempo of Ansons resulted in the matter being dropped.

In the meantime, negotiations were well underway for the procurement of more Hudsons for the RAAF. In April 1940, the War Cabinet approved the purchase of 49 additional Hudsons, of which 18 would be allocated to a new general reconnaissance (GR) squadron and the remainder to replace Ansons in other GR squadrons. The Avro aircraft would then be transferred to EATS units and the cost of the Hudsons was put at £2.277m ($4.554m) including spare parts and engines.

These Hudsons (Mk.IVs, with Twin Wasp engines) never served with the RAAF as in May 1940 and following requests from the

British government, the Australian Prime Minister Mr R G Menzies agreed to their retention by the Royal Air Force.

It wasn't until March 1941 that more Hudsons were ordered for the RAAF, their acquisition prompted by the fact that the Australian Beaufort production programme was falling behind schedule and aircraft were required as an interim measure. This, of course, was reminiscent of the reason the first 100 Hudsons had been ordered.

The March 1942 approval was for 52 additional Hudsons at a total cost of £2.348m ($4.696m), but this was increased to 146 aircraft when Mr Menzies, in London at the time, was able to convince the British government to divert the Hudsons from RAF orders and/or Lend-Lease allocations. Unofficially, this was considered to be a gesture of thanks in recognition of the RAAF's contributions to the Royal Air Force's efforts in Britain and North Africa. An extra aircraft found its way into the equation – A16-222, the former Royal Air Force AE488 – and the number of Hudsons ultimately delivered to the RAAF was 247. AE488 was a survivor of the Singapore campaign which was evacuated by a RAAF crew to Australia in March 1942 where it was taken onto RAAF strength and renumbered A16-222.

A Basis for Confusion

The extra 147 Hudsons were delivered to the RAAF between December 1941 and May 1942 and were allocated the serial numbers A16-101 to A16-247. The first 52 (A16-101/152) were Mk.IV aircraft with Pratt & Whitney engines and the remainder were a mixture of Wright Cyclone engined Mk.IIIAs and Pratt & Whitney engined

Mk.IVs – at least according to published accounts.

Confusion arises with a study of individual aircraft histories through their RAAF status cards, photographic evidence and cross reference of previous USAAF and RAF identities.

According to previous assumptions, A16-153 to -163 should be Mk.IIIs, A16-164 to -169 Mk.IVs, A16-170 a Mk.III, A16-171 a Mk.IV and A16-172 to -247 Mk.IIIs.

Further examination reveals that *all* of the RAAF's Hudsons from A16-153 onwards are in fact Mk.III aircraft (or Mk.IIIA to be absolutely correct as they are Hudsons originally allocated to the RAF under Lend-Lease) and a summary of models and deliveries might appear as below:

RAAF HUDSONS SUMMARY OF DELIVERIES				
RAAF Nos	Mark	Qty	Delivery	Remarks
A16-1/50	I	50	01-03/40	equivalent to RAF Mk.IV
A16-51/100	II	50	03-06/40	similar but c-s props
A16-101/152	IV	52	12/41	RAF mark number
A16-153/247	III	95	01-05/42	RAF mark number

Notes: As mentioned in the text, the above differs substantially from previously published listings where Hudsons A16-153 to -247 are concerned. There are considerable inconsistencies among official records and on the aircraft's status cards, including in the latter one type of engine crossed out and another pencilled in, often with serial numbers. All the Hudson IIIs as listed above which previously wore RAF serial numbers were regarded by the British Air Ministry as that model. Refer to the aircraft tables at the end of this section for details. The author notes that due to the confusion, the above is not necessarily definitive, merely a 'line of best fit' from the available evidence.

RAAF HUDSONS MONTHLY DELIVERIES			
	1940	1941	1942
January	9	–	7
February	33	–	–
March	29	–	32
April	8	–	30
May	12	–	26
June	9	–	–
July	–	–	–
August	–	–	–
September	–	–	–
October	–	–	–
November	–	–	–
December	–	52	–

No 2 Squadron Hudsons A16-12 and A16-73 at Laverton in May 1941. A16-12 was destroyed by enemy action in February 1942. (Murray Lawson via Ken Hutchison)

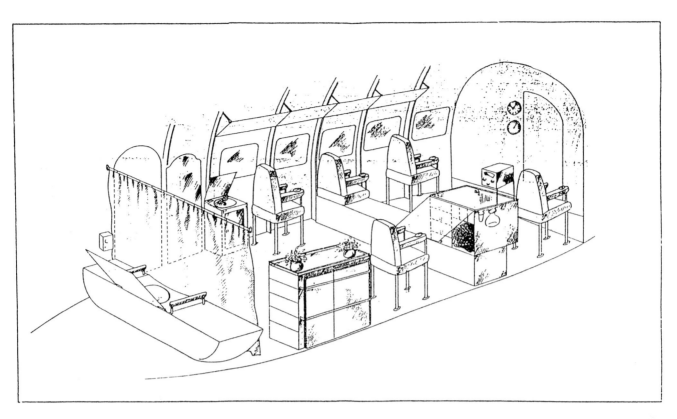

Drawing of the interior of Hudson A16-99 as proposed for use by General Blamey as his personal transport. Some of the special items of equipment were costed thus: 1 toilet fixture 16 shillings and sixpence (16/6 or $1.65), 1 carafe and cup 1.5 pints 1/6 ($0.15), 1 wash hand basin 13.5in stainless steel 42/6 ($4.25), basin plug and washer 1.25in 6/9 ($0.68), 1 soap holder Trader Horn pattern 8/6 ($0.85).

DITCHING OF HUDSON AIRCRAFT (MKS. I, III, & IV) ON THE SEA.

42A

INTRODUCTION.

This bulletin details the results of ditching tests carried out on scale models and a comparison made between the tests and the actual ditching of an R.A.A.F. Hudson aircraft on the sea.

SCALE MODEL DITCHING TESTS.

The following table gives a resume of the results of using various flap settings for a landing, at low speeds with the tail down as much as possible on smooth water. The model nose window was open and the model flaps were made to break at approximately the correct strengths in all cases, but in some instances there is a possibility that the brittle breaking of the model flaps may not have represented sufficiently closely the large plastic deformations which the tracks of Fowler flaps might in practice undergo before complete failure.

Under these conditions the results as tabulated may be somewhat optimistic.

The loading of the models approximated 17,500 lbs. gross weight.

Flaps	Approx. indicated air speed at impact	REMARKS	TABLE I.
Up	85 Knots	Nose window momentarily submerged. Probably as safe a landing as can be made, especially if the nose window does not break.	
Down 50%	75 Knots	Violent dive after impact.	
Down 70%	75 Knots	Violent dive after impact.	
Down 100%	60 Knots	Doubtful failure of flaps. Difficulty of getting tail down.	

It will be seen that the probability of a safe landing is greatest with the flaps up. Additional tests on the Hudson were therefore confined to the flaps up condition.

Since in normal practice the Hudson is landed on aerodromes at speeds well above the stall, model tests were made to find the effect of landing on the sea at high speeds. The results are given in the following table.

Flaps	Approx. indicated air speed at impact	Nose Window.	REMARKS TABLE II.
Up	85 Knots	Closed	As safe as possible. Maximum deceleration 0.9G.
Up	85 Knots	Open	Maximum deceleration 1.1G.
Up	100 Knots	Closed	Maximum deceleration about 3G. Possible dangerous directional instability.
Up	100 Knots	Open	Dangerous porpoising. Maximum deceleration 5 to 6½ G's. Possible violent directional instability.

These results indicate that the Hudson is likely to encounter least trouble when landed slowly. If the glide is checked very harshly so that the tail is well down on striking the sea, the risk of breaking the bomb aimer's window should be very much reduced and the deceleration becomes less violent.

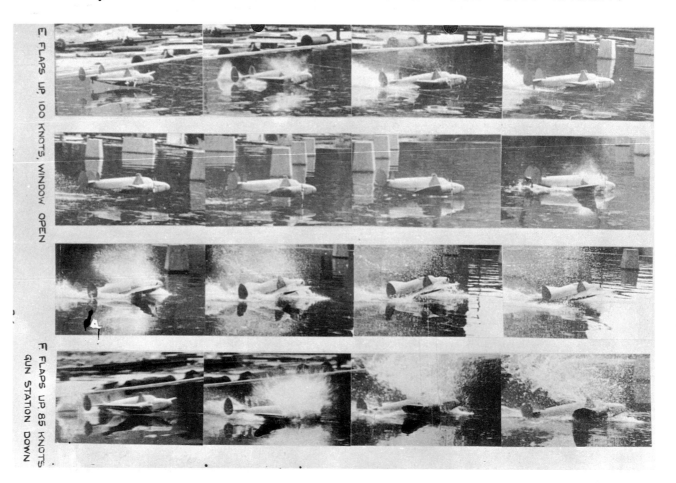

E. FLAPS UP, 100 KNOTS, WINDOW OPEN

F. FLAPS UP, 85 KNOTS, GUN STATION DOWN

The next series of tests were concerned with the bomb doors, as it was desired to know what risks the aircraft would run if in attempting to jettison the bombs the pilot should be forced to alight with the bomb doors open.

Further, it was found by means of full scale static dropping tests with a Hudson fuselage, that not only would the normal Hudson nose window almost certainly break on hitting the sea, but also the bomb doors would bend inwards.

Model landings were made under these two conditions, namely with the bomb doors open, and also with them collapsed. In addition a few experiments were made to see whether or not it would be dangerous to land on the sea with the retractable lower gun platform extended.

Where reference is made to the nose window being open, this is applicable only to R.A.F. Hudson aircraft in which the window is hinged.

TABLE III.

Flaps	Indicated air speed	Variation from normal condition.	REMARKS
Up	85 Knots	Nose Window open gun platform extended.	Dangerous, should be avoided if at all possible.
Up	85 Knots	Nose Window open bomb doors open.	Very dangerous.
Up	85 Knots	Nose Window open Bomb doors closed but broken inwards.	Rather dangerous

CONCLUSIONS:

When landing the Hudson on the sea, it seems best to check the glide as heavily as possible so that the aeroplane hits the sea as slowly as possible with the tail well down, with flaps and undercarriage retracted. It is so important to get the tail down that the general safety of the landing is likely to be increased even if some risk of wing dropping is taken. The crew should brace themselves well before landing, and should be careful not to release their holds too soon, as in fast landings especially there may be two impacts separated by a second or two, and the second impact will be the more severe.

Table II gives some idea of the maximum decelerations to be encountered.

G
FLAPS UP
85 KNOTS
BOMB DOORS
OPEN

HUDSON

INTERVAL ²/5TH·SEC.

H
FLAPS UP
85 KNOTS
BOMB DOORS
COLLAPSED

During actual forced landings on the sea, it was observed that as soon as the tail touched the water, the nose was thrown in heavily and then the deceleration became violent.

The bomb aimers' window seems to have withstood the impact, but it was found that water came rapidly through the floor.

The heavy inrush of water and the quick dropping of the nose would indicate that the bomb doors failed.

In tests of a model with damaged bomb doors it has been possible to reproduce the sudden downward pitching motion on impact and also the subsequent heavy deceleration.

As far as the model experiments can show however, a Hudson should run fairly smoothly on water if landed near the stall. Damage to the bomb doors due to the landing may also tend to prevent the kind of porpoising found in high speed model landings and may therefore allow landings to be made at high speeds than the results would indicate.

It seems almost certain, however, that a safe landing becomes much more probable as the speed is reduced nearly to the stall.

DITCHING OF R.A.A.F. HUDSON ON THE SEA:

The following table details the conditions under which the successful ditching of a R.A.A.F. Hudson was accomplished.

Weight	18,500 lbs. gross weight (Bomb jettisoned and fuel down to 30 gallons);
Weather Conditions	Normal. Slightly "choppy" sea running;
Crew	Four, with pilot, observer and wireless operator strapped in their normal positions. The rear gunner was holding himself well braced near the rear spar and received slight injuries when thrown forward on impact;
Landing	Speed was 80 knots with flaps, undercarriage and tunnel gun platform retracted. Just before "touch down" the control column was brought hard back to ensure the tail striking first;
Damage	The only reported damage was the stoving in of the Perspex panels in the tunnel gun platform;
Flotation	The aircraft floated for approx. 4 to 5 mins. which was ample time for the crew to abandon the aircraft by means of the pilot's escape hatch.

a RESULT OF FULL SCALE DROPPING TEST   b MODEL REPRESENTATION OF DAMAGE

A comparison of R.A.F. results of model tests and the actual ditching of the R.A.A.F. Hudson indicates that the conclusions arrived at should be used as the basis of ditching this type of aircraft on the sea to ensure maximum safety and to enable the crew to abandon the aircraft with a minimum of trouble.

The actual time the aircraft floats is ample for the crew to abandon the aircraft and prepare the emergency dinghy for use. However the time is not sufficient to allow important items of equipment to be salvaged.

Although no reports of actual forced ditchings or model tests have been received concerning Ventura or Lodestar aircraft it is considered that, as these are very similar in construction and aerodynamic features to Hudson aircraft, they could be successfully ditched using the same procedure as that adopted for Hudson aircraft.

Attached as Appendix I are photographs of model ditching tests, also one photograph of the result of the full scale dropping test with a Hudson fuselage.

REFERENCES: R.A.E. Report (Aero 1713)
               R.A.A.F. File 9/19/446.

DATE OF ISSUE: September, 1943.

A Hudson which survives today, A16-112 or VH-AGS as it was best known during its civil days. The photographs were both taken at Sydney Airport in December 1966 (top) and February 1969 (bottom) and show two colour schemes used by Adastra Aerial Surveys. The gentleman with the red jacket and white beard in the co-pilot's seat of the upper shot looks a little suspicious, although it is December! (Eric Allen)

Another view of VH-AGS at Sydney in 1969 (top) while VH-SMO (ex A16-105) is photographed at the same airport in 1966 (bottom). This Hudson also survives. (Eric Allen)

HUDSON IN RAAF SERVICE

The Crash of A16-97

The entry of the Hudson into RAAF service during the course of 1940 brought a touch of history with it. It was, after all, the first American combat aircraft to be ordered for the RAAF and by contemporary standards, one of the most modern types in RAAF service.

The early months of Hudson operations were not without flaw. Five were lost by the end of 1940, and one of those losses brought with it an enormous amount of publicity and speculation.

On 13 August 1940, Hudson A16-97 departed Melbourne for Canberra. On board was the aircraft's skipper, Flt Lt Robert Hitchcock and his three crew members along with some very important passengers – the Minister for Air, J V Fairbairn; the Minister for the Army and Repatriation, Brigadier G A Street; the Vice President of the Executive Council, Sir Henry Gullett, the Chief of the General Staff, General Sir Brudenall Bingham White; Lt Col Francis Thornthwaite and Richard Elford, private secretary to Mr Fairbairn. It was an impressive passenger list, a fine collection of 'top brass'.

The Hudson approached Canberra airport to land, perhaps a little low and distinctively nose up. The Hudson momentarily disappeared behind one of the hills which surround Canberra airport, then reappeared. There was the sound of engines being gunned, then the aircraft disappeared again. Then an explosion and the sight of a large plume of black smoke. All on board the Hudson died.

A witness later said the aircraft appeared to drop its left wing and then dip its nose

steeply, classic symptoms of a stall too close to the ground for recovery.

An enquiry was held, but in camera, with the result that for many close to the subject, the findings didn't go far enough. It was found that the probable cause was a stall and loss of control below a height sufficient to recover. Recommendations were made regarding reminding pilots of the Hudson's stall characteristics, to keep ample speed in hand and that pilots converted to the Hudson have a wide background of experience, particularly on twin engined aircraft.

The latter alluded to what many thought, and still do – that Fairbairn himself was at the controls of the aircraft during the approach and that the sudden burst of power was applied by Hitchcock when he realised the aircraft was too low and too slow.

Fairbairn was a pilot who had flown with the Royal Flying Corps in World War I and who, at the time of his death, owned and flew his own aircraft. Some weeks before the accident, Fairbairn had said to Mr H J Storey, headmaster of the Commonwealth Defence Training Centre: "I will be using a Hudson for my departmental travelling and on every possible occasion I'll practice landings ..." He also discussed the known tricky stalling characteristics of the aircraft with Mr Storey, but when this information was presented, it was filed as deeply in the bowels of the bureaucracy as was possible.

The Defence of Singapore

Two of the RAAF's Hudson squadrons were among the first to encounter the juggernaut which was Japan in December

1941 and the first half of 1942. Nos 1 and 8 Squadrons, based at Laverton and Canberra, respectively, were moved to the Malaya/Singapore area in 1940 as part of a general build up of British and Commonwealth forces there. A secure Singapore had long been a vital part of the defence of the British Empire.

By 7 December 1941, some 160 British, Australian and to a lesser extent New Zealand and Dutch first line aircraft were based in Malaya and Singapore, divided about equally between the two. The RAAF component comprised No 453 Squadron's Brewster Buffalos at Sembawang in Singapore and No 21 Squadron's Buffalos and Wirraways at Sungei in Northern Malaya. Also in Malaya were the 12 Hudsons from No 8 Squadron at Kuantan and No 1 Squadron's similar number at Kota Bharu. The Royal Air Force had Catalinas, Blenheims, Vickers Vildebeests and Beauforts defending Singapore and Malaya, the defence of the latter being necessary to the security of the strategically more important Singapore.

Before moving to this area of South East Asia, both Australian Hudson squadrons had been performing the usual roles associated with RAAF general reconnaissance squadrons – shipping reconnaissance and protection, anti submarine patrols, search and rescue, naval co-operation and so on.

No 1 Squadron was established in Singapore by early July 1940 and moved to Northern Malaya in May 1941; No 8 Squadron arrived in Singapore during August 1940.

The period between the squadrons' arrival and the outbreak of war with Japan in

Hudsons of No 1 Squadron, the first RAAF unit to fly the type. The Wirraway at the bottom of the formation belongs to 21 Squadron; both were involved in the defence of Malaya and Singapore. (via Neil Mackenzie)

Hudson A16-76 of No 8 Squadron photographed in Singapore during August 1940, shortly after arrival. Note the lack of dorsal turret – these were fitted a few weeks later. (via Neil Mackenzie)

December 1941 was spent performing general reconnaissance and transport missions, much the same as they had been doing in Australia but with greater urgency as Japan's intentions became more obvious as 1941 wore on. Orders included the necessity to report and shadow any convoy comprising more than three ships and both squadrons moved base on several occasions during the year, to be finally deployed as noted above when the Japanese assault began. Kota Bharu, where No 1 Squadron was finally based, was the point first attacked by the Japanese.

On 6 December 1941 (Eastern Australian Time), a 1 Squadron Hudson flown by Flt Lt J C Ramshaw reported a Japanese convoy of one battleship, five cruisers, seven destroyers and 22 transports some 260 miles (400km) distant. Other aircraft were sent out to shadow the ships, but failed to find them, mainly because of dreadful monsoonal weather in the area. The next day, small groups of Japanese seaborne forces were discovered and shadowed.

The assault began in the early hours of 8 December (Eastern Australian and local time) and it's interesting to note that using this time as the measure (it was December 7 in Hawaii due to the effects of the International Date Line), the attacks on Malaya and southern Thailand were launched one hour and twenty minutes *before* the first Japanese aircraft hit Pearl Harbour. On the same morning, the Philippines, Guam, Hong Kong and Wake Island were also attacked.

The attack on Kota Bharu began with shelling the shore defences and 1 Squadron's Hudsons were sent out to attack. Flt Lt J Lockwood struck the first blow by any Commonwealth airman against the Japanese on this strike.

The Hudsons continued to attack during the night, the Japanese transport ships being the primary targets. Some success was achieved with one of these ships blown up, another set on fire, a third damaged and at least 26 barges destroyed or put out of action by morning. The cost was two Hudsons lost and several others damaged.

No 8 Squadron continued to attack the invasion force from daylight, using all 12 of its Hudsons in four flights of three. Their efforts were heroic, but two of the aircraft were badly damaged and three were seriously holed by small arms fire.

Despite the fact the battle was being fought against colossal odds, the remaining serviceable Hudsons from the two Australian squadrons continued to attack not only the larger transport ships but also the accompanying small craft. None of this, nor the efforts of other Allied aircraft and troops prevented the Japanese from landing and by the end of the first day and following a series of low level air raids, Kota Bharu had been taken and 1 Squadron evacuated to Kuantan. By then only five of the squadron's original 12 Hudsons remained.

The evacuation was by necessity hurried, even desperate, with as many men as possible being loaded into the Hudsons. Anything which couldn't be taken was burned. An example of the tenacity required for a successful withdrawal was provided by Flt Lt J K Douglas, who saw one of the loaded Hudsons parked near a concentration of Japanese soldiers.

Knowing the Hudson's hydraulic system was out of order, meaning that neither the flaps (which were fully down) nor the undercarriage could be retracted and that takeoff would have been impossible in this condition, Douglas grabbed some wire, ran the gauntlet of Japanese fire to the Hudson and wired its flaps up. With the enemy fire following him, he taxied the Hudson along the runway and picked up nine other men as he rolled past. He managed to takeoff, fly to Kuantan with the undercarriage down and then perform a flapless landing on arrival.

Kuantan was attacked the next day with the loss of three of 8 Squadron's aircraft on the ground. Further withdrawal became necessary, both squadrons going to Sembawang on Singapore, the surviving Hudsons flying out and the ground crews following by train.

Between them, the two Australian Hudson squadrons could muster only 11 aircraft when they regrouped in Singapore. They had left behind them a story of valiant defence, accounting for an estimated 15,000 Japanese troops. Casualties had been so heavy among the Japanese brigades tasked with the landing they had been reformed into a single brigade.

At Singapore, it was decided to combine the resources of the RAAF Hudson squadrons pending the arrival of replacement aircraft and equipment. Eight new Hudsons arrived on Christmas Day. Seaward patrols and convoy protection flights were carried out through the remainder of December 1941 and into the new year, along with strikes on Japanese shipping and aerodromes, often in conjunction with RAF aircraft and usually without fighter protection.

But the situation grew steadily worse. Singapore was now under constant attack including a raid on the airfield at Sembawang on 17 January with the loss of three Hudsons. At the end of the month the combined Hudson squadrons took their 17

No 1 Squadron Hudsons at Kota Bharu, Malaya (top) and an 8 Squadron aircraft in trouble. (via Mike Kerr/Neil Mackenzie)

The end of a 1 Squadron Hudson at Palembang with Japanese troops showing their pleasure. (RAAF Historical)

'Tojo Busters', Hudson A16-211 of No 2 Squadron photographed in May 1943 after its undercarriage collapsed on landing at Milingimbi following combat with enemy fighters. A16-171 was shot down in the same action. (via Bob Piper)

Hudsons to Palembang in Sumatra. Of these, seven were of no further use. The remainder bombed Japanese bases in Malaya, hit convoys and flew reconnaissance over Sumatran waters.

In mid February, Palembang itself faced invasion, and the Hudsons flew 'shuttle' bombing and strafing sorties against Japanese troops, many of whom were killed in their barges. Despite this, their landings were successful and another withdrawal became necessary. On 16 February (the day after Singapore surrendered) the Hudsons moved to Semplak in Java, from where they bombed the Palembang oil fields and shipping around the coast of Sumatra.

No 8 Squadron ceased to exist the following week, disbanded temporarily with many of its ground crew transferred to 1 Squadron and aircrews sent to Darwin. The squadron remained inactive until March 1943 when it was reformed at Canberra and equipped with Beauforts.

No 1 Squadron battled on, bombing the invasion forces and dropping back as airfields were overrun. At the end of February the squadron was on Java and by 4 March only three Hudsons remained serviceable. These were flown to Australia. Remaining personnel attempted to reach the mainland but only 120 succeeded and included in those taken prisoner by the Japanese was the commanding officer, Wng Cdr R H Davis.

During the three months of the Singapore campaign, No 1 Squadron had flown 1,318 operational hours, sunk 15 ships and numerous barges and small vessels as well as killing thousands of Japanese troops. But against an overwhelming force, its and 8 Squadron's efforts were in vain.

No 1 Squadron was reduced to a cadre unit on its return to Australia and reformed in December 1943 equipped with Beauforts.

2 Squadron RAAF

No 2 Squadron began replacing its Ansons with Hudsons in June 1940 and was soon fully operational on the type. Under the command of Sqdn Ldr F W Thomas, the squadron remained based at Laverton for the moment, continuing the main activities it was tasked to perform when equipped with Ansons – seaward patrols, shipping protection and so on.

These included flying safety perimeter patrols around troopships, the *Queen Mary*, *Queen Elizabeth*, *Aquitania* and *Mauretania* among them. These ships were given continuous air cover whilst in Australian waters, the 'clearance search' patrols involving long flying hours over large expanses of ocean. One such patrol in December 1940 saw four of 2 Squadron's Hudsons fly 3,452 miles (5,555km) and cover 52,000 square miles in the space of 24 hours.

The generally worsening situation in the Malay Peninsula, Borneo and Netherlands East Indies areas in the second half of 1941 caused No 2 Squadron's routine to be changed irrevocably. By then, Japan's intentions were clear to most if not actually

Two shots of 2 Squadron Hudsons on operations near Timor in July 1943. The extended ventral guns can be made out. (Ken Hutchison)

declared, and considerable general strengthening of resources was carried out in the north of Australia and beyond.

In October 1941, four of 2 Squadron's Hudsons were detached to Darwin with the intention of making a reconnaissance of the Netherlands East Indies bases at Laha, Namlea and Koepang. This exercise was successfully carried out and repeated the following month.

On 3 December 1941 it appeared that hostilities with Japan were imminent, and the squadron was ordered to stand by for a move to Darwin at short notice. The order was received just two days later and the

squadron's 12 Hudsons were flown to Australia's northern capital between December 5 and 7, the latter the day *before* the Japanese attack on Pearl Harbour in Australian time. Immediately, a flight of four Hudsons moved further north and began operating from the previously surveyed base of Koepang in Dutch Timor. This detachment was under the command of Flt Lt R W B Cuming, and later in December, he established the flight at Namlea on the island of Buru as the squadron's advanced operational base.

The squadron's main base remained Darwin and the CO was Wng Cdr F Head-

Hudsons from No 2 Squadron formate for the camera. (via Neil Mackenzie)

lam, who had taken over the previous April. Other squadrons based at Darwin in mid December 1941 were Nos 12 (Wirraways) and 13 (Hudsons), the latter also with a detachment on Ambon.

Into Battle

Koepang provided some difficulties and few comforts for crews stationed there. A lack of anti aircraft defences, dispersal areas, camouflage and shelter pens didn't help, nor did the fact that supply was poor and repair and maintenance of the Hudsons had to be carried out back at Darwin.

No 2 Squadron recorded its first strike of the Pacific war on 8 December when some of its aircraft attacked the Japanese radio ship *Nanyo Maru* off the north coast of Timor. The ship was damaged, abandoned by its crew and finally ran aground near Dili.

Anti submarine patrols and convoy protection duties occupied much of the remainder of December and in early January 1942 three Hudsons from the Namlea detachment attacked and damaged a destroyer, which unfortunately turned out to be the USS *Perry*. No blame was attached

to No 2 Squadron for this incident, because the ship had previously been shadowed by a US Navy Catalina and had been declared hostile as a result of reports issued from that aircraft.

Successful attacks on enemy shipping at Manabo in the Celebes were made during the course of January 1942, but later in the month the tide began to turn against the Hudson squadron as the Japanese started a series of air raids on its advance bases (Namlea with Amboina by now added) with the loss of aircraft on the ground. Evacuation became necessary with the approach of a large enemy convoy but Koepang was the next target, with heavy damage to the squadron.

With invasion imminent, Koepang was also abandoned and the squadron withdrew to Darwin on 19 February. This was unfortunate timing as that was the date of the first Japanese raid on Darwin. A skeleton volunteer group remained at Koepang to dispose of equipment and records which couldn't be taken with the Hudsons, and most of these were rescued two months later.

Within three hours of No 2 Squadron arriving in Darwin, the Japanese raid on the city was underway. Destroyed were the squadron's headquarters at the RAAF base (along with all of its records and considerable equipment) and four of its Hudsons. Between them Nos 2 and 13 Squadrons had five Hudsons destroyed in the raid – A16-6, -57, -72, -78 and -135, while A16-63 was severely damaged and written off. To add to these already substantial losses, A16-141 crashed that same night.

The squadron was withdrawn further south to Daly Waters the next day in order to give its exhausted air and ground crews a chance to recover and to repair and replace equipment. New aircraft began to arrive, along with fresh crews, and although it was not fully up and running again until May, the squadron in the meantime carried out some small scale raids on Dili and Koepang along with reconnaissance sorties over Timor. These were conducted in conjunction with the Hudsons of No 13 Squadron.

Wng Cdr A B McFarlane took over command in May 1942 and Wng Cdr R H Moran in October. The squadron remained at Daly

Hudson A16-66 (minus turret and forward guns) was delivered in March 1940 and spent its entire life with 13 Squadron until lost in January 1942, strafed on the ground in company with three others. (RAAF Historical)

Hudsons of 2 Squadron (A16-160 and -238 visible) at Milingimbi in 1943. When aircraft from Hughes or Batchelor had to attack some targets in the Netherlands East Indies or New Guinea, they bombed up at their home bases and topped up with fuel at Milingimbi, flying to the targets the next day. Hudsons from 2 and 13 Squadrons had extra fuel tanks in the fuselage. (Ken Hutchison)

Waters until August when it moved to Batchelor, also in the Northern Territory.

Intensive activity began again in May 1942, the first major raid of this new period in the squadron's history taking place on 13 May when nine Hudsons set out from Darwin before dawn to attack enemy shipping, wharves, power houses and water tanks in the Ambon area.

From a unit history which describes a typical Hudson raid of the period: "Five of the aircraft crossed the coast south-east of the town, skimming over the tops of the hills behind it. Past the hills the formation opened out, each aircraft taking a different ship and attacking it from mast height with four 250lb GP bombs fitted with 7-second delay fuses.

"Immediately following these, three other Hudsons came in from the east at 1,000 feet and released five 250lb SAP bombs with 1-second delay fuses. The attack was a complete surprise, and no anti aircraft fire was met until the first flight was already on its way down the bay. Some firing came from a destroyer and some merchant vessels, but no enemy aircraft were encountered during the attack.

"Plt Off Venn's aircraft made its attack on a 3,000 ton ship from masthead height, the ship blew up and the aircraft was seen to explode in mid air at the same time. The result of this strike was that one 3,000 ton vessel was sunk, one 2,000 ton hit and damaged, another of 3,000 tons hit and damaged and a near miss was scored on a 5,000 ton vessel.

"In addition to this devastation a fire was left burning on the coal wharf. The ninth Hudson, having been delayed 10 minutes on takeoff and climb and failing to make contact with the attacking force, and not wishing to jeopardise its attack did not go near Ambon but dropped its bombs on Namlea aerodrome. All aircraft were absent from base for about ten hours".

Another attack on Ambon by eight Hudsons later in the same month brought slightly different results. This was a dive bombing attack on shipping, but this time the Japanese were fully prepared. The targets – a destroyer and two merchant vessels – were underway when the Hudsons arrived and their guns were blazing as the aircraft attacked. The bombs all overshot and as the Hudsons flew away, two stragglers were bounced by Zero fighters. One Hudson was seen to be shot down and the other was last seen being chased by one of the Japanese fighters.

No 2 Squadron then entered into a period of intense activity with its Hudsons. It moved to Hughes airfield in April 1943 and retained its Hudsons until January 1944 when Beauforts were received. These in turn were quickly replaced by B-25 Mitchells.

The squadron's activities in the interim are perhaps best summarised by a citation it received from the President of the United States of America on the recommendation of General Douglas MacArthur. Dated 4 January 1943, it read: "Number 2 Squadron, Royal Australian Air Force, is cited for outstanding performance of duty in action during the period April 18th, 1942, to August 25th, 1942.

"Operating from bases in north-western Australia, this squadron, equipped with airplanes highly vulnerable to enemy fighter airplanes, made repeated attacks on enemy shipping, airdromes, troops and installations on and near Timor, Amboina and other islands in the Banda Sea, inflicting heavy damage to enemy material and causing numerous casualties. It successfully maintained continuous long range reconnaissance over the waters to the north-west of Australia.

"The courage of its members in combat and the high morale of this unit under hazardous combat situations contributed greatly to the success of the operations in this area".

A vice-regal occasion as Hudson A16-71 of 2 Squadron and its crew meets the Governor General, Lord Gowrie, at Darwin in July 1941. (RAAF Historical)

COMMONWEALTH OF AUSTRALIA.

Headquarters,
   Allied Air Forces,
     Victoria Barracks,
      MELBOURNE. S.C.1. (Copy to Air Board).

Royal Australian Air Force,
Headquarters,
North Western Area,
Allied Air Forces,
DARWIN. N.T.
4th July, 1942.

LOADING Mk.III and Mk. IV HUDSON AIRCRAFT.

The loading of the above aircraft to justify attacks on its most distant target,(AMBON), exceeds the operational necessity figure of the Air Board Weight Sheet Summary 24/4/42. (21,892 lbs with 2 x 250 lb bombs) and is well in excess of the maximum figure laid down in R.A.A.F. Publication No. 133B May 1942.

2.   The attached Weight Sheet Summary, (29/5/42), as used by No. 2 Squadron gives a normal all up weight with 4 x 250lb G.P. bombs of 20, 614.5 lbs. As the practice is to carry an extra observer in the loaders and deputy leader's aircraft the load increases by 200lbs.i.e. 20,814.5 lbs. With full auxiliary tanks the weight is further increased by 1,563 lbs. giving a total of 22,377 lbs. all up weight.

3.   Further, if the excess load is carried the aircraft is structurally endangered. At the same time single engine performance at that load is problematical and the operation of the aircraft is again extremely hazardous should an engine fail during take off.

4.   The following loads are required to be carried in N.W. Area:-

Location.	Operation.	Aux.Tank.	Crew.	Bombs.	Total.
Koepang	Recon.	One Full	5	2x250lbs	21,127 lbs
Koepang	Strike	One Full	5	4x250lbs	21,627 "
Koepang	Strike	One Full	5	5x250lbs	21,877 "
Ambon	Recon	Both Full	5	- -	21,377 "
Ambon	Strike	Both Full	5	4x250lbs	22, 377 "
Ambon	Strike	Both Full	5	5x250lbs	22,627 "
Ambon	Strike	Both Full	5	6x250lbs	22,877 "

5.   It is noted from practical observation that the Mk. IV Hudson single engine performance is not good beyond 20,600lbs though the Mk. III still gives single engine performance beyond that figure.

6.   In view of the undercarriage failures which have occurred through handling error it is considered that the aircraft could become predisposed towards these failures through overloading which must be done if strikes are to be worth while.

7.   The following policy in relation to operation of Hudson aircraft has therefore been adopted by this Headquarters:-

(a)   Aircraft on reconnaissance in the AMBON area carry 2x250lb bombs only.

(b)   Hudson aircraft are not used to attack targets in the AMBON area except when the importance of the targets in relation to enemy fighter defences justifies such a course.

(c)   When targets at AMBON are attacked as stated in para 7b a bomb loading of 4x250 or 5x250lb bombs is carried and the overloading is accepted as a justifiable risk of war.

8.   Comment upon or concurrence with the above policy is requested.

Air Commodore,
AIR OFFICER COMMANDING.
NORTH WESTERN AREA.
ALLIED AIR FORCES.

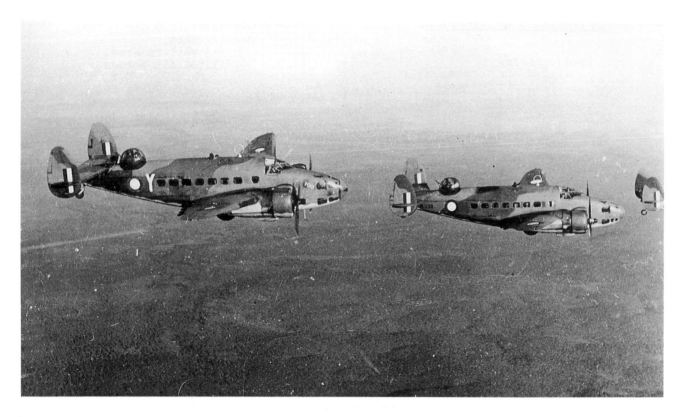

Hudsons A16-233 and -236 of No 2 Squadron near Hughes NT in 1943. These were later production aircraft, delivered to the RAAF in May 1942. (via Mike Kerr)

Bombing up a Northern Territory based Hudson, the crew in standard dress for the conditions. (via Neil Mackenzie)

No 13 Squadron received a similar citation from the United States President, its activities paralleling those of No 2 Squadron to a large extent.

13 Squadron RAAF

No 13 Squadron was formed at Darwin in June 1940 by absorbing most of the personnel and all of the aircraft (Ansons and Wirraways) of No 12 Squadron. The first commanding officer was Flt Lt J R Balmer. Later in the same month the squadron's first ten Hudsons (A16-7, -8, -63, -64, -66, -67, -68, -69, -71 and -72 were on strength and these were joined by three more in July.

The squadron operated Hudsons for a period of three years before they were replaced by Beauforts and then Venturas in the second half of 1943. In the meantime it operated from Darwin, conducting coastal patrol and security sorties as well as exercises with the Navy.

These continued into 1941, but in May there was an indication of things to come when a series of familiarisation flights to the Netherlands East Indies was begun. A particularly significant flight was conducted on 5 July when A16-68, flown by Wng Cdr Balmer, began a three day tour and reconnaissance of Koepang, Ambon and Namlea.

In August, Wng Cdr Balmer was replaced as 13 Squadron's commanding officer by Sqdn Ldr J R G McDonald, but he and his crew were lost on 10 December when Hudson A16-69 crashed into the sea off Ambon. Sqdn Ldr J P Ryland was appointed in his place.

On 2 December 1941, the squadron was placed on 36 hours notice of movement to the Netherlands East Indies area. The order to do so was received two days later, six Hudsons immediately flying to Laha on Ambon while the remaining six remained at Darwin awaiting orders to move to Namlea.

The arrival of the Hudsons at Ambon coincided with the start of the Pacific war and the beginning of a period in 13 Squadron's history which would see tragedy and triumph in the face of overwhelming odds from the rampaging Japanese. The remainder of December 1941 was relatively quiet for the squadron as it established itself at Ambon and carried out patrols in the area. Things began to warm up just before Christmas, and the following notes give an indication of the desperate events which took place over the next few weeks, resulting in the squadron withdrawing to Darwin from Ambon:

30 December 1941: The Hudsons recalled from Namlea to reinforce Laha and to be prepared for Japanese flying boat attack at any time. Namlea advised to prepare aerodrome and buildings for destruction in the event of evacuation.

6 January 1942: Laha – during the early hours of the morning seven enemy Type 97 flying boats bombed and strafed the aerodrome and building area and damaged a number of buildings and workshops belonging to the Dutch. No RAAF casualties. Native villages also bombed. The raid had an adverse effect on morale. The knowledge that no warning facilities were available almost caused a general evacuation of camp area at night. Trenches dug into side of hill adjacent to camp area. Most personnel went to these at night but without protective mosquito netting which resulted in considerable increase in incidence of malaria.

10 January: At Laha a Hudson made two attacks on a Type 97 flying boat over the Molucca Sea. After scoring hits on the enemy aircraft, Hudson forced to break off due to lack of fuel.

11 January: Laha again raided by 27 bombers escorted by Zero fighters. Runway badly holed, Zeros strafed aerodrome igniting one of the fuel dumps.

12 January: Hudsons A16-7 (Flt Lt G Sattler) and A16-67 (Flt Lt A R Barton) posted missing on operations at Manado in the Celebes Islands.

15 January: Zero fighters and bombers attack Laha. Attack lasted two hours and two Buffalo fighters which attempted interception were shot down. One Hudson destroyed on ground, two US Catalinas destroyed on water, runway rendered temporarily unserviceable, damage caused to fuel dumps, quarters and aircraft on ground. Dutch quarters destroyed by fire.

16 January: Further air raids, no RAAF losses.

20 January: A day of heavy losses with Hudson A16-64 (Flt Lt M P Willing) missing on photo reconnaissance sortie to Kena Bay and three Hudsons (A16-66, -125, -71) strafed and destroyed on ground by Zeros.

Hudson A16-117 in the Northern Territory. (via Neil Mackenzie)

21 January: Three raids on Laha, one of which put radio station out of action.

22 January: Laha camp areas evacuated overnight.

23 January: 17 flying boats and 18 Zeros attack Ambon, damage to aircraft and runways and 3,000 gallons of fuel destroyed. Anti aircraft fire ineffective.

25 January: Auxiliary base at Babo evacuated due to intense enemy action. Personnel returned to Darwin.

25-27 January: Further heavy raids on Ambon, serious damage to fuel, buildings and runways but no aircraft lost. Conditions deplorable and base rapidly becoming untenable. Maintenance of aircraft neglected and many operations flown by aircraft well past inspection periods.

28 January: Evacuation of Ambon ordered due to the increasingly difficult situation, the lack of air cover and an approaching convoy of enemy ships. 42 personnel returned to Darwin by air in Hudsons and Short Empire flying boats, the latter also carrying the sick, most of whom were suffering from malaria. The enemy convoy comprised 22 vessels – one heavy cruiser, three cruisers, five destroyers and 13 transports.

29 January: Evacuation continued. Further 62 personnel flown out to Darwin.

30 January: Complete evacuation preparations continued. All unsalavagable equipment destroyed including tractors and boxes of rifles. Volunteers selected to remain behind to carry out demolition work, they then trekked 100km to Tifu on the south coast where they were picked up six weeks later by an Empire flying boat. Members of 'Gull Force', the Australian 2/21 Battalion remained behind in attempt to hold off Japanese, but losses then and afterwards were horrendous.

With the withdrawal of what was left of No 13 Squadron from Ambon to Darwin, it was decided to move the squadron south to Daly Waters, although operations continued to be controlled from Darwin, at least for the moment. Daly Waters was used mainly as a maintenance base in the second half of February, looking after Hudsons from both 13 and 2 Squadrons, but in early March squadron headquarters also moved to there. One flight of Hudsons remained in Darwin.

No 2 Squadron was still operating from Koepang in Dutch Timor, but it too would soon be evacuated to Darwin. This was done on 19 February with the assistance of 13 Squadron, but as noted above, this was also the date of the first Japanese air raid on

Darwin. Both squadrons lost Hudsons in the raid and that in combination with the previous losses sustained and the serviceability problems meant that between them the two squadrons sometimes only had two or three operational aircraft.

The Japanese conducted many raids on targets in the Northern Territory during March and April 1942, striking as far south as Katherine as well as hitting Broome in Western Australia.

This period was used to replenish both the aircraft and personnel strengths of 13 Squadron and from April to September the squadron embarked on an intensive period of raids on enemy shipping and ground installations throughout the Netherlands East Indies and Timor, many of them in conjunction with No 2 Squadron. At the beginning of May the squadron moved again, this time to Hughes, just south of Darwin.

13 Squadron retained its Hudsons until April 1943 when the unit was moved to Canberra, wound down and then re-established equipped with Beauforts and Venturas.

The post Ambon period had seen the squadron fight its way back from near oblivion, in conjunction with 2 Squadron striking

Wing Commander Balmer and officers of No 13 Squadron at Darwin in June 1941. (RAAF Historical)

targets effectively. As noted both squadrons earned a Presidential Citation for their efforts.

6 Squadron RAAF

Based at Richmond NSW, No 6 Squadron began replacing its Ansons with Hudsons in April 1940 and its primary roles over the next 28 months were anti submarine and convoy protection patrols. The squadron as a whole did not move to a northern operational area until August 1942 when it played an important part in what became known as the battle of Milne Bay, fought during the last week of August and the first week of September. The move of the whole squadron to the northern area had been preceded by a detachment to the New Guinea area in January 1942, more of which below.

In the meantime, the generally monotonous sea patrols off the New South Wales Coast continued, with usually little result despite the known presence of enemy submarines. An exception occurred on 5 June 1942 off Newcastle when a 6 Squadron Hudson flown by Flt Lt Hitchcock spotted something suspicious on the surface, something which would soon be confirmed as a submarine.

A 6 Squadron Hudson (A16-37) in 1940, shortly after delivery and before the dorsal turret had been fitted. At this stage the squadron was conducting patrols off the New South Wales coast. (Jim Moore via Mike Kerr)

Hudsons of No 6 Squadron on patrol in the Milne Bay area. The squadron played an important role in the decisive battle at Milne Bay. (via Neil Mackenzie)

Hitchcock attacked in a medium dive and dropped four 250lb anti submarine bombs from 700 feet. The bombs were seen to explode in the wake created by the submarine's periscope. Debris was thrown high into the air, a column of water rose 35 to 40 feet and the Hudson was jolted some 200 feet upward by the blast.

A dark brown patch was observed on the water a few minutes after the attack, and this gradually spread to the accompaniment of large bubbles. It is considered that this submarine was at least damaged.

In late December 1941, No 6 Squadron received an operational order which briefed a most secret mission: "Long range Hudsons are to carry out photographic reconnaissance of Truk [a major Japanese base in the Caroline Islands] at the earliest opportunity. Long range tanks have been fitted to two Hudsons of No 6 Squadron together with special cameras".

The Hudsons IVs had two extra 105imp gal (477 litre) fuel tanks fitted in their cabins and a pair of 20-inch cameras installed – one in the nose and one in the standard camera well near the door. The aircraft were flown by Flt Lt R A Yeowart and Flg Off R M Green and were nicknamed *Tit Willow* and *Yum Yum*, respectively.

Only one of the Hudsons – Yeowart's – undertook the mission because Green's aircraft suffered a carburettor problem which was discovered when the pair reached their planned starting point, Rabaul.

Concerned about enemy raids on Rabaul, Yeowart flew his Hudson to Kavieng on the northern tip of New Ireland which took some distance off the 1,300 miles (2,000km) round trip from Rabaul. He departed at first light on 9 January 1942 and four and a half hours later found himself over Toll, the harbour of the main island.

In it were 12 warships (including an aircraft carrier), three merchant vessels and a hospital ship along with several float planes, eight 'Mavis' flying boats and 27 bombers parked on the nearby airstrip.

Yeowart conducted two photographic runs at 13,000 feet, encountering anti aircraft fire at the end of the first one and enemy aircraft during the second. He dived into a rain squall and returned to Kavieng, his mission successfully completed. The force Yeowart had discovered at Truk was part of that which would shortly be used in the successful Japanese assault on Rabaul.

No 6 Squadron moved from Richmond to Horn Island off the northern tip of Australia in late August 1942 and immediately began operations. The CO at this stage was Wng Cdr A A Barlow. The first attack occurred on 24 August when A16-205 (Plt Off Law) sighted an enemy convoy of three cruisers, four merchant ships and minesweepers. Law attacked with four 250lb general purpose and three 100lb anti submarine bombs from 100 feet, scoring no hits but one or two near misses and receiving intensive anti aircraft fire for his trouble.

Shortly after arriving at Horn Island a flight of 6 Squadron Hudsons was moved to Milne Bay on the south-eastern tip of New Guinea to carry out anti submarine patrols,

A photograph taken from Flt Lt Yeowart's Hudson during his reconnaissance of Truk in January 1942. To that point, this was the longest sea reconnaissance undertaken by the RAAF and the flight gave warning of the forthcoming Japanese assault on New Britain and New Ireland. (RAAF)

provide air cover for friendly shipping and to perform reconnaissance of the Milne Bay as well as providing support for the ground forces there.

On the night of 25 August, Japanese troops landed on the northern shore of Milne Bay, thus beginning an epic battle involving troops on the ground and several RAAF squadrons including No 6's Hudsons and the Kittyhawks of Nos 75 and 76, which were effectively used for both air-to-air combat and for strafing enemy barges and installations. In addition, Hudsons from No 32 Squadron were involved in the battle, which was vital to the defence of Port Moresby.

Milne Bay provided an extremely significant milestone in Australian military history as it was fought and won entirely by Australian airmen and soldiers from the 2nd AIF.

No 6 Squadron's Hudsons played their part, carrying out photographic and reconnaissance missions in dreadful weather as well as attacking Japanese shipping, barges and dumps.

The Flight Commander of the Milne Bay detachment, Sqdn Ldr D W (David) Colquohoun, was awarded the Distinguished

Flying Cross for his actions during the battle, one of them involving a solo attack against an enemy force of one cruiser and eight destroyers which were entering the Bay. Despite encountering a barrage of anti aircraft fire, Colquohoun pressed home his attack and scored a direct hit on the stern of the destroyer.

The Australians held out at Milne Bay despite the odds, and by the end of the first week of September 1942, the Japanese began to withdraw.

The main part of No 6 Squadron remained at Horn Island until October when it moved to Ward's Strip, Port Moresby, while the Milne Bay detachment remained in place. In the meantime the squadron shouldered a heavy workload patrolling the approaches to Milne Bay and areas far out to sea. In fact the entire responsibility of keeping the New Guinea sea lanes open to Allied shipping fell onto the shoulders of 6 Squadron's Hudsons and 100 Squadron's Beauforts for some months, mixed with another vital activity; the dropping of supplies to the Allied land forces in New Guinea.

In November 1942 the squadron flew 17 supply missions to Buna, two to Ioma and one to Kokoda as well as to other points, dropping 40,000lb (18,144kg) of supplies. These missions continued into 1943, as did the occasional night bombing sortie.

Despite ever more difficult to maintain and war weary aircraft, a lack of spares and Japanese air raids, 6 Squadron continued operating the Hudsons well into 1943, with anti submarine work becoming more frequent, many of these sorties resulting in attacks.

In August 1943, the squadron relinquished its tired Hudsons and replaced them with Beauforts.

7 Squadron RAAF

No 7 Squadron had its origins in World War I when it was formed in the United Kingdom as a training unit for the purpose of training Australian officers of the Australian Flying Corps. It disbanded in 1919 in its original form and re-established in June 1940 at Laverton Vic, equipped with Hudsons on loan from No 24 Squadron along with personnel from that unit to assist in training.

In October 1940 the 24 Squadron aircraft and personnel departed, leaving 7 Squadron with no aircraft of its own and only a core of personnel. They were attached to No 2 Squadron, also at Laverton, to gain operational experience on Hudsons, but this lack of separate identity continued for more than a year until January 1942 when 7 Squadron achieved its independence and began receiving its own Hudsons.

Between January and June 1942 the squadron's main activity was that of an Operational Training Flight, although seaward patrols were also conducted including anti submarine patrols.

The squadron moved to Bairnsdale Vic in May 1942 and it was during a patrol from there the following month that Flt Lt C Williams' Hudson sighted a ship off Gabo Island. Later identified as the *Iron Crown*, the ship exploded as the Hudson's crew watched, and shortly afterwards an enemy submarine surfaced nearby. The Hudson dived to attack, dropping two anti submarine bombs which apparently damaged the submarine. It eventually submerged and escaped.

7 Squadron again temporarily lost its identity in the same month when it was absorbed into No 1 Operational Training Unit. In September 1942 it was re-established at Nowra NSW, equipped with Beauforts.

14 Squadron RAAF

Based at Pearce WA, No 14 Squadron began replacing its Ansons with Hudsons in April 1940 and by the following month the Lockheed type was the squadron's sole equipment. It operated Hudsons until December 1942 when Beauforts were brought on strength and in the intervening years remained based in Western Australia. Detachments were occasionally based at other airfields around the state (mainly Geraldton, Carnarvon and Albany) and 14 Squadron aircraft also operated from Darwin from time to time.

One of these occasions arose in December 1940 when eight of the squadron's Hudsons were allocated to extended operations from Darwin, involving lengthy patrols covering an area stretching from Broome WA to Milingimbi on the north coast of Arnhem Land.

For the most part, the squadron's seaward patrols were routine, comprising clearing searches for convoys and troop ships as well as anti submarine and general reconnaissance patrols.

There were some interesting sidelights, however, such as participating in the search for the overdue HMAS *Sydney* in November 1941 and conducting, in July 1941, pigeon release trials! A 'Mr Burge of the Metropolitan Pigeon Club and several of his charges were taken up in a Hudson and the birds were released at various points ranging from 20 to 50 miles away from their lofts and at altitudes between 2,000 and 8,000 feet, including from above cloud. All the pigeons but one – which got caught in power lines – returned safely to their lofts.

The exercise was repeated, but at more extreme ranges of up to 150 miles and all the pigeons made it home, some of them the next day.

The declaration of war on Japan in December 1941 had little immediate effect on 14 Squadron's main activities, except that the frequency of seaward patrols was increased. The Japanese raid on Broome on 3 March cost the squadron one Hudson when A16-119 was destroyed on the ground after being strafed. A fire started and the Hudson's bombs exploded. Throughout 1942 there were a few encounters with enemy aircraft whilst patrolling but with no result for either side.

14 Squadron's first encounter with a submarine was an unfortunate one. On 4 March 1942 Hudson A16-122 (Flt Lt L R Trewren) was ordered to locate and attack a submarine which had failed to answer signals or in any way identify itself. The submarine was

Unhappy landing for A16-31 of 14 Squadron at Pearce. (via Neil Mackenzie)

A lovely panorama with three Hudsons from No 14 Squadron featured. (via Neil Mackenzie)

14 Squadron personnel at Pearce WA. (RAAF Historical)

Four more of 14 Squadron's Hudsons. Note the early 'inverted bathtub' dorsal guns. A16-30 (third from left) became VH-ASV after the war. (RAAF Historical)

duly attacked and damaged but turned out to be the USS *Sargo*. It limped into Fremantle for repairs and the Hudson's captain was naturally exonerated from any blame.

23 Squadron RAAF

No 23 Squadron began receiving Hudsons in August 1940 and operating from Archerfield, Brisbane, continued the activities it had begun with its Ansons, namely clearing searches for shipping, anti submarine and mine patrols, security patrols and co-operation exercises with the Army and Navy.

These remained the squadrons primary roles for its Australian based component until August 1942 when the squadron re-equipped with Bell Airacobras, supplemented by Wirraways. In the meantime, 23 Squadron moved from Archerfield to Amberley Qld in May 1942 and then to Lowood Qld the following month.

24 Squadron RAAF

No 24 Squadron was formed at Amberley Qld in June 1940 equipped with a mixed fleet of Wirraway and Moth Minor aircraft with Hudsons joining from August. These and the Wirraways became the squadron's

main equipment for the time being, the Wirraways being used for training in gunnery and dive bombing and the Hudsons for their usual sea patrol work. A considerably mixed fleet remained however, and it's interesting to note that in October 1941 it comprised five Hudsons, 11 Wirraways, three Moth Minors and a single Fairey Battle.

In October, the squadron moved to Townsville and began conducting reconnaissance flights between the mainland and New Guinea.

In December 1941 with the declaration of war on Japan, 24 Squadron was deployed forward to the New Britain area for use as an advanced strike force with one flight of Wirraways and one of Hudsons based on Rabaul. In late January 1942 Rabaul began to come under intensive attack from the Japanese, beginning an assault which was to see the heroic but desperately inadequately armed 24 Squadron Wirraway pilots attempt to stave off large Japanese air raids. The Wirraways were being used as interceptors – a role for which they were never designed – due to a lack of anything else. Against overwhelming odds there was only one possible outcome to the battle.

It reached its peak on 20 January with the result that 24 Squadron was all but wiped out with only two Wirraways escaping and wounded aircrew transported out in a Hudson. The hopeless defence of Rabaul cost 24 Squadron dearly in terms of personnel and aircraft, the latter including ten Wirraways and Hudsons A16-13, -19 and -146 along with A16-145 which was missing in action. The Japanese began landing on Rabaul on 23 January, the day after 24 Squadron evacuated, an adventure in itself.

32 Squadron RAAF

No 32 Squadron was unusual among RAAF Hudson squadrons in that it was formed after war with Japan began and at what was virtually the front line – 21 February 1942 at Port Moresby. Flights of Hudsons from Nos 6, 23 and 24 Squadrons had been operating informally as a composite unit for some weeks and its core comprised four Hudsons from No 6 Squadron including the two aircraft and crews which had been assigned to the Truk reconnaissance mission, Flt Lt Yeowart and Flg Off Green and their long range camera equipped Hudsons.

Hudsons A16-3, -38 and -47 of No 23 Squadron during its period of operation from Archerfield Qld (RAAF)

Hudson A16-155 of an Operational Training Unit. (via Neil Mackenzie)

A16-120, the Chief of Air Staff's Hudson at Milne Bay in February 1945. (via Neil Mackenzie)

numerous and often heavy enemy raids, with Seven Mile coming in for its fair share of attention. The result was the dispersal of the squadron's aircraft to Horn Island, from which they flew to Port Moresby to refuel and fly on to their targets. Even Horn Island wasn't immune, however, as it suffered numerous raids, one of which – on 7 July – destroyed several buildings and vehicles.

In early March 1942 the Japanese were close to mounting their first assaults on the New Guinea mainland and it was a 32 Squadron Hudson flown by Flg Off A S Hermes which spotted an enemy convoy in the Solomon Sea heading in the general direction of Buna. The date was 7 March and the convoy comprised one medium cruiser, four destroyers and six transports of various sizes.

32 Squadron Hudsons were the first aircraft to attack Japanese forces landing at Lae and Salamaua in early March, with some success.

The confusion of that period, when New Guinea was being defended from invasion by Japan – with obvious implications for Australia's own security – is illustrated by the variety of missions being undertaken by 32 Squadron's Hudsons, and indeed many other RAAF squadrons generally ... attacks on shipping, attacks on flying boat bases, reconnaissance, anti submarine patrols, night attacks, supply dropping, convoy protection, conventional bombing of land targets and so on, all usually with Japanese fighters paying close attention to the Hudsons.

The last week of July 1942 witnessed 32 Squadron's final offensive operations

Sqdn Ldr D W Kingwell was transferred from No 23 Squadron at Archerfield to command the new squadron which initially comprised 10 Hudsons, 29 officers and 176 other ranks. The squadron's establishment was seen as a necessary strengthening of Australian forces in and around Port Moresby.

Operations began from Port Moresby's Seven Mile aerodrome on the day of 32 Squadron's formation when Flt Lt Hampshire took A16-102 out to search for a submarine which had been reported off Murray Island. The search was unsuccessful.

The squadron's first bombing mission was carried out on 27 February when five Hudsons were sent out to attack Gasmata on New Britain. On this occasion three of the aircraft successfully bombed Gasmata's airstrip but one had to return to Port Moresby with engine problems and another failed to locate the target. Gasmata and other targets in New Britain would remain 32 Squadron's 'bread and butter' between then and the following September, when it would return to Australia.

The first few weeks of 32 Squadron's tenancy at Port Moresby saw it subject to

Hudson A16-112 of the RAAF Survey Flight, photographed at Busselton WA in 1946. The flight was one of the few RAAF units to fly Hudsons postwar. This particular aircraft was operated by East-West Airlines and Adastra Airways from 1949 as VH-BNJ, EWA and AGS, its latter guise photographing the New Guinea/West Irian border area as late as 1963. (via Neil Mackenzie)

"A bit late on the roundout, Hoskins!" An OTU Hudson (A16-47) with its nose to the grindstone. (via Neil Mackenzie)

before it returned to Australia at the beginning of September. The only RAAF aircraft to participate in attacks against the Japanese at Gona on the 23rd was 32 Squadron's Flt Lt Manning in A16-218 and Sgt Clarke also attacked targets in the Gona area on the following day.

The squadron's final offensive mission was on 30 July when one of its Hudsons along with aircraft from Nos 4 and 6 Squadrons attacked a Japanese convoy near Kitava Island, en route to Milne Bay.

32 Squadron participated in some supply dropping and convoy protection sorties in August, operating from Horn Island and preparatory to returning to Australia. This was achieved in early September, the squadron re-establishing at Richmond NSW and then Camden NSW later in the same month.

From Camden, anti submarine patrols, convoy protection flights and seaward reconnaissance sorties were flown off the New South Wales coast for the remainder of 1942 and the early months of 1943. The Hudsons were replaced by Beauforts in March of that year.

Miscellaneous Hudsons

Several other RAAF units operated Hudsons, among them No 38 (Transport) Squadron, formed at Richmond NSW in September 1943. The Hudson was the squadron's initial equipment and was operated on general freight, passenger and VIP duties from Richmond to points all over Australia until May 1944 when the Hudsons were replaced with Dakotas.

Other RAAF units which operated Hudsons included Nos 1, 3, 4 and 6 Communications Units at Laverton Vic, Mascot NSW, Archerfield Qld and Darwin NT, respectively, along with the Survey Flight and Operational Training Units.

The critical overall situation and the demand for more transport capability in New Guinea during 1942 resulted in the formation of the RAAF Special Transport Flight, comprising 15 Hudsons drawn from No 1 OTU at Bairnsdale Vic, one Douglas DC-2 from the Paratroop Training Unit and a variety of impressed civil aircraft – one DC-2, three DC-3s, two Lockheed 10s, two Stinsons, one Lockheed 14 and two de Havilland DH.86s.

The Special Transport Flight operated from Ward's Strip, Port Moresby, and only for a period of four weeks from mid December 1942. During that time some extremely hazardous flying was undertaken whilst dropping stores, stern opposition coming from not only Japanese fighters but also the New Guinea weather. One Hudson was shot down by Japanese anti aircraft fire on only the second day of operations and others were damaged by both AA fire and attacking enemy fighters.

One Hudson attracted the attention of no fewer than seven Zeros but its skipper, Sqdn Ldr O B Hall (the unit's CO) used low level evasion tactics and got away, albeit with a badly damaged aircraft. Hall's gunner managed to shoot down one Zero, probably destroy another and damage a third.

Even supposedly 'friendly' forces had a go at the Special Transport Flight. On the same day that Sqdn Ldr Hall's aircraft was attacked by seven Zeros, Sqdn Ldr N G Hemsworth's was attacked by several fighters just after takeoff from Dobodura. On board was a number of wounded Australian soldiers. Hemsworth flew low, sought out

The crew of a 459 Squadron Hudson walks back to debriefing after a sortie. From the left: Warrant Officers J Leathearn, Campbell, M E Gisz and W Robinette. (via Neil Mackenzie)

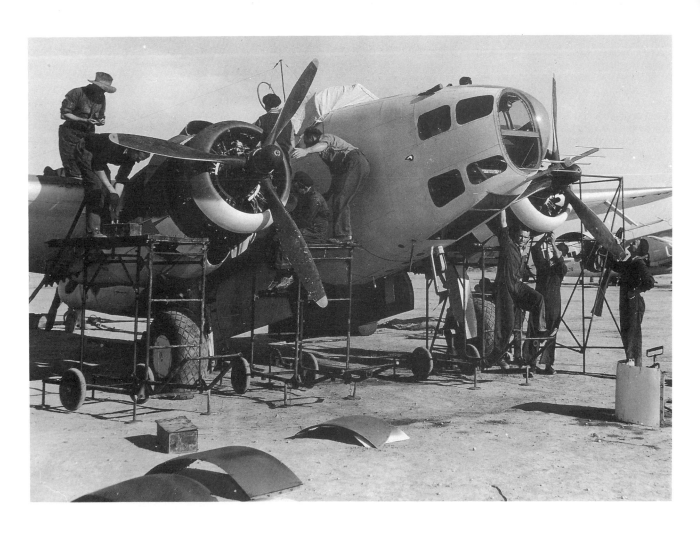

Good detail in these shots of 459 Squadron Hudsons being overhauled during the Western Desert campaign. This Australian squadron operated Cyclone engined Hudson IIIs. (via Neil Mackenzie)

the protection of a nearby Allied warship but on the way was fired upon by an American anti aircraft battery which misidentified the low flying Hudson. The Hudson was hit and forced to ditch, with the loss of two of the soldiers.

The Special Transport Flight's Hudsons flew 645 sorties over the rugged Owen Stanley Mountains during its four weeks existence, logging 1,020 flying hours, carrying 1,107 troops and some 780 tons of supplies.

Hudsons in the Middle East

One Australian squadron flew Hudsons with the Royal Air Force in the Middle East – No 459 – operating in Egypt and the Mediterranean mainly as a maritime patrol unit but also carving a reputation for itself in the anti shipping role.

No 459 Squadron RAAF was originally intended to be a flying boat unit attached to the British No 201 Naval Co-operation Group, but the character, operational style and equipment was changed prior to its formation in Egypt at Burg-el-Arab, about 45 miles (70km) west of Alexandria on 10 February 1942.

The philosophy behind the formation of 459 Squadron was explained thus: "To meet the growing air requirements over the Eastern Mediterranean, Air Ministry authorised an expansion of 201 Naval Co-operation Group in August 1941. This expansion took the initial form of providing more reconnaissance units; and to this end, 459 Squadron was formed.

"With the view that there was always a possibility that Australia might someday be faced with a similar problem around her coasts, it was further decided to man the unit entirely with RAAF personnel, thus providing Australia with a reserve of her own personnel trained in GR [general reconnaissance] work".

The initial establishment of the squadron was planned to be 16 Hudsons, but diversions of aircraft to the Malaya/Singapore region meant that its first equipment was just two Hudsons and four Bristol Blenheims. The commanding officer was Sqdn Ldr P W Howson and the squadron initially operated as a part of 203 Squadron RAF, from which the Blenheims were seconded.

The relative lack of aircraft restricted 459 Squadron's operations in the early months, but no time was wasted in getting underway with the first two operational sorties taking place four days after formation. Sqdn Ldr Howson in one of the Hudsons had an eventful first trip, but Flt Lt I L Campbell, in the other, had anything but.

Campbell and his crew first sighted and photographed a convoy bound for Malta which was being shadowed by a Junkers Ju 88, then a submarine's periscope was spotted and they attacked it with four bombs, but without result as two of them failed to explode and the other pair narrowly missed.

The Blenheims were used mainly for training and only occasionally flown on operations over the next couple of months before being returned to 203 Squadron, while the two Hudsons flew anti shipping patrols, transport sorties and on one occasion as navigation leaders for a group of Hurricanes flying to Malta.

By May 1942 the squadron had received a further 12 Hudsons and was operating as an independent unit, flying mainly anti submarine and Malta convoy protection patrols until July when attacks on German F-boats (heavily armed tank landing craft) and other enemy vessels began. The squadron sank 12 F-boats during the month, the result of swapping the usual offensive load of depth charges for ten 100lb bombs. The cost was heavy – six aircraft and crews lost, although the RAF average at the time was the loss of no fewer than four aircraft for every F-boat sunk.

By now, the squadron was based at its own landing ground at Idku in Egypt. It suffered its first casualty in late June when one of the Hudsons crashed near the aerodrome.

Three aircraft were detached from the main body of the squadron in September 1942 and sent to Aden, while at the same time six were moved to St Jean in Palestine.

A 459 Squadron Hudson gives away the origin of its crew with the words 'Southern Cross' appearing on the nose between the windows, accompanied by the appropriate symbol. (via Neil Mackenzie)

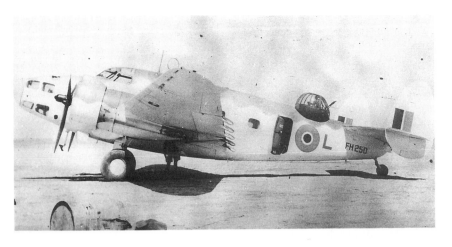

Australian Hudsons on active service: FH250 (top) in the Western Desert and FH428 (bottom) on patrol over Crete. (via Neil Mackenzie)

Disposals and Civil Use

It is not the intention of this book to delve into the story of postwar commercial use of ex-RAAF Lockheed Hudsons, but as the type was originally developed as a civil airliner as the Model 14, it is not surprising that several found their way onto the Australian civil register after World War II.

Although some Hudsons remained in service with the RAAF until 1949, most of the survivors were withdrawn from use at war's end and offered for sale by the Commonwealth Disposals Commission in 1946-47. Stored at East Sale, Richmond, Werribee, Canberra, Pearce and Laverton, the aircraft – nearly 50 in all – were offered at the bargain basement price of £1,000 ($2,000) each on a first come first served basis, this price featuring in the sales information which emphasised the original cost of £42,000 ($84,000) each.

According to the blurb: "The value is obvious. With the machine's ability for being converted to fulfil a necessary role in the present rapid expansion of civil aviation in Australia and overseas, the value becomes even more obvious ... these machines provide a splendid opportunity to obtain a really good speedy aircraft capable of being converted for passenger or freight purposes or for comfortable executive travel ..."

Flying hours on the airframes were generally low; few had more than 2,000 hours on the clock and one – A16-214 – had flown just 343 hours. A typical Hudson had 1,400-1,600 hours in its log book and perhaps 200 hours since its last major inspection. Engine lives varied but 200-300 hours since last major inspection was typical.

Forty-eight Hudsons were sold including 11 which were sold for scrap. Of the others major purchasers included European Air Transport (7), the Macquarie Grove Flying School (11) and Godden Board Godden (6).

Many of these were resold to other operators. Seventeen former RAAF Hudsons found their way onto the Australian civil register, operated by such notable organisations as East-West Airlines, John Fairfax & Sons (Herald Newspapers) and Adastra Airways/Adastra Aerial Surveys.

Four of these are extant in 1992: A16-105 and -112 with Malcolm Long at Coolangatta Qld, A16-122 with Bob Eastgate at Melbourne Vic and A16-199 which is on display at the Royal Air Force Museum, Hendon.

For the record, a summary of the civil careers of the 17 Australian registered Hudsons follows, noting owners, dates and registration letters:

A16-30: H W G Penny 7/47 (VH-ASV); cancelled 4/48.

A16-105: Curtis Madsen Aircrafts 10/49 (VH-BKY); East-West Airlines 10/50 (VH-BKY, EWB, EWS); John Fairfax & Sons 10/62 (VH-SMO); Sepal Pty Ltd 6/66 (VH-SMO/AGP); Adastra Aerial Surveys 10/69 (VH-AGP).

A16-110: Curtis Madsen Aircrafts 12/47 (VH-JCM); East-West Airlines 11/50 (VH-EWE, BPT, EWR); Sepal Pty Ltd 8/62 (VH-AGE) crashed Tennant Creek NT 9/66.

Both detachments were to help protect the British supply line. The aircraft still in Egypt performed general maritime operations in the lead-up to the decisive Battle of El Alamein.

A major 'kill' was recorded by 459 Squadron in September 1942 when an enemy destroyer was left ablaze following a low level attack by Plt Off Beaton and his Hudson. Beaton released ten 100lb bombs from only 40 feet, causing a large explosion.

The squadron moved to Gambut in December 1942 to begin a lengthy period of day and night convoy protection patrols. Detachments were occasionally sent to Nicosia in Cyprus, St Jean and Berka (Libya), but there was little excitement for some months due to the retreat and then surrender of the Axis forces in North Africa in May 1943.

An exception to this occurred on 16 June 1943 when the squadron scored its first submarine kill. Flt Sgt D T Barnard and his crew were responsible, attacking from behind and dropping four depth charges, one of which scored a direct hit. The U-boat sank in about five minutes, stern first, but the explosion which accompanied the direct hit threw the Hudson violently upwards, damaging its wings, fuselage and tail surfaces. The Hudson returned safely.

By the end of June 1943, 459 Squadron had flown 1,445 sorties and 7,681 operational hours.

A new phase of operations began in September 1943 when the squadron was taken off maritime work and tasked with the day and night bombing of enemy airfields in Greece and Crete, as part of the Aegean campaign. These operations were carried out for a month before routine maritime patrol work was reverted to for the remainder of the year. One enemy vessel was sunk by the squadron during this period, the 700 ton *Santoriai*.

In January 1944 the squadron exchanged its Hudsons for their bigger brothers – Venturas.

Same Hudson, different registration. The former A16-199 was first registered VH-SMM when bought by John Fairfax & Sons in 1950. It was purchased by Adastra in 1966 and the registration was changed to VH-AGJ later in the same year. These photographs were taken at Sydney in April 1966 (top) and February 1967. A16-199 now resides in the Royal Air Force Museum, Hendon. (Eric Allen)

Adastra Hudsons VH-AGS and VH-AGX (ex A16-122) both photographed at Sydney in 1965. (Eric Allen)

Another prominent postwar civil Hudson operator was East-West Airlines. Here, VH-EWB (A16-105) has a moment. The aircraft was repaired and survives today.

A16-105, one of four surviving former RAAF Hudsons. (RAAF Historical)

The Anson, Hudson & Sunderland, In Australian Service   133

A16-112: East-West Airlines 12/49 (VH-BNJ, EWA); Adastra Airways 7/53 (VH-AIU, AGS).

A16-114: John Fairfax & Sons 5/48 (VH-SMK), crashed 1950.

A16-115: Mandated Airlines 8/47 (VH-BDN); Fawcett Aviation 6/49, crashed Lae, New Guinea 3/50.

A16-120: John Fairfax & Sons 2/49 (VH-SML), lost off north coast of NSW 9/54.

A16-122: Adastra Airways 11/54 (VH-AGX); Sepal Pty Ltd 6/62; Adastra Aerial Surveys 10/69.

A16-147: C R Penny 6/48 (VH-BIH), delivered to India 2/49 then Palestine.

A16-155: European Air Transport 12/47 (VH-BFQ), delivered to India 2/49 then Palestine.

A16-192: European Air Transport 12/47 (VH-BIB), withdrawn from service 12/48.

A16-199: John Fairfax & Sons 12/50 (VH-SMM); Sepal Pty Ltd 6/66 (VH-AGJ); Adastra Aerial Surveys 10/69.

A16-214: Lionel Van Praag 5/47 (VH-ALA), crashed Markham River New Guinea 4/48 (37 people on board!).

A16-215: Adastra Airways 5/53 (VH-AGO), withdrawn from service 1957.

A16-219: Lionel van Praag 7/48 (VH-BLA); Adastra Airways 7/50 (VH-AGG), crashed off, Lae New Guinea 6/58.

A16-222: T Brain 11/48 (VH-BLB), left Australia for Palestine 2/49.

A16-226: European Air Transport 12/47 (VH-BIA); R Jorio 11/48; N Marcello 1/49, delivered to India 2/49 then to Palestine.

Adastra Aerial Surveys is probably the best known postwar operator of former RAAF Hudsons. From the top: VH-AGS (ex A16-112), VH-AGX (A16-122) and VH-SMM (A16-199). (via Bob Livingstone)

RAAF LOCKHEED HUDSONS

Abbreviations: w/o – written off; t/o – takeoff; soc – struck off charge; wfu – withdrawn from use; cvtd – converted; compnts – components; deliv – delivery; e/a – enemy action; AA – anti aircraft fire; u/c – undercarriage; prev i/d – previous identity; ops – operations; a/c – aircraft; NEI – Netherlands East Indies.

Notes: In some cases, the mark number listed here for Hudsons in the A16-153 to A16-247 serial range are different to those previously published. Refer to the main text for details. The RAAF called its first 100 Hudsons Mks.I and II (50 of each), equivalent to the RAAF's Mk.IV with Pratt & Whitney Twin Wasp engines. Those listed as Mk.IIIs (Wright Cyclone engines) and Mk.IVs are as per their RAF equivalents.

RAAF No	Prev I/D	Mark	Deliv	Disposal/Remarks
A16-1	–	I	02/40	sold for scrap 09/49
A16-2	–	I	01/40	destroyed by fire 09/46
A16-3	–	I	01/40	crashed into sea 12/42
A16-4	–	I	01/40	soc 02/42 after accident
A16-5	–	I	01/40	demolished by Army, w/o 09/42
A16-6	–	I	01/40	destroyed air raid Darwin 02/42
A16-7	–	I	01/40	missing on ops over Celebes 01/42
A16-8	–	I	01/40	crashed Darwin gunnery range 08/41
A16-9	–	I	01/40	lost at sea and w/o 02/42
A16-10	–	I	01/40	sold for scrap 03/48
A16-11	–	I	02/40	lost and w/o 02/42
A16-12	–	I	02/40	destroyed by enemy action 02/42
A16-13	–	I	02/40	destroyed by enemy action 01/42
A16-14	–	I	02/40	w/o in Far East 07/41
A16-15	–	I	02/40	w/o 02/42
A16-16	–	I	02/40	soc 02/49
A16-17	–	I	02/40	w/o 03/42
A16-18	–	I	02/40	w/o 10/42
A16-19	–	I	02/40	w/o 01/42
A16-20	–	I	02/40	lost to enemy action, w/o 01/42
A16-21	–	I	02/40	w/o in Far East 03/42
A16-22	–	I	02/40	sold Guinea Airways 03/46
A16-23	–	I	02/40	w/o in Far East 03/42
A16-24	–	I	02/40	lost to enemy action 12/41
A16-25	–	I	02/40	soc 09/41
A16-26	–	I	02/40	cvtd to compnts 08/44
A16-27	–	I	02/40	lost near Stradbroke Is Qld 08/40
A16-28	–	I	02/40	lost in Far East 03/42
A16-29	–	I	03/40	crashed in sea near Ambon 01/42
A16-30	–	I	02/40	sold Godden Board Godden 06/46
A16-31	–	I	03/40	cvtd to compnts 07/40
A16-32	–	I	02/40	w/o 07/43
A16-33	–	I	02/40	w/o 01/42
A16-34	–	I	02/40	cvtd to compnts 08/44
A16-35	–	I	02/40	lost in Far East 03/42
A16-36	–	I	02/40	shot down by AA fire Soputa 12/42
A16-37	–	I	02/40	w/o 03/42
A16-38	–	I	02/40	w/o 11/42
A16-39	–	I	02/40	cvtd to compnts 07/42
A16-40	–	I	02/40	w/o 02/42
A16-41	–	I	02/40	w/o Malaya 12/41
A16-42	–	I	02/40	w/o 03/42
A16-43	–	I	02/40	w/o 02/42
A16-44	–	I	02/40	lost in Far East, w/o 03/42
A16-45	–	I	03/40	cvtd to compnts 08/44
A16-46	–	I	03/40	w/o 02/42
A16-47	–	I	03/40	lost Lowood-Bowen Qld flight 07/45
A16-48	–	I	03/40	w/o 03/42
A16-49	–	I	03/40	crashed into sea off Malaya 02/41
A16-50	–	I	03/40	w/o 07/41
A16-51	–	II	03/40	w/o 03/42
A16-52	–	II	03/40	w/o 01/42
A16-53	–	II	03/40	lost to enemy action, w/o 01/42
A16-54	–	II	03/40	lost to enemy action, w/o 01/42
A16-55	–	II	03/40	soc 09/49

RAAF No	Prev I/D	Mark	Deliv	Disposal/Remarks
A16-56	–	II	03/40	lost in Far East, w/o 03/42
A16-57	–	II	03/40	destroyed air raid Darwin 02/42
A16-58	–	II	03/40	cvtd to compnts 07/40
A16-59	–	II	03/40	destroyed by enemy a/c Namlea 01/42
A16-60	–	II	03/40	w/o 03/42
A16-61	–	II	03/40	crashed Koepang 02/42
A16-62	–	II	03/40	w/o 03/42
A16-63	–	II	03/40	damaged air raid Darwin 02/42, w/o
A16-64	–	II	03/40	missing over Tondawa 01/42
A16-65	–	II	03/40	w/o 04/42
A16-66	–	II	03/40	strafed by enemy a/c Laha 01/42
A16-67	–	II	03/40	missing over Celebes 01/42
A16-68	–	II	03/40	crashed Richmond NSW 12/44
A16-69	–	II	03/40	crashed into sea off Ambon 12/41
A16-70	–	II	03/40	lost to enemy action, soc 12/41
A16-71	–	II	03/40	strafed by enemy a/c Laha 01/42
A16-72	–	II	04/40	destroyed air raid Darwin 02/42
A16-73	–	II	04/40	sold for scrap 09/48
A16-74	–	II	04/40	sold for scrap 09/49
A16-75	–	II	04/40	w/o 03/42
A16-76	–	II	04/40	w/o 03/42
A16-77	–	II	04/40	crashed Fishermen's Bend 10/43
A16-78	–	II	04/40	destroyed air raid Darwin 02/42
A16-79	–	II	04/40	w/o 03/42
A16-80	–	II	05/40	cvtd to compnts 03/42
A16-81	–	II	05/40	lost in Far East, w/o 03/42
A16-82	–	II	05/40	w/o 03/42
A16-83	–	II	05/40	crashed on t/o Broome WA 09/40
A16-84	–	II	05/40	sold for scrap 09/49
A16-85	–	II	05/40	lost in Far East, w/o 03/42
A16-86	–	II	05/40	w/o 07/41
A16-87	–	II	05/40	w/o 01/42
A16-88	–	II	05/40	sold for scrap 09/49
A16-89	–	II	05/40	cvtd to compnts 08/42
A16-90	–	II	05/40	soc 12/41
A16-91	–	II	05/40	w/o 02/42
A16-92	–	II	06/40	w/o 12/41
A16-93	–	II	06/40	w/o 03/42
A16-94	–	II	06/40	w/o Malaya 12/41
A16-95	–	II	06/40	w/o 03/42
A16-96	–	II	06/40	lost at Koepang 01/42
A16-97	–	II	06/40	crashed Canberra ACT 08/40
A16-98	–	II	06/40	sold for scrap 09/49
A16-99	–	II	06/40	cvtd to compnts 08/44
A16-100	–	II	06/40	w/o 04/42
A16-101	41-23171	IV	12/41	w/o 03/42
A16-102	41-23172	IV	12/41	cvtd to compnts 03/44
A16-103	41-23173	IV	12/41	cvtd to compnts 10/44
A16-104	41-23174	IV	12/41	cvtd to compnts 02/42
A16-105	41-23175	IV	12/41	sold European Air Transport 12/47, extant M Long
A16-106	41-23176	IV	12/41	cvtd to compnts 10/43
A16-107	41-23177	IV	12/41	cvtd to compnts 10/43
A16-108	41-23178	IV	12/41	crashed Timor 06/42
A16-109	41-23179	IV	12/41	shot down off Timor 03/42
A16-110	41-23180	IV	12/41	sold V J Madsen 04/47
A16-111	41-23181	IV	12/41	cvtd to compnts 02/44
A16-112	41-23182	IV	12/41	sold Godden Board Godden 10/47, extant M Long
A16-113	41-23183	IV	12/41	lost at sea
A16-114	41-23184	IV	12/41	sold Herald Flying Services 04/47
A16-115	41-23185	IV	12/41	sold W R Carpenter & Co 05/47
A16-116	41-23186	IV	12/41	sold MacRobertson Miller Aviation 01/47
A16-117	41-23187	IV	12/41	sold Herald Flying Services 04/47
A16-118	41-23188	IV	12/41	crashed into sea, w/o 03/45
A16-119	41-23189	IV	12/41	w/o Broome WA 03/42

RAAF No	Prev I/D	Mark	Deliv	Disposal/Remarks
A16-120	41-23190	IV	12/41	sold Macquarie Grove Flying School 03/48
A16-121	41-23191	IV	12/41	w/o 02/42
A16-122	41-23192	IV	12/41	sold Godden Board Godden 08/47, extant R Eastgate
A16-123	41-23193	IV	12/41	destroyed by enemy a/c Laha 01/42
A16-124	41-23194	IV	12/41	sold Macquarie Grove Flying School 06/48
A16-125	41-23195	IV	12/41	destroyed by enemy a/c Laha 01/42
A16-126	–	IV	12/41	strafed NEI 01/42
A16-127	–	IV	12/41	sold Macquarie Grove Flying School 09/47
A16-128	–	IV	12/41	oxygen/explosion hazard test a/c, soc 10/43
A16-129	–	IV	12/41	cvtd to compnts 09/43
A16-130	–	IV	12/41	sold Macquarie Grove Flying School 09/47
A16-131	–	IV	12/41	cvtd to compnts 10/45
A16-132	–	IV	12/41	missing on ops 06/42
A16-133	–	IV	12/41	cvtd to compnts 10/43
A16-134	–	IV	12/41	sold W G Stuart 09/47
A16-135	–	IV	12/41	destroyed air raid Darwin 02/42
A16-136	–	IV	12/41	w/o 03/42
A16-137	–	IV	12/41	missing on ops Koepang 04/42
A16-138	–	IV	12/41	sold Herald Flying Services 09/47
A16-139	41-23209	IV	12/41	cvtd to compnts 06/42
A16-140	41-23210	IV	12/41	cvtd to compnts 03/42
A16-141	41-23211	IV	12/41	crashed near Darwin 02/42
A16-142	41-23212	IV	12/41	cvtd to compnts 01/43
A16-143	–	IV	03/42	sold Macquarie Grove Flying School 09/47
A16-144	41-23214	IV	12/41	cvtd to compnts 01/42
A16-145	41-23215	IV	12/41	w/o 01/42
A16-146	41-23216	IV	12/41	w/o 02/42
A16-147	41-23217	IV	12/41	sold Godden Board Godden 04/47
A16-148	41-23218	IV	12/41	sold Macquarie Grove Flying School 09/47
A16-149	41-23219	IV	12/41	sold Godden Board Godden 04/47
A16-150	41-23220	IV	12/41	cvtd to compnts 11/43
A16-151	41-23221	IV	12/41	cvtd to compnts 05/42
A16-152	41-23222	IV	12/41	cvtd to compnts 02/43
A16-153	BW681	III	03/42	w/o 10/42
A16-154	BW736	III	03/42	cvtd to compnts 08/45
A16-155	BW737	III	03/42	sold Godden Board Godden 09/47
A16-156	BW738	III	03/42	sold European Air Transport 09/47
A16-157	BW739	III	03/42	sold Mr Williams 07/46
A16-158	BW740	III	03/42	cvtd instructional airframe 08/43
A16-159	BW741	III	03/42	w/o 04/42
A16-160	BW742	III	03/42	cvtd to compnts 12/45
A16-161	BW743	III	03/42	cvtd to compnts 05/45
A16-162	BW744	III	03/42	cvtd to compnts 07/42
A16-163	41-23275	III	12/41	sold European Air Transport 09/47
A16-164	41-23276	III	01/42	cvtd to compnts 05/42
A16-165	41-23277	III	01/42	w/o 03/42
A16-166	41-23278	III	01/42	missing on ops Timor 12/42
A16-167	41-23279	III	01/42	w/o 03/42
A16-168	41-23280	III	01/42	cvtd to compnts 04/42
A16-169	41-23281	III	01/42	w/o 04/43
A16-170	BW745	III	03/42	w/o 11/42
A16-171	41-23283	III	01/42	shot down 05/43
A16-172	BW746	III	03/42	w/o 09/42
A16-173	BW747	III	03/42	cvtd to compnts 11/42
A16-174	BW748	III	03/42	w/o 07/42
A16-175	BW668	III	03/42	cvtd to compnts 07/42
A16-176	BW669	III	03/42	cvtd to compnts 02/43
A16-177	BW670	III	03/42	sold Aircrafts Pty Ltd 08/46
A16-178	BW671	III	03/42	missing on ops off NT coast 10/43
A16-179	BW672	III	03/42	w/o 07/42
A16-180	BW673	III	03/42	sold Macquarie Grove Flying School 09/47
A16-181	BW674	III	03/42	w/o 08/43
A16-182	BW675	III	03/42	w/o 12/42
A16-183	BW676	III	03/42	cvtd to compnts 11/43
A16-184	BW661	III	03/42	cvtd to compnts 09/42
A16-185	BW662	III	03/42	cvtd to compnts 11/43
A16-186	BW663	III	03/42	crashed Hughes NT 06/43
A16-187	BW664	III	03/42	w/o 07/42
A16-188	BW665	III	03/42	cvtd to compnts 10/42
A16-189	BW666	III	03/42	sold Macquarie Grove Flying School 09/47
A16-190	BW667	III	03/42	w/o 07/42
A16-191	BW677	III	04/42	w/o 07/42
A16-192	BW678	III	04/42	sold European Air Transport 09/47
A16-193	BW679	III	04/42	w/o 07/42
A16-194	BW680	III	04/42	w/o 07/42
A16-195	FH169	III	04/42	w/o 07/43
A16-196	FH171	III	04/42	w/o 10/42
A16-197	FH172	III	04/42	cvtd to compnts 09/43
A16-198	FH173	III	04/42	w/o 07/42
A16-199	FH174	III	04/42	sold Macquarie Grove Flying School 09/47, extant RAF Museum Hendon
A16-200	FH177	III	04/42	sold European Air Transport 09/47
A16-201	FH178	III	04/42	w/o 07/42
A16-202	FH179	III	04/42	cvtd to compnts 10/43
A16-203	FH180	III	04/42	w/o 04/44
A16-204	FH182	III	04/42	cvtd to compnts 08/45
A16-205	FH183	III	04/42	w/o 12/42
A16-206	FH184	III	04/42	cvtd to compnts 02/43
A16-207	FH186	III	04/42	sold Macquarie Grove Flying School 09/47
A16-208	BW754	III	04/42	cvtd to compnts 01/43
A16-209	FH195	III	04/42	w/o 09/42
A16-210	BW752	III	04/42	w/o 01/43
A16-211	BW751	III	04/42	cvtd to compnts 07/43
A16-212	FH191	III	04/42	crashed in storm Hughes NT 02/43
A16-213	BW753	III	04/42	cvtd to compnts 10/43
A16-214	FH170	III	04/42	sold Lionel van Praag 11/46
A16-215	BW750	III	04/42	sold Sqn Ldr B E Hughes 06/48
A16-216	BW755	III	04/42	w/o 09/42
A16-217	FH192	III	04/42	cvtd to compnts 03/44
A16-218	FH194	III	04/42	w/o 09/42
A16-219	FH196	III	04/42	sold Lionel van Praag 01/48
A16-220	FH197	III	05/42	w/o 09/42
A16-221	–	III	04/42	cvtd to compnts 04/43
A16-222	AE488	III	03/42	sold Lionel van Praag 04/47
A16-223	FH176	III	05/42	cvtd instructional airframe 03/43
A16-224	FH181	III	05/42	crashed Laverton Vic 10/42
A16-225	FH185	III	05/42	cvtd to components 12/42
A16-226	FH187	III	05/42	sold European Air Transport 09/47
A16-227	FH188	III	05/42	cvtd to compnts 11/43
A16-228	FH189	III	05/42	cvtd to compnts 10/43
A16-229	FH200	III	05/42	sold Macquarie Grove Flying School 09/47
A16-230	FH201	III	05/42	w/o 04/44
A16-231	FH202	III	05/42	sold European Air Transport 09/47
A16-232	FH190	III	05/42	cvtd to compnts 10/43
A16-233	FH193	III	05/42	w/o 09/43
A16-234	FH212	III	05/42	w/o 10/42
A16-235	FH211	III	05/42	sold for scrap 11/48
A16-236	FH213	III	05/42	cvtd to compnts 08/45
A16-237	FH214	III	05/42	cvtd to compnts 04/43
A16-238	FH198	III	05/42	cvtd to compnts 10/43
A16-239	FH199	III	05/42	cvtd to compnts 02/43
A16-240	FH203	III	05/42	soc 08/45
A16-241	FH204	III	05/42	w/o 10/42
A16-242	FH205	III	05/42	cvtd to compnts 11/43
A16-243	FH206	III	05/42	w/o 10/42
A16-244	FH207	III	05/42	cvtd to compnts 02/44
A16-245	FH208	III	05/42	crashed in sea off East Cape 02/43
A16-246	FH209	III	05/42	w/o 11/42
A16-247	FH210	III	05/42	cvtd to compnts 07/43

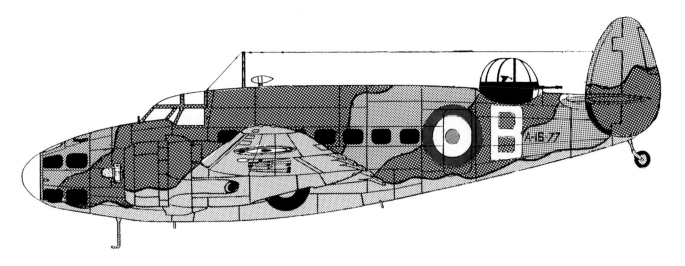

Hudson MkI A16-77/B of No 2 Sqn, 1940
Medium green and sand upper surface with silver undersurface. Medium grey code and black serial.

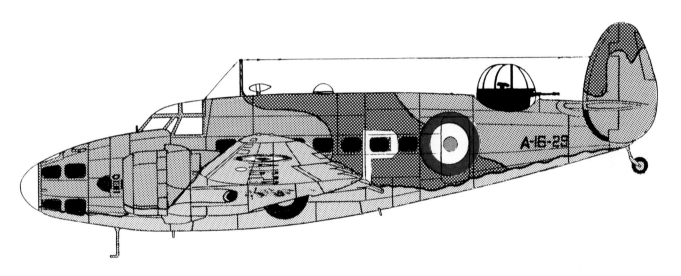

Hudson MkI A16-29/P of No 14 Sqn, 1940
Medium green and sand upper surface with silver undersurface. Medium grey code and black serial.

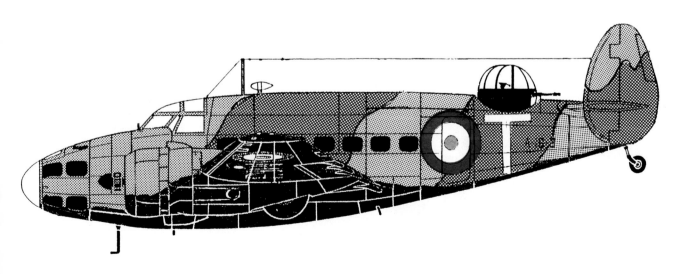

Hudson MkI A16-3/T of No 23 Sqn, late 1940
Medium green and sand upper surface with night (black) undersurface. Medium grey code and black serial.

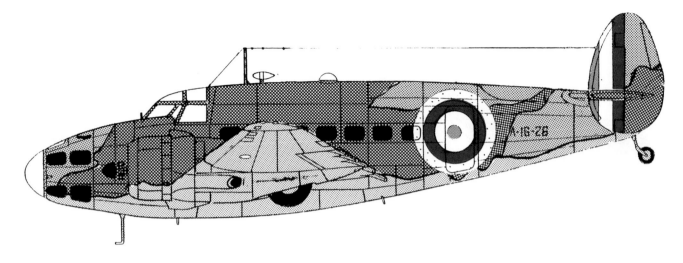

Hudson MkI A16-26 of No 1 Sqn, en route to Malaya, 1941
Medium green and sand upper surface with silver undersurface. No underwing roundels.

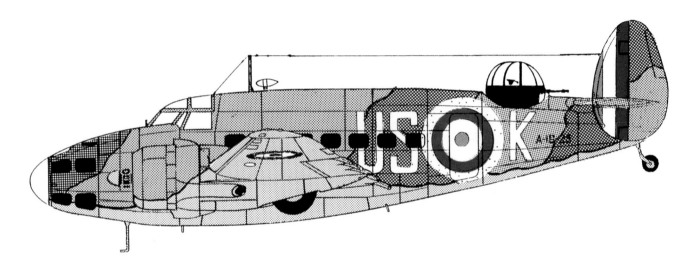

Hudson MkI A16-25/US-K of No 1 Sqn, Malaya, 1941
Medium green and sand upper surface with silver undersurface. Medium grey codes and black serial. Silver spinner.

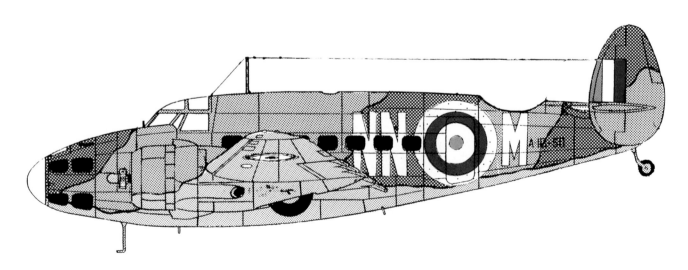

Hudson MkI A16-50/NN-M of No 8 Sqn, Malaya, 1941
Medium green and sand upper surface with silver undersurface. Medium grey codes and black serial.

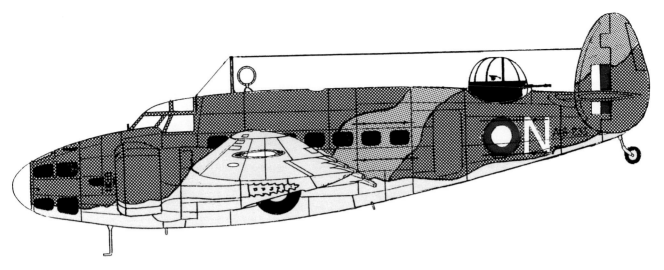

Hudson MkIII A16-233/N of No 2 Sqn, 1943
Medium green and sand upper surface with sky blue undersurface. Light grey code and black serial.

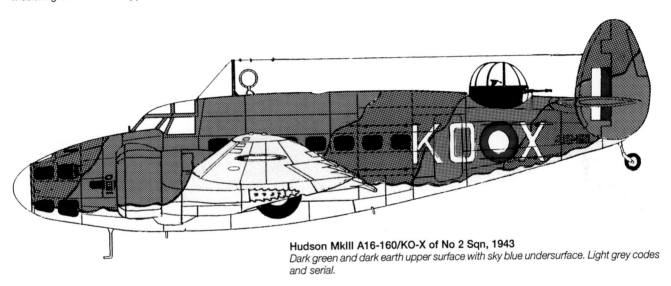

Hudson MkIII A16-160/KO-X of No 2 Sqn, 1943
Dark green and dark earth upper surface with sky blue undersurface. Light grey codes and serial.

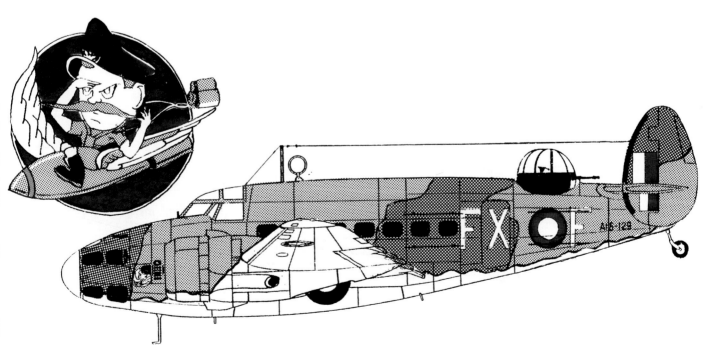

Hudson MkIV A16-129/FX-F of No 6 Sqn, New Guinea, 1943
Medium green and sand upper surface with sky blue undersurface. Light grey codes and black serial. Artwork on the nose shows a caricature of the squadron CO. The figure probably has flesh coloured skin with sand clothes and blue cap and is riding on a light brown bomb with a red stripe on nose. Disc is probably blue with white outline. All details in black.

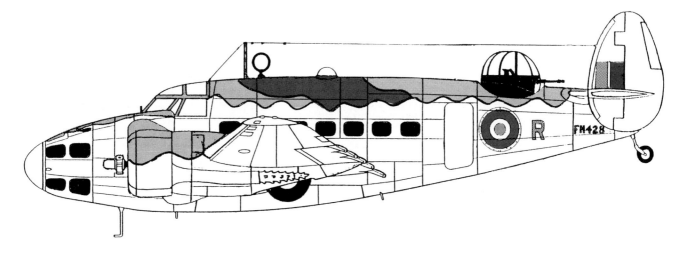

Hudson MkIII FH428/R of No 459 Sqn, Mediterranean area, 1944
Extra dark sea grey and dark slate grey upper surface with white sides and undersurface. Red code and serial.

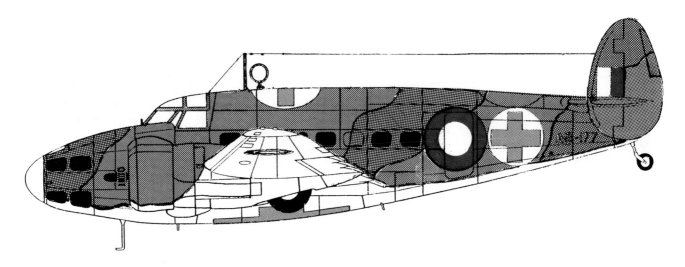

Hudson MkIII A16-177 of No 2 AAU, 1945
Dark green and dark earth upper surface with white undersurface. Red cross on white disc with red cross on fuselage undersurface. Medium grey serial.

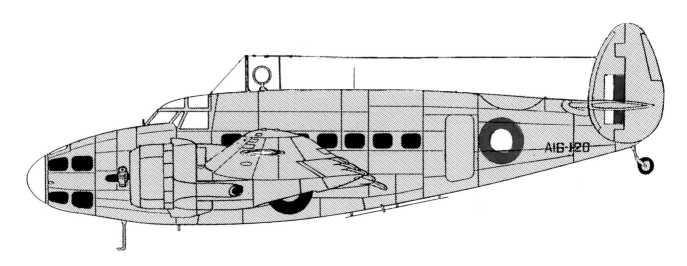

Hudson MkIV A16-120 of Chief of Air Staff, 1945
Natural metal overall with black serial.

Hudson MkIV A16-122/SU-P of Survey Flight, 1945
Foliage green overall with white codes and serial.

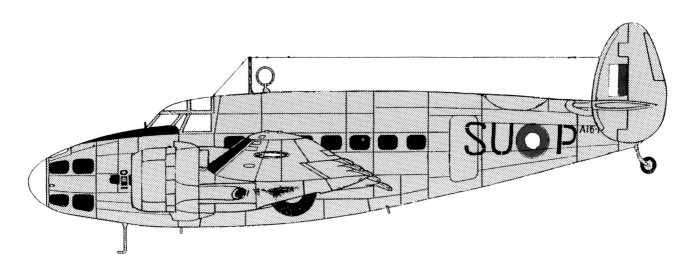

Hudson MkIV A16-122/SU-P of Survey Flight, 1946
Natural metal overall with black codes, serial and anti-glare panel on nose.

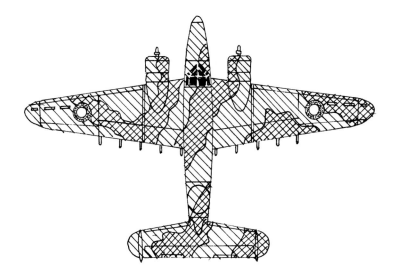

Scheme A upper surface camouflage pattern

Scheme B upper surface camouflage pattern

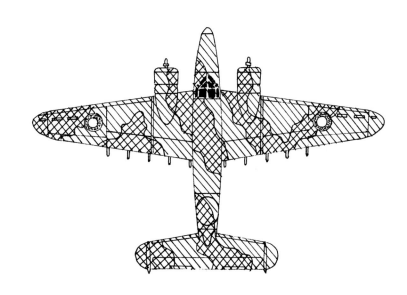

*Dark
Green*

*Dark
Earth*

*Medium
Green*

Sand

Silver

Sky Blue

*Insignia
Blue*

*Insignia
Red*

Yellow

*Extra Dark
Sea Grey*

*Dark Slate
Grey*

*Foliage
Green*

SHORT
SUNDERLAND

No 10 Squadron RAAF's first Sunderland I, N9048/RB-A, delivered on 11 September 1939. It was destroyed 14 months later during an air raid on its base at Mount Batten, Plymouth.

SHORT SUNDERLAND

Some military aircraft attract more than their fair share of attention because of the perception of 'glamour' attached to their roles. Fighters and bombers have traditionally been the favourites of small boys, their fathers, modellers, authors and airshow crowds, but occasionally a combat aircraft of a different ilk also achieves fame due to its exploits in action and the success of its design.

The Short S.25 Sunderland is one of these and with the American Consolidated Catalina, shares the title of the best known flying boat of World War II.

Built initially to a Royal Air Force requirement, the Sunderland served with Britain, Australia, Canada and South Africa during World War II and New Zealand and France after it. Its country of origin, Britain, operated the Sunderland for 21 years from 1938 and apart from its designed role of long range maritime patrol/reconnaissance bomber, the big boat was also used extensively as a transport and many aircraft were converted to civilian standards after the war as Sandringhams. Wartime transport activities included the evacuations of Greece, Crete and Norway as they were overrun by the Germans.

First flown in 1937, the Sunderland remained in production until 1946 by which time 749 examples had come off Short production lines at Belfast (Northern Ireland), Rochester (Kent) and Lake Windemere (Cumbria) and from the Blackburn Aircraft factory at Dumbarton in Scotland. As a point of order, the Belfast Sunderlands were built by a company called Short & Harland Ltd, a joint venture established by the aircraft manufacturer and the shipbuilders Harland & Wolff Ltd in 1936.

The original English company had been formed as a partnership between the brothers Horace, Eustace and Oswald Short. All three had engineering backgrounds and Eustace and Oswald had built and flown a balloon as early as 1902. The company acquired a licence to build six examples of the Wright brothers' 'Flyer', and as such became the world's first aircraft manufacturer in the commercial sense as all six aircraft were built to fulfil customer orders.

The Sunderland's contribution to Britain and the Allies' war effort was of the greatest importance. Patrolling the Atlantic, Indian and Pacific Oceans as well as the Mediterranean and North Seas, it protected shipping, attacked and sunk enemy ships and submarines and was used for countless rescue missions. Sunderlands were responsible for damaging or destroying more than 60 U-boats, many of them in the early days of the Battle of the Atlantic when the packs of German submarines threatened to cut Britain's shipping lifeline.

The Sunderland's ability to protect itself earned it the nickname 'Flying Porcupine', a sobriquet bestowed upon it by the Germans and resulting from an action over the Bay of Biscay in April 1940 when a Sunderland from No 204 (RAF) Squadron was

A Sunderland in its element – somewhere over the cold Atlantic Ocean protecting a convoy. This aircraft is from No 201 Squadron RAF. (via Neil Mackenzie)

The Shorts S.23 'C' Class 'Empire' flying boat and the Sunderland were developed in parallel and shared many features. The first Empire flew in July 1936 and the Sunderland in October 1937. (Shorts)

The 'G' Class Empire boat, larger, heavier and more powerful than its predecessors. The first example flew in July 1939 and only three were built. (Shorts)

attacked by several waves of Junkers Ju 88s. The result was one of the heavily armed Junkers shot down, another one crashing on the way home and the remaining six being driven off. The Sunderland was peppered with holes from the Junkers' 20mm cannon, some of which punctured fuel tanks, but the flying boat made it home with only slight injuries to some of the crew. There were several other examples of Sunderlands fighting off hordes of German fighters, usually Ju 88s.

The Royal Australian Air Force's operational use of the Sunderland began shortly after the declaration of war on Germany on 3 September 1939. The type had been ordered by the RAAF for use at home, but while personnel from No 10 Squadron were in Britain to collect their aircraft, the war started and it was decided to put the squadron to good use 'over there'.

Number 10 was joined by another RAAF squadron, No 461, in 1942, and between them the two units played a major role in the European maritime war. By the end of it all they had each destroyed (or shared in) six U-boats and left at least a further eight damaged. The two squadrons operated a total of 147 Sunderlands between them, all of them RAF aircraft carrying British serial numbers.

In contrast, only six Sunderlands were taken on RAAF charge in Australia and issued with local serial numbers. These aircraft were delivered in 1944 and operated by No 40 Squadron as transports until 1947 when the five survivors were sold.

Developing the Sunderland

Throughout its history, Shorts had manufactured several different types of flying boat and floatplane for both civil and military use. Experience with these and with the manufacture of metal hulls led to several famous flying boat designs from the late 1920s and through most of the 1930s, including the twin engined S.5 Singapore I, the S.8 Calcutta trimotor, the derivative Rangoon, the S.12 Singapore II and S.19 Singapore III with four engines (two tractor and two pusher in tandem) and the six engined Sarafand with stainless steel wing spars. All of these were biplanes with metal hulls but fabric covered wings. The most numerically successful was the Singapore III, 37 of which were built for the Royal Air Force between 1935 and 1937.

The company gained its chance to move into all metal construction of its flying boats in 1933 with the issue of two requirements – one military and one civil – which would result in the S.23 'C' Class 'Empire' boat for Imperial Airways and the S.25 Sunderland for the Royal Air Force.

As these two designs were developed in parallel, with the Empire emerging first, it is sometimes said that the Sunderland was merely a military derivative of the civilian aircraft. This is not entirely accurate even though they shared similar basic structures and powerplants, the Bristol Pegasus nine cylinder single row radial engine. The Empire was slightly longer than the Sunderland and had a marginally greater wingspan although the latter operated at considerably higher weights.

Even though the requirement which resulted in the Empire boat was issued slightly after that which resulted in the Sunderland, the civil aircraft was always intended to be developed first, with a resulting degree of 'spinoff' from one design to the other. The first S.23 Empire boat flew in July 1936 and 31 were subsequently built along with nine more powerful and heavier S.30s and two S.33s, a hybrid of the two.

Sunderland Defined

In November 1933 the British Air Ministry issued Specification R.2/33 for a new long range four engined general purpose flying boat for the Royal Air Force. Among its requirements were a range of 1,400 nautical miles (2,600km) at 2,000 feet with full load, a service ceiling of 15,000 feet, the ability to fly on three engines at maximum weight and on two at reduced weight.

The specification suggested a crew of six (with sleeping accommodation for each along with catering facilities) and a fixed armament of four single 0.303in Lewis machine guns located at different points around the aircraft.

Shorts submitted its S.25 design to the Air Ministry and in 1934 it was accepted and a prototype ordered. The design bore no relationship to the company's earlier biplanes, although chief designer Arthur Gouge and his team had initially looked at an enlarged development of the Sarafand, itself a very large aeroplane for its time, spanning 120 feet (36.5m) and featuring a maximum weight of 70,000lb (31,752kg) or 75% more than the first Empire boats. The

The 'Maia' and 'Mercury' composite aircraft of 1938, collectively known as the 'Mayo'. Designed for long range flight, the combination flew 5,997 miles (9,651km) from Dundee to Orange River, South Africa in October 1938. 'Mayo' carried sufficient fuel to fly 3,800 miles (6,115km) on its own.

Sunderland, even in its later and heavier variants, had a maximum weight notably less than this.

Design work on the Empire dictated the final configuration of the Sunderland as Arthur Gouge gradually moved away from the traditional biplane flying boat and observed the development of all metal monoplane commercial aircraft in the USA and elsewhere. Thus was established the form of the Empire boat and as a result, that of the Sunderland as well.

There was some shuffling of the aircraft's gun armament before a configuration was finally settled on and this resulted in some changes to its detail design. Consideration was given to installing a massive 37mm Vickers cannon in the bow but this idea was dropped as it was realised that rear defence was more important. As a result, the Air Ministry called for a Frazer Nash FN13 turret housing four 0.303in machine guns be installed in the aircraft's rear and at the same time it was decided to replace the big Vickers cannon in the nose with an FN11 turret containing a single Lewis or Vickers 0.303in gun.

The installation of the heavy rear turret moved the aircraft's centre of gravity a long way aft and to compensate, the previously straight wing had to be given some sweepback. The engines moved back with the wings, resulting in them pointing slightly outwards when viewed in plan and giving the Sunderland one of its distinguishing features.

This change resulted in the need for modifications to the lower hull, which suffered altered hydrodynamic properties during takeoff and landing.

Specification 22/36 was issued in 1936, covering the aircraft as presented by Shorts (before the changes listed above were introduced) and orders were placed for 21 production aircraft as the Sunderland I. As construction of the prototype was well under way when the design changes were

A Sunderland's 'bridge', with the captain and second pilot in their seats. The overhead console houses (front to rear) the fuel jettison, slow running cutout, engine master cocks, elevator trim and rudder trim controls. (RAAF Historical)

Sunderlands and a Stirling at a Shorts factory in 1941 at the earliest, the date dictated by the presence of dorsal turret equipped aircraft in the photograph. The aircraft in the foreground is L2163, the seventh Sunderland built. (Shorts)

Well worn Sunderland I of No 210 Squadron RAF, clearly showing the open dorsal gun positions. Sunderland operations were tough on exterior finishes. This particular aircraft, L2163, later served with No 10 Squadron RAAF.

Sunderland III W4004 of No 10 Squadron RAAF on its beaching trolleys and being brought indoors for some maintenance. Note the aerials associated with the ASV radar. (via Neil Mackenzie)

settled upon, it was decided to leave this aircraft in the original configuration and modify it later on. All production Sunderlands featured the swept back wings and modified hull from the start.

The prototype was given the RAF serial K4774 and was rolled out from Short's Rochester factory on 14 October 1937. After completing taxying trials on the adjacent River Medway, the first Sunderland recorded its maiden flight two days later. On board were the company's chief test pilot, John Lankester Parker, co-pilot Harold Piper and engineer George Cotton. K4774 was initially fitted with 950hp Pegasus X engines and flew only four times before it was withdrawn to be modified to production standard with the swept back wings, modified hull and 1,010hp Pegasus XXII engines.

The prototype resumed flying in early March 1938 and was joined the following month by the first production Sunderland, L2158. The first production batch of 11 aircraft had all flown by early August 1938 and manufacture continued at a steady rate from there.

By the standards of the time, the Sunderland was a very large aircraft, spanning 112ft 9.5in (34.38m) and measuring 85ft 4in (26.01m) in length. The cavernous interior was of a double deck arrangement complete with an officer's wardroom, sleeping quarters, galley and workshop. A crew of seven was standard early on but this increased to ten with the addition of extra guns and operational equipment – two pilots, navigator, ASV radar operator, radio operator, nose gunner/bomb aimer, engineer, rear gunner, and mid upper gunner/s.

The aircraft was of all metal construction. The high cantilever wing structure comprised four extruded T-sections which formed the corners of a box girder which were braced in the lift section by tubular struts and in the drag bays by built up rib members. With the exception of the trailing edges of the ailerons, the whole wing was metal covered including the large, retractable Gouge flaps. The tail surfaces featured metal structures but were fabric covered aft of the leading edges.

The hull was built up from channel section frames interconnected by Z-section stiff-

eners and was entirely metal covered using countersunk rivets. The upper deck consisted of the forward cockpit area (perhaps 'bridge' would be a better word) accommodating the two pilots, the radio operator, the engineer and the navigator. Aft of the wing spar frames equipment stowage space was provided.

The extreme nose housed the nose gunner/bomb aimer and the turret retracted aft to provide space for a crewmember to assist in mooring. Behind and below the turret, on the lower deck, was the mooring compartment and behind that were housed the toilet, wardroom, galley, crew quarters and bomb storage area.

Sunderland Is were delivered with gun armament as described above, although this was added to in service. Some aircraft were fitted with a two gun nose turret and most had two separate hand operated Vickers machine guns installed in the upper rear fuselage in open positions with the gunners protected by metal fairings.

Offensive armament comprised up to 2,000lb (908kg) of bombs, depth charges or mines which were stored in the hull and

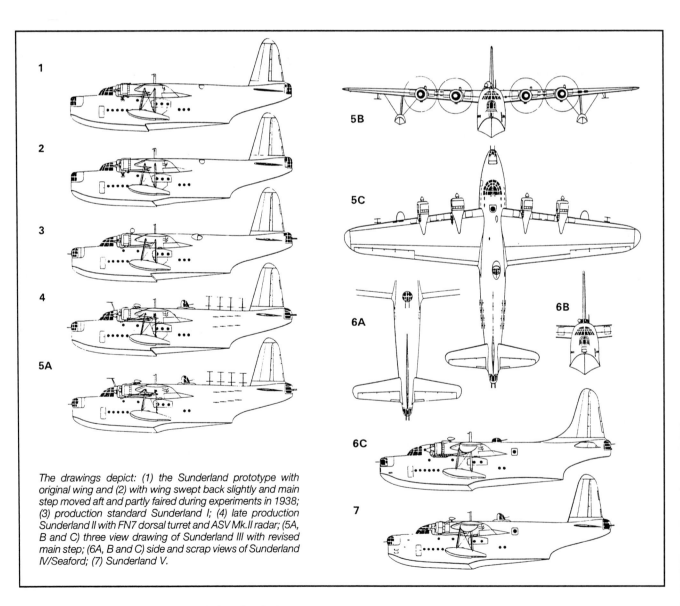

The drawings depict: (1) the Sunderland prototype with original wing and (2) with wing swept back slightly and main step moved aft and partly faired during experiments in 1938; (3) production standard Sunderland I; (4) late production Sunderland II with FN7 dorsal turret and ASV Mk.II radar; (5A, B and C) three view drawing of Sunderland III with revised main step; (6A, B and C) side and scrap views of Sunderland IV/Seaford; (7) Sunderland V.

winched up and out to under the wing through hatches when required.

The Sunderland I's four 1,010hp Pegasus XXII poppet valve radial engines drove three bladed de Havilland two pitch propellers and allowed the aircraft to cruise at 170mph (274km/h) over a range of 2,110 miles (3,396km). At a lower 'patrol' speed of 136mph (219km/h), the Sunderland's 2,025imp gal (9,205 l) fuel capacity in six wing tanks gave a maximum range of 2,500 miles (4,023km) and an endurance of 18 hours. Normal maximum takeoff weight of the Sunderland I was 45,210lb (20,507kg) with 49,000lb (22,226kg) available as a maximum overload.

Orders for the Sunderland I were placed in dribs and drabs between 1936 and 1940, production of this model finally amounting to 89, of which 74 were built by Shorts at Rochester and the remainder by Blackburn Aircraft.

The first RAF squadron to receive Sunderlands was No 230 in Singapore which had its first aircraft ferried out by No 210 Squadron personnel in June 1938. No 210 Squadron, based at Pembroke Dock in South Wales, received its own first aircraft in the following month and by the time war broke out in September 1939 the RAF had 39 Sunderlands in service, equipping three squadrons in Britain and one at Singapore. No 10 Squadron RAAF received its first aircraft a week after war was declared. Ultimately, 18 RAF, three RAAF, two RCAF, three RNZAF, one SAAF and five *Aero-navale* squadrons operated Sunderlands.

For the record, the first U-boat sinking in which a Sunderland played a part was that of the U-55 in January 1940. The submarine was scuttled by its skipper after receiving the attentions of a 228 Squadron aircraft and two Royal Navy ships. The first submarine sunk by a Sunderland acting alone was the Italian *Argonauta*, destroyed by a 230 Squadron aircraft in June 1940.

Developing the Sunderland

A converted prototype and 43 production Sunderland IIs followed, with deliveries beginning in May 1941. This variant featured Pegasus XVIII engines fitted with two speed superchargers and rated at 965hp for takeoff and 1,000hp at 3,000 feet when running on 87 octane fuel or 1,050hp for takeoff and 1,065hp at 1,250 feet on 100 octane.

Defensive armament was upgraded to include a two gun FN11 nose turret as standard, a four gun FN4A rear turret with twice the ammunition (1,000rpg) of the previous FN13 and in later aircraft, a two gun FN7 mid upper turret in place of the two open beam guns fitted to most Sunderland Is.

Operationally, the Sunderland II featured a marked improvement in capability with the fitting of ASV (air-surface vessel) radar with its associated masts, antennae and transmitting loops. The 43 Sunderland IIs were built by Shorts Rochester (23), Shorts Belfast (15) and Blackburn (5).

The Sunderland II was a temporary expedient and was quickly replaced in produc-

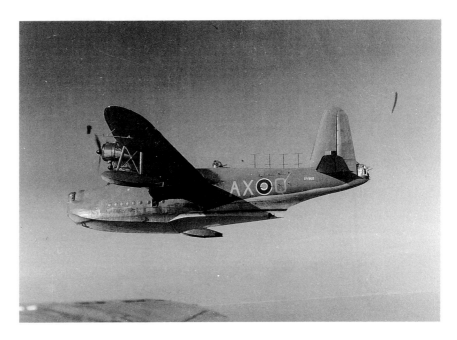

Shots of a Sunderland II (top) and III (bottom) clearly show the revised main step introduced on the later model. Also evident is the different dorsal gun layout and ASV radar aerials on the Mk.III. (via Neil Mackenzie)

tion by the most numerous of all Sunderland variants, the Mk.III. A prototype converted from a Mk.I was flown in June 1941 and was followed in December 1941 by the first of 462 production aircraft which were built at Rochester (186), Belfast (71), by Blackburn at Dumbarton (170) and at a new Shorts facility on Lake Windemere (35) which had been established mainly to carry out maintenance and repair tasks on Sunderlands.

The Sunderland III retained the Pegasus XVIII engines of its immediate predecessor in combination with two extra fuel tanks per wing giving a total capacity of 2,552imp gal (11,600 l) and either two pitch or constant-speed de Havilland propellers.

Initially, armament remained as before but later aircraft were fitted with four fixed Browning 0.303in machine guns in the nose (two on each side) and others acquired twin

0.50in guns in the hatches on either side of the aft hull. Prior to this the Australian Sunderland squadrons had developed a field modification which allowed the fitting of a single swivelling Vickers gun in each galley hatch on the sides of the hull and this also became a standard fitting. The Australians were also responsible for the first fixed nose guns experiments, the aim being to provide better defensive and offensive firepower. The result was that a Sunderland could be fitted with no fewer than 18 machine guns – 'Flying Porcupine' indeed!

The Sunderland III retained the ASV radar, mainly in its improved Mk.III form which had been developed from the H2S radar bombing equipment fitted to many Lancasters and Halifaxes. The installation of this radar had become necessary due to German countermeasures against the ear-

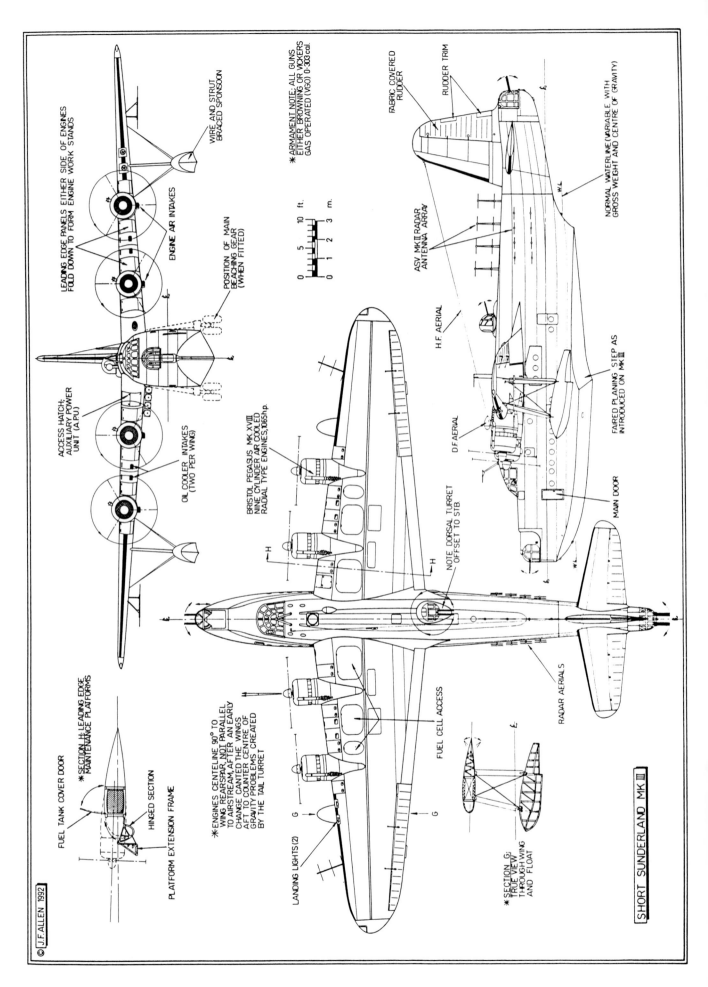

WIRE AND STRUT BRACED SPONSOON

LEADING EDGE PANELS EITHER SIDE OF ENGINES FOLD DOWN TO FORM ENGINE WORK STANDS

ENGINE AIR INTAKES

* ARMAMENT NOTE: ALL GUNS EITHER BROWNING OR VICKERS GAS OPERATED (VGO) 0.303 cal.

RUDDER TRIM

FABRIC COVERED RUDDER

NORMAL WATERLINE (VARIABLE WITH GROSS WEIGHT AND CENTRE OF GRAVITY)

POSITION OF MAIN BEACHING GEAR (WHEN FITTED)

ACCESS HATCH; AUXILIARY POWER UNIT (A.P.U.)

OIL COOLER INTAKES (TWO PER WING)

ASV MK II RADAR ANTENNA ARRAY

H.F. AERIAL

D.F. AERIAL

FAIRED PLANING STEP AS INTRODUCED ON MK III

MAIN DOOR

BRISTOL PEGASUS MK XVIII NINE CYLINDER AIR COOLED RADIAL TYPE ENGINES,1065hp.

NOTE DORSAL TURRET OFFSET TO STB

RADAR AERIALS

FUEL TANK COVER DOOR

HINGED SECTION

PLATFORM EXTENSION FRAME

* SECTION H: LEADING EDGE MAINTENANCE PLATFORMS

* ENGINES CENTRELINE 90° TO WING REARSPAR, NOT PARALLEL TO AIRSTREAM, AFTER AN EARLY CHANGE CANTED THE WINGS AFT TO COUNTER CENTRE OF GRAVITY PROBLEMS CREATED BY THE TAIL TURRET

LANDING LIGHTS (2)

FUEL CELL ACCESS

* SECTION G: TRUE VIEW THROUGH WING AND FLOAT

© J.F. ALLEN 1992

SHORT SUNDERLAND MK III

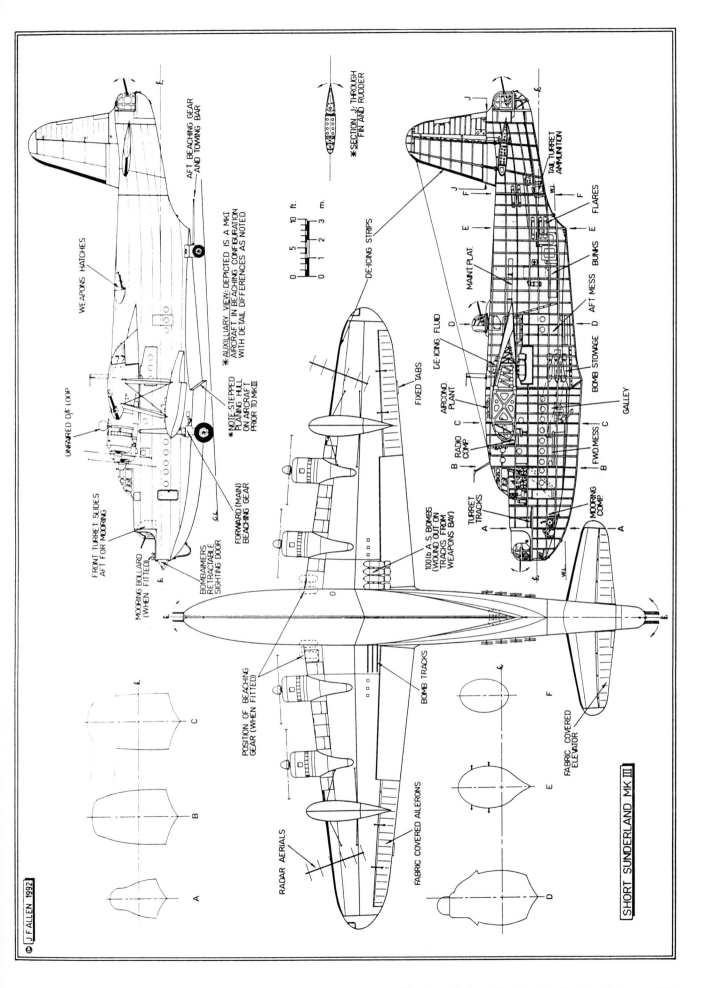

AFT BEACHING GEAR AND TOWING BAR

WEAPONS HATCHES

✱ AUXILLIARY VIEW: DEPICTED IS A MKI AIRCRAFT IN BEACHING CONFIGURATION WITH DETAIL DIFFERENCES AS NOTED.

✱ NOTE STEPPED PLANING HULL ON AIRCRAFT PRIOR TO MKIII

UNFAIRED D/F LOOP

FORWARD (MAIN) BEACHING GEAR

FRONT TURRET SLIDES AFT FOR MOORING

BOMBAIMERS RETRACTABLE SIGHTING DOOR

MOORING BOLLARD (WHEN FITTED)

✱ SECTION J: THROUGH FIN AND RUDDER

TAIL TURRET AMMUNITION

DE-ICING STRIPS

DE-ICING FLUID

MAINT. PLAT.

FLARES

AIRCOND. PLANT

BOMB STOWAGE

AFT MESS BUNKS

RADIO COMP.

FWD MESS

GALLEY

MOORING COMP.

TURRET TRACKS

FIXED TABS

100lb A.S. BOMBS (WOUND OUT ON TRACKS FROM WEAPONS BAY)

POSITION OF BEACHING GEAR (WHEN FITTED)

BOMB TRACKS

FABRIC COVERED AILERONS

RADAR AERIALS

FABRIC COVERED ELEVATOR

0 5 10 ft.
0 1 2 3 m.

SHORT SUNDERLAND MK III

What the Sunderland was all about. A very close up view of a U-boat under attack from a Royal Canadian Air Force Sunderland. This particular attack resulted in a kill for the Canadians of No 423 Squadron in April 1944. (RAAF Historical)

Coastal Command's last convoy escort for the Royal Navy in World War II was carried out by this Sunderland V of 201 Squadron on 4 June 1945. (via Neil Mackenzie)

lier equipment which had its transmissions detected by U-boats fitted with responders, giving ample warning of an approaching Sunderland. ASV Mk.III nullified this advantage.

The Sunderland III also incorporated a redesigned main step which was faired to remove the characteristic transverse step of earlier variants. The new design provided improved performance and handling in the air (at the expense of some qualities on the water) and became a standard feature of all subsequent Sunderlands. The Sunderland III remained in production until early 1945.

Further Improvement

The designation Sunderland IV was given to a faster and heavier derivative developed for the Pacific theatre. Featuring 1,800hp Bristol Hercules radial engines, a lengthened and widened planing bottom and substantially increased weights, the first of two Sunderland IV prototypes (factory designation S.45) flew in August 1944 after a protracted development period which had begun more than two years earlier.

The Sunderland IV never went into production as such, but instead was renamed Seaford I and was externally distinguishable by its very tall fin and rudder assembly and larger horizontal tail surfaces with increased dihedral. Only eight Seafords were completed before the war ended and as a result production of the 26 S.45 variants eventually completed was mainly postwar, the majority of them appearing as Solent civil transports with passenger windows and different versions of the Hercules engine installed.

A rather more urgent need was met by the Sunderland V, investigations into which began in early 1942. Sunderland crews had

---

SHORT S.25 SUNDERLAND I and V

Powerplants: (I) Four Bristol Pegasus XXII nine cylinder single row air cooled radial engines with single speed superchargers each rated at 1,010hp for takeoff and 865hp at 6,500ft; de Havilland three bladed two-pitch metal propellers of 12ft 9in (3.89m) diameter; fuel capacity 2,025imp gal (9,206 l) in six wing tanks.
(V) Four Pratt & Whitney R-1830-90 Twin Wasp 14 cylinder two row air cooled radial engines with two speed superchargers each rated at 1,200hp for takeoff and at 4,900ft and 1,050hp at 13,100ft; de Havilland three bladed constant-speed and feathering propellers of 12ft 9in (3.89m) diameter; fuel capacity 2,552imp gal (11,601 l) in ten wing tanks.
Dimensions: (I/V) Wing span 112ft 9.5in (34.38m); length 85ft 4.1in (26.01m); height (on beaching trolleys) 32ft 2in (9.79m); wing area 1,487sq ft (138.14sq m).
Weights: (I) Empty 30,600lb (13,880kg); normal loaded 45,210lb (20,507kg); max overload 49,000lb (22,226kg); max wing loading 32.95lb/sq ft; max power loading 12.12lb/hp.
(V) Empty 36,900lb (16,738kg); max takeoff 60,000lb (27,216kg); max wing loading 40.34lb/sq ft; max power loading 12.5lb/hp.
Armament: (I, defensive) One (or two) 0.303in Vickers machine gun(s) in Frazer Nash FN11 nose turret; two 0.303in Vickers machine guns in open dorsal positions; four 0.303in Browning machine guns in FN13 rear turret with 500rpg.
(V, defensive) Two 0.303in Browning machine guns in Frazer Nash FN11 nose turret with 500rpg; two 0.50in fixed Browning machine guns in nose with 2,000rpg; two 0.303in Browning machine guns in FN7 dorsal turret with 1,000rpg; four 0.303in Browning machine guns in FN4A rear turret with 1,000rpg; one 0.50in Browning machine gun per side in beam position with 400rpg.
(I/V, offensive) Maximum load of 2,000lb (908kg) comprising depth charges, mines and bombs.
Performance: (I) Max speed 209mph (336km/h) at 5,000ft; cruising speed 170mph (274km/h) at 5,000ft; time to 5,000ft 7.2min at normal loaded weight; service ceiling 15,000ft (4,572m); range with max load 1,790 miles (2,880km); range with max fuel 2,110 miles (3,396km) at 170km/h, 2,500 miles (4,023km) at 136mph.
(V) Max speed 207mph (333km/h) at sea level, 213mph (342km/h) at 5,000ft; long range cruise 133mph (214km/h) at 2,000ft; initial climb 814ft (248m)/min; service ceiling 17,900ft (5,456m); max range 2,690 miles (4,329km) at 133mph.
Note: Sunderland III performance: Max speed 210mph (338km/h) at 6,500ft; economical cruise 178mph (286km/h) at 5,000ft; initial climb 720ft (219m)/min; service ceiling 16,000ft (4,877m); normal range 1,780 miles (2,864km), max range 2,900 miles (4,667km).

A Sunderland V of the 'Aeronavale' photographed in the late 1950s and displaying the underwing pods housing its ASV Mk.Vlc radar. This Pratt & Whitney Twin Wasp powered Sunderland variant came about largely due to the efforts and influence of No 10 Squadron RAAF. (Shorts)

indicated the need for better and more reliable engine performance than was being provided by the Pegasus units installed in the first three marks of the flying boat. The problem stemmed from the fact that the Pegasus needed to be run at constant high power settings to achieve the desirable performance, resulting in high fuel consumption, short overhaul lives and numerous failures.

As had been the case with the fitting of extra guns, it was the Australians (through No 10 Squadron) who first pressed the need for more powerful engines. They were given permission to convert a Sunderland III to accept four Pratt & Whitney R-1830-90 Twin Wasp 14 cylinder radial engines equipped with two speed superchargers and rated at 1,200hp for takeoff. Shorts undertook a similar conversion at the same time and offered the Australians technical assistance.

The Shorts conversion first flew in March 1944 followed by the 10 Squadron aircraft the following month. The result was the Sunderland V, 154 production examples of which were built at Rochester (47), Belfast (47) and Dumbarton (60), the first of them being handed over to the RAF in October 1944. A further 33 Sunderland IIIs were converted to Mk.V configuration.

The new engines gave the Sunderland greatly improved engine out performance and more endurance at the cruise due to the lower power settings which could be used. It was now possible to maintain height at maximum weight (60,000lb/27,216kg) with two engines out and the practical endurance at normal power settings was about 15 hours, a figure which could be increased to no less than 20 at a more leisurely patrol speed. Also fitted to Sunderland Vs was improved 9 centimetre ASV Mk.VIc radar with the large aerials of the previous installations replaced with neat split scanners in flush fitting radomes under each wingtip.

With the introduction of RAF role designation prefixes, the Sunderland V became the GR ('general reconnaissance') Mk.V. Postwar, the RAF replaced Roman numerical designations with Arabic figures, so this final Sunderland production variant became the GR Mk.5.

Perhaps ironically, No 10 Squadron RAAF, which had got the Sunderland V programme underway, had to wait some months before it received the new variant, with several RAF and the other RAAF Sunderland squadron in Britain – No 461 – taking delivery first. By then, the European war was over!

Civil Variants

The Sunderland's large interior made it suitable for transport duties and numerous such versions were created by conversion. The first was 24 new production Sunderland IIIs delivered to BOAC in 1943/44 and used on services between Poole and Lagos and then Poole-Cairo.

Near the end of the war and immediately afterwards, further Sunderland IIIs were converted to civil transports for BOAC as the Hythe while other Mk.IIIs and Mk.Vs for both civil and military use retained the name Sunderland.

Civil Sunderlands: the famous VH-BRF 'Islander' (top) of Ansett Flying Boat Services started out as Sunderland III ML814 and after serving with the RAF, RCAF and RNZAF, became the last of its type converted to civil specifications in 1963. It survives in 1992. F-OBIP (bottom) began as Sunderland III JM719 and was converted to a Sandringham 7 in 1947. In civil guise it served with BOAC, P G (Sir Peter) Taylor as VH-APG and finally with RAI in Tahiti.

Perhaps the best known civil transport conversions were those called the S.25/V Sandringham, all but one of which were fitted with Pratt & Whitney Twin Wasp engines regardless of the mark (either III or V) from which they were derived. The exception was the first and only Sandringham 1, converted from a Sunderland III and revealed in its new configuration in November 1945 with turrets removed and replaced with recontoured fairings and rectangular windows inserted in the fuselage. Sandringhams normally accommodated 21 or 22 passengers for medium/long range operations or up to 43 over short stages.

The Sandringham 2, 3, 4, 5, 6 and 7 were sub-variants developed for specific operators and the total number of conversions performed amounted to 25 aircraft, many of which found their way to the South Pacific area for service with Qantas, TEAL, New Zealand National Airways, Barrier Reef Airlines, Trans Oceanic Airways and Ansett.

The final Sunderland civil conversion was performed for Ansett Flying Boat Services in 1963, using a former RNZAF GR.5 as its basis. This aircraft (the famous VH-BRF 'Islander') was not given the name Sandringham but instead remained a Sunderland.

Sunderland VH-BRF 'Islander' (ex RAF ML814) served with Ansett between 1963 and 1973. It is photographed here at Sydney's Rose Bay in November 1964 (top) and departing Sydney Harbour (bottom) exactly eight years later. (Eric Allen)

Sandringham IV VH-BRC 'Beachcomber' put in more than two decades' service with Ansett from 1953. It makes a magnificent sight as it takes off from Sydney Harbour. Both these shots were taken near the end of the flying boat's career. (Eric Allen)

AUSTRALIA'S SUNDERLANDS

Sometimes, significant events in the history of an entity – whether it be a person, a country, a branch of the services or an air force squadron – come about as much by accident as design. The circumstances which resulted in the Royal Australian Air Force's significant and often heroic use of the Short Sunderland in Britain during World War II could be classed under former heading, although subsequent events were certainly indicative rather more of skill and determination than what may be described as 'luck'.

In a nutshell, when personnel from the RAAF's No 10 Squadron began arriving in Britain in July 1939 to prepare for the collection of their new Sunderlands and the flight back to Australia, little did they know that the declaration of war on Germany just six weeks later would result in the aircraft, the squadron and the personnel remaining 'over there' for the duration of hostilities.

The circumstances created a unique honour for No 10 Squadron – it was the first RAAF squadron to see overseas service in World War II.

In April 1942 No 10 was joined by another RAAF squadron equipped with Sunderlands, No 461, formed around a nucleus of personnel from No 10 Squadron. Between them, the two Australian squadrons operated 147 Sunderlands, played a part in the sinking of 12 U-boats and were responsible for armament and powerplant innovations which made their aircraft more effective and reliable. These developments benefited all Sunderland squadrons operating in the United Kingdom, both Australian and British.

By comparison, the RAAF's use of the Sunderland in waters closer to home was limited, with only six aircraft being taken on charge from March 1944 and operating on mainly transport duties in the South West Pacific Area in the hands of No 40 Squadron.

Sunderlands Ordered

As part of the RAAF's general expansion of the middle and late 1930s, the Minister for Defence (Mr G A Street) announced in May 1939 that a new RAAF seaplane station would be established at Rathmines (Lake Macquarie) NSW and that two squadrons would be based there. These were named as No 9 (Fleet Co-operation) and No 10 (General Reconnaissance) Squadrons. No 9 had been formed the previous January while No 10 was yet to be established.

Later in the same month it was announced that a number of Sunderlands would be purchased from Britain to equip 10 Squadron, operating from Rathmines and also Port Moresby in New Guinea. On 23 June 1939 the purchase of nine Sunderlands for Nos 10 and 11 Squadrons was announced at a cost of £49,225 ($98,450) each plus spare parts.

The Sunderlands were allocated the RAAF serial numbers A18-1 to A18-9, although these were never applied to the aircraft due to their remaining in the United Kingdom.

Empire Boats Impressed

The same circumstances resulted in No 11 Squadron never receiving any Sunderlands, but shortly after the declaration of war it was allocated two Short S.23 'C' Class (Empire) flying boats which had been impressed from QANTAS to help satisfy Australia's immediate coastal reconnaissance needs. These aircraft were G-ADUT *Centaurus* and G-AEUA *Calypso*, and were given the RAAF serials A18-10 and A18-11,

Sunderland I N9048, the first aircraft delivered to No 10 Squadron in the United Kingdom on 11 September 1939 and displaying the squadron codes 'RB'.

respectively. Two more Empire boats were impressed in June 1940 (VH-ABC/A18-12 *Coogee* and VH-ABB/A18-13 *Coolangatta*), the aircraft operating on a contract basis with QANTAS supplying some crew members and performing major servicing. A fifth Empire boat (VH-ACD/A18-14 *Clifton*), an S.33 model, joined the RAAF in March 1942.

The Empire boats were used on coastal patrol and transport duties until replaced by Lockheed Hudsons and during their time with the RAAF served with Nos 11, 13, 20, 33 and 41 Squadrons. *Calypso* and *Coogee* were involved in the desperate evacuation of Rabaul in January 1942 but neither of them survived beyond that year. *Calypso* was destroyed in August when its hull collapsed whilst landing on a rough sea

at Daru in New Guinea and *Coogee* crashed on landing at Townsville after a test flight in February.

A third Empire boat was also lost: *Centaurus* was sunk at its moorings at Broome WA as a result of Japanese bombing in March 1942.

10 Squadron Prepares

No 10 Squadron was formed at RAAF Point Cook as a general reconnaissance squadron on 1 July 1939. The first commanding officer was Sqdn Ldr L V Lachal, who went on to command the squadron in the United Kingdom until early 1940. The squadron absorbed the seaplane element of No 1 Flying Training School and its first equipment was a pair of Supermarine Seagulls.

On 11 July, a party of 14 airmen (fitters, riggers and radio operators) departed Australia on board the RMS *Strathard*, bound for England and their new charges. Within a fortnight, the CO and six pilots (Flt Lts W H Garing, W N Gibson, C W Pearce, J A Cohen and Flg Offs I S Podger and H M Birch) had also left for the UK, in their case flying and arriving near the end of July. The pilots then went to the RAF Flying Boat Training School at Calshot to undergo conversion training on four engined boats, using Short Singapore IIIs.

The airmen arrived in mid August and were posted to Pembroke Dock in South Wales for training on the Sunderland. Pembroke was the home of two RAF Sunderland squadrons, Nos 210 and 228, and the Australian airmen were attached to the

Five Shorts Empire flying boats were impressed into RAAF service, the first pair shortly after hostilities with Germany began. They were used on coastal patrol and transport duties and three were destroyed whilst flying with the RAAF.

former for familiarisation and training on the new aircraft.

The first Sunderland I handed over to No 10 Squadron at Short's Rochester factory was N9048/RB-A on 11 September followed by N9049/RB-B on 19 September and N9050/RB-D on 3 October. While they were waiting for their new aircraft to be readied, four of the pilots (Pearce, Cohen, Podger and Birch) temporarily joined the RAF's No 210 Squadron for some operational experience, flying convoy and anti submarine patrols over the Atlantic and St George's Channel, the stretch of water separating Wales and Ireland.

The intention, of course, was to ferry these initial three Sunderlands back to Australia and take up duties there, but with the declaration of war on 3 September, fate took a hand in 10 Squadron's history.

Until 7 October, plans to take the Sunderlands to Australia remained in place as far as 10 Squadron's personnel were concerned, but on that day the order was received that the detachment was to remain in Europe and the squadron would operate as a 'lodger' unit at Pembroke attached to No 210 Squadron. Three days later, the Australian Sunderlands flew their first operational flight, when Flt Lts Garing and Gibson and their crew took Sunderland N9049

Being a member of the ground crew on a flying boat squadron meant lots of pushing and shoving of aeroplanes, in this case 10 Squadron's N9050. This Sunderland was one of the first batch handed over in late 1939. The photographs were taken on 30 December 1939. (RAAF Historical)

to Bizerta in Tunisia. On board was a spare Pegasus engine for a stranded 228 Squadron (RAF) Sunderland.

The decision to keep No 10 Squadron in Britain meant the hasty recruitment of volunteer air and ground crews from RAAF ranks in Australia to bring the squadron up to operational status and keep it there. By the last week of November two officers and 183 airmen were on their way to Pembroke on board the SS Orontes from Fremantle, attracting considerable attention from politicians and the press as they departed.

As the first squadron from any of the Dominions' air forces to see active service and to be deployed overseas, No 10 Squadron became something of a 'celebrity' unit with regular visits from distinguished guests occurring in late 1939 and early 1940.

More important matters had to be addressed as well, particularly the putting into place of the logistics required to run the squadron. Borrowed RAF facilities helped a great deal, as did the arrival on Boxing Day 1939 of the Orontes and her valuable cargo of skilled personnel.

Miscellaneous, mainly transport flights were undertaken while the squadron was working up in January 1940, among them a trip to Alexandria carrying Air Chief Marshall Sir Charles Burnett (the RAF Inspector General and shortly to become the RAAF Chief of Air Staff) and Air Vice Marshall R (later Air Marshall Sir Richard) Williams.

In early January No 10 Squadron was formally incorporated into RAF Coastal Command's No 15 Group which was charged with anti submarine patrol duties mainly to the west and north-west of the British Isles in the North Atlantic.

After intensive training and working up, the squadron was made operationally active on 1 February 1940 and performed its first sortie – a convoy escort – under its new status five days later. The Sunderland involved was flown by the squadron's new commanding officer, Flt Lt Pearce.

10 Squadron's Sunderlands

Delivery of Sunderland Is to No 10 Squadron continued after the first three had been handed over and ten had been delivered to the unit by the end of 1939, of which

one was only on strength for a matter of days before being moved on. A further three Sunderland Is were allocated to the squadron during the course of 1940.

No 10 received first allocation (to the Australian squadrons) of a total of 71 Sunderlands during the course of war, comprising 21 Mk.Is, 12 Mk.IIs and 38 Mk.IIIs. Other aircraft were passed from No 461 Squadron to the original unit, including all of the 11 Mk.Vs it operated. Refer to the tables at the end of the Sunderland section of this book for details.

No 10's first Sunderland II was taken on strength in January 1941 and the first Mk.III was allocated 12 months later. The Mk.Vs were transferred from No 461 Squadron in June 1945, too late to see action in the European war.

No 10 Squadron briefly operated one other type of Short flying boat in 1941, the S.26 'G' Class, a larger and heavier development of the original Empire boat. Only three were built – G-AFCI 'Golden Hind', G-AFCJ 'Golden Fleece' and G-AFCK 'Golden Horn' – all of which were impressed into RAF service and given the

No 10 Squadron's first commanding officer, Wng Cdr L V Lachal (left) at Pembroke Dock shortly after the outbreak of war. With him are members of the first group of pilots to go to Britain (left to right): Sqdn Ldr W N Gibson, Sqdn Ldr C W Pearce, Sqdn Ldr I S Podger and Sqdn Ldr W H Garing. Gibson scored the squadron's first U-boat kill in July 1940 while Pearce succeeded Lachal as CO. (RAAF Historical)

A 10 Squadron Sunderland II (W3983) is launched at Pembroke in the second half of 1941. Mk.IIs had ASV radar fitted from new, but early examples were delivered with the open dorsal gun positions. (via Neil Mackenzie)

More manual labour for 10 Squadron's ground crews as a Sunderland is pulled ashore for maintenance. (RAAF Historical)

10 Squadron Sunderland I P9600 roars over a scene which if were not for the times (and the Catalinas moored on the water) could be any quiet fishing village anywhere in Britain. (via Neil Mackenzie)

serial numbers X8275, X8274 and X8273, respectively.

Tail and dorsal Boulton Paul gun turrets and provision for the carriage of depth charges were installed in the aircraft, and in June 1941 all three were allocated to the Australian squadron with the intention of forming a long range communications flight within the unit.

Transport duties had hitherto been one of 10 Squadron's tasks, a job which meant that Sunderlands had to be taken off submarine patrols in order to perform these tasks.

The 'G' Class boats proved unsuitable for the task as they suffered performance limitations and were a headache for the squadron's hard pressed maintenance crews with their Bristol Hercules engines and numerous other characteristics which were vastly different from the Sunderlands.

They were quickly withdrawn, but not before 'Golden Fleece' crashed into open sea after suffering failures of two engines off Cape Finisterre on the north-west tip of Spain. Lives were lost in this incident but five survivors were picked up by a German seaplane. One of them – Corporal L G Corcoran – became 10 Squadron's only prisoner of war.

Despite the squadron codes, this Sunderland I belongs to No 10 Squadron RAAF and was delivered in November 1939. It crashed at Lismore, Scotland, in September 1940 whilst attempting to land in fog. (via Neil Mackenzie)

ML839, the Sunderland III converted by No 10 Squadron to Pratt & Whitney Twin Wasp engines and first flown as such in early May 1944. This shot was taken shortly after the conversion was completed, a conversion which led to the production Sunderland V. Other Pegasus powered Sunderlands were also converted to the more reliable Twin Wasps. (RAAF Historical)

461 Squadron's Sunderlands

The second Australian Sunderland squadron to join the fray in Britain was No 461, formed at Mount Batten on 25 April 1942 and incorporated as part of No 19 Group, RAF Coastal Command. By now, No 10 Squadron was also operating under the control of 19 Group, so the two squadrons were operating the same type of aircraft from the same base.

The original intention was to equip 461 Squadron with Catalinas, but the supply of sufficient Sunderlands allowed it to be equipped with the larger flying boat, allowing commonality with No 10 Squadron. No 19 Group's principal activity was anti submarine patrols and it operated in the North Atlantic to the south-west of Britain, its area of responsibility including the vitally important Bay of Biscay area.

The squadron was formed around a nucleus of personnel from No 10 Squadron including the first (temporary) commanding officer, Sqdn Ldr R B Burrage. 461's first Sunderlands were Mk.Is T9090, T9085 and T9109, all of which were delivered between April 22 and 24. Air and ground crew graduates of the Empire Air Training Scheme joined the squadron through May and June 1942 as it was working up to operational readiness, and this was achieved in early July with two Sunderlands and their crews available. By the end of the month the squadron was at full strength, albeit with generally inexperienced personnel, and its first 'permanent' commanding officer was Wng Cdr N A R Halliday, RAF.

Of the two Australian Sunderland squadrons, No 461 received first allocation of 76 aircraft, comprising eight Mk.Is (from April 1942), five Mk.IIs (from July 1942), 49 Mk.IIIs (from October 1942) and 14 Mk.Vs (from February 1945). As was the case with No 10 Squadron, 461 operated a couple of Sunderlands which had first served with its 'sister' unit, but No 461 was the only one of the pair to receive Sunderland Vs as first allocations, and of the 14 taken on strength, 11 were subsequently passed on to the other squadron.

RAAF SUNDERLANDS FIRST ALLOCATIONS TO SQUADRONS			
Mark/Sqdn	10	461	Total
Mk.I	21	8	29
Mk.II	12	5	17
Mk.III	38	49	87
Mk.V	–	14	14
Total	71	76	147

Note: the above refers only to first allocations of aircraft; a small number served with both squadrons including 11 of the Mk.Vs.

Improving the Odds

Mention was made in the previous chapter of modifications to the Sunderland which were intended to improve the effectiveness of the aircraft and which were pioneered by the Australian squadrons. Defensive and offensive gun armament was an example of

this, as was the fitting of Pratt & Whitney Twin Wasp engines in place of the original Bristol Pegasus, the latter resulting in a new Sunderland production model, the Mk.V. Additionally, older Mk.I Sunderlands were progressively fitted with ASV radar from mid 1941.

The need for extra guns became manifest as operations progressed in 1941 and into 1942, firstly as defence against the daily menace of heavily armed Junkers Ju 88 fighters, particularly in the important Bay of Biscay area, and secondly as an offensive strafing weapon against submarines and other enemy targets on the surface.

Australian ingenuity rose to the occasion here with the fitting by No 461 Squadron of swivel mounted Vickers 'K' 0.303in machine guns in the galley hatches (Mk.III EJ134 was the first Sunderland so equipped), the four fixed nose 0.303in Brownings installation first developed by 10 Squadron and subsequently incorporated in production aircraft, and the twin gun belt fed FN 5 nose turret installation developed by 461 Squadron. The firepower of the galley installation was later increased by the installation of 0.50in Brownings (following the development of suitable mounts) while the fixed battery of nose guns served the dual purpose of offensive weapon and sighting tool to eliminate line error when carrying out a depth charge attack, the splashes of the rounds on the water providing an orientation clue.

The Pratt & Whitney engine installation grew from a need for more reliable perfor-

Sunderland III EK575 of No 461 Squadron RAAF and delivered to them at Pembroke Dock in August 1943. It later served with No 10 Squadron. 461's squadron codes were either '2' (as shown here) or 'UT'. (via Neil Mackenzie)

mance than the Pegasus engines could provide. This was an observation noted by most Sunderland operational squadrons and the manufacturer, but it was No 10 Squadron which set in motion the process which would result in the Pratt & Whitney powered Sunderland V.

In early 1944 and following a stress analysis which determined the heavier American engines would not cause structural problems, permission was given to No 10 Squadron to convert a Sunderland III (ML839) to accept R-1830-90 Twin Wasp engines fitted with two speed superchargers and rated at 1,200hp for takeoff. At the same time, Shorts began work on its conversion, also using a Mk.III aircraft (ML765).

The manufacturer provided technical assistance to the Australians, who were given engines by the British Ministry of Aircraft Production which were originally intended for experiments in Bristol Beauforts, while engine nacelles came from Shorts and other bits and pieces were scrounged or made as required.

The factory conversion beat the Australian effort into the air by a few weeks, recording its first flight in March 1944. ML839 first flew in its new guise on 4 May 1944 and completed 100 hours of test flying before being approved for operations. The result was a Sunderland which was able to fly at lower power settings for a given result, meaning fewer engine failures, longer times between overhauls, lower fuel consumption (and therefore greater endurance) and better performance when the extra power provided by the Twin Wasps was exploited.

In its production form the Twin Wasp Sunderland was called the Mk.V, and deliveries began in February 1945. Strangely, No 10 Squadron was not the first to receive Mk.Vs but had to wait until June 1945 before it received the first examples of what was its brainchild, and even then the aircraft involved had first seen service with 461 Squadron.

Pacific Sunderlands

More than four years later than intended, Sunderlands were finally delivered to the RAAF in Australia in March and June 1944 for service with No 40 Squadron. Formed on 31 March 1944 at Townsville Qld, this new squadron's intended role was transport between Australia and New Guinea.

The six Sunderland IIIs which equipped the squadron were the only examples of the famous flying boat to wear RAAF serial numbers, A26-1 to A26-6. The serials allocated to the original nine Sunderlands ordered in 1939 (A18-1 to -9) but not used were not reallocated.

After preparation by No 10 Squadron maintenance crews for their long journey to Australia and the selection of experienced, mainly tour expired crews from Nos 10 and 461 Squadrons, the first two aircraft (A26-1/ML730 and A26-3 (ML732) left Mount Batten on 27 January 1944 commanded by Sqdn Ldr T Egerton DFC and Flt Lt G G Rossiter DFC. These were followed by A26-2 (ML731) and A26-6 (DP192) on 14 February and A26-4 (ML733) and A26-5 (ML734) on 1 March.

The epic 17,000 mile (27,350km) ferry flights were routed via Gibraltar, West Africa, Brazil, the Caribbean, San Francisco and on to Australia. The Sunderlands served with No 40 Squadron until October 1945 when regular operations ceased. The final flight was recorded in February 1946 and the squadron disbanded five months later.

A Sunderland III of No 10 Squadron undergoing maintenance at Mount Batten. Note the fixed gun ports in the nose and underwing radomes for the ASV Mk.VIc radar which has been retrofitted. PP142/RB-L in the background is also a Sunderland III. This photograph is dated April 1945. (RAAF Historical)

A peaceful scene as No 40 Squadron's A26-2 rests at Fitzroy Island, near Cairns Qld. 40 Squadron's six Sunderland IIIs operated a transport service between Queensland and New Guinea in 1944-46. (via Neil Mackenzie)

'Islander' again, this time departing Sydney for Lord Howe Island on 4 December 1973. (Eric Allen)

AUSTRALIAN SUNDERLAND OPERATIONS

The Battle of the Atlantic

It is impossible to overstate the importance of Royal Air Force Coastal Command to Britain during World War II. Here was an island nation dependent to a very large extent on its Merchant Navy to provide all manner of goods essential to its very survival, especially at a time of war. Home production was inadequate to its needs, whether the goods required be guns or whether they be food.

For Germany, what would be known as the Battle of the Atlantic was an attempt to starve Britain to death. Against the ships providing the lifeline to Britain was ranged the might of the German U-boat fleet: against them Britain employed aircraft, warships, the convoy system and ever improving technology to finally win the battle, but at a very high price.

The British Merchant Navy suffered the greatest losses in human terms of any branch of the services. All its personnel were volunteers and poorly paid; some 145,000 British merchant seamen served during World War II, of which more than 32,000 – or 22 per cent – died at sea.

The cost in lost shipping was commensurately great – more than 2,800 Allied merchant ships were sunk by U-boats during the war, representing 36% of the total British merchant fleet.

In the early years of battle the advantage lay very much with the U-boats but from 1943 gradually swung the other way. Victory in North Africa was a major help, as it provided bases from which long range aircraft could operate, narrowing what was

referred to as the 'Atlantic Gap', the mid-Atlantic area out of range of aircraft based on both sides of the ocean. The USA's entry to the war also helped here, but there was always a large section of water which was unprotected by aircraft.

The first eight months of World War II have been described as the 'Phoney War' because not much happened in the way of land activities. On the oceans, the story was quite different with naval actions taking place from the very beginning, actions which would see the powerful German surface fleet removed from the equation by sinking or by forcing the capital ships to remain hidden.

On the other hand, the U-boats, under the command of Admiral Karl Doenitz, remained an effective force for a large proportion of the war and were quickly into action, sinking 26 British merchant ships in September 1939, the first one the passenger liner *Athenia* on the very day war was declared, killing 112 civilians, 28 of them Americans.

Military sinkings quickly followed including the aircraft carrier *Courageous* in September and the battleship *Royal Oak* the following month. The latter was sunk at its moorings in the supposedly safe waters of Scapa Flow and the action well illustrated what an audaciously commanded U-boat was capable of.

The German submarines held the ascendancy until 1943 when the benefits of the centimetric radar fitted to some ships, Sunderlands and other aircraft began to be felt.

That radar is considered to be *the* item of equipment which swung the battle.

March 1943 had been the Allies' worst month with 43 ships sunk in the first 20 days. But the tide completely turned in April and May with the U-boats suffering their heaviest losses (about 30% of those at sea each month) and a relatively small number of Allied ships sunk. So marked was the turnaround that Allied losses to German submarines in the Atlantic were *nil* in June, July, August and September 1943.

From that point the Germans had lost the Battle of the Atlantic although it continued, the U-boats being fitted with the *Schnorkel*, a breathing device which enabled them to recharge their batteries without having to surface and the homing torpedo which used an acoustic device to home onto the sound of the target ship's propeller. This was quickly countered by the ships towing a contraption called the 'foxer', which generated more noise than the propellers.

The U-boats were responsible for the sinking of 2,828 Allied merchant ships and 145 warships during the war – the Germans built 1,162 submarines and lost 785 of them.

The Royal Air Force Sunderland squadrons played a significant part in the winning of the Battle of the Atlantic, a part in which the two Australian squadrons had leading roles.

10 Squadron 1940

After becoming fully operational in February 1940, No 10 Squadron spent the next

Atlantic convoy – from a 10 Squadron Sunderland. (Roy Winston via Keith Western)

A 10 Squadron Sunderland watches as the battle cruiser HMS 'Hood' eases past. 'Hood' was sunk in May 1941 by Germany's 'Bismark' with the loss of all but three of its crew of 1,477.

two months operating from Pembroke Dock. Under the command of Sqdn Ldr C W Pearce, the squadron was charged with the heavy responsibility of protecting Allied shipping in the south-west approaches to Britain from U-boat attack.

Patrols were mainly routine during this period with little contact with the enemy. Indeed, the squadron's most difficult problems seemed to be associated with the logistics involved in keeping the Sunderlands operational.

Pembroke dock was a crowded place, with two RAF Sunderland squadrons sharing the base with the Australians and a lack of tools and the need to perform maintenance on the aircraft out of doors made life difficult for the ground crews, particularly in the early cold months of the year. The fact they were dealing with a still unfamiliar aircraft added to the difficulties.

This adversity developed a high level of skill and resourcefulness among the ground crews who operated independently from RAF maintenance resources – even for major overhauls – and established their own schedules, methods and parts/replacement control systems. The result was a highly efficient squadron which reflected the quality of both its air and ground crews and its administration. Aircraft 'turned around' during maintenance very quickly indeed.

The significant modifications to the Sunderland's armament and powerplants referred to in the previous chapter are indicative of this and the fact they were adopted as production line modifications by the manufacturer further underlines the point. The other RAAF Sunderland squadron in Britain – No 461 – also contributed to these field modifications after its establishment in April 1942, although its aircrafts' maintenance was performed under the RAF system with the result that Sunderlands were usually away from the squadron for some considerable time while they underwent major inspections and overhaul at RAF facilities.

Move to Mount Batten

No 10 Squadron's independence in this area developed strongly from April 1940 when it moved from Pembroke Dock to Mount Batten near Plymouth, a much better base from which to operate with its excellent maintenance facilities and improved living conditions. In addition, at that time No 10 was the only squadron in residence at Mount Batten.

The move coincided with the start of the 'real' war and the first few months of operations from the new base were conducted when Britain was under serious threat. Denmark, Norway and the Low Countries would be overrun in April, quickly followed by France in the same month and that country's capitulation in June. The Allied withdrawal from Dunkirk took place in late May and from July to September the Battle of Britain raged.

In June, Italy declared war on Britain and France and by October had invaded Egypt and Greece, precursors to the North African campaign which would not be finally resolved in the Allies favour until mid 1943.

All these goings on required the squadrons to operate at maximum effort, and the situation provided the Australians with an opportunity to display an early example of their ingenuity and their reluctance to blindly follow the established 'rules'.

In May 1940, Sqdn Ldr Pearce decided to use his primary resource – the aircraft – not in the prescribed manner but in a way

Dressed in the necessary wading suits, two of 10 Squadron's ground crew (Sgt W B Granger and Cpl J A Pinkerton) brings the tail beaching carriage ashore after launching a Sunderland in early 1940. (RAAF Historical)

10 Squadron ground crews move Sunderland I W4004 at Mount Batten. (via Neil Mackenzie)

which got the most out of them. According to the book, the normal establishment of nine Sunderlands were to be used thus: six for normal operations, two as initial reserves and one for training. Pearce used all nine for normal operations and the squadron's sortie rate increased accordingly. Predictably, officialdom frowned on this and after a short time it was forbidden by both the Australian Air Board and by Coastal Command.

No 10 Squadron's previous routine of basically uneventful patrols changed dramatically during the May-June 1940 period when the Sunderlands were covering Allied shipping leaving French ports. Vastly increased U-boat activity provided the crews with plenty of action to watch, but for a time no direct contact with the enemy. Nevertheless, the squadron's sortie rate was impressive and English co-pilots were temporarily recruited to give the hard pressed Australian pilots some relief. There was no such relief for the ground crews; for most of them it was a matter of being on call 24 hours a day in order to keep all nine Sunderlands in the air.

In June 1940 the squadron flew 88 sorties and 728 hours, most of them over the English Channel but some travelling further afield, such as to Brest to carry out anti submarine patrols in areas which under different circumstances would have been covered by the French. Important transport sorties were also flown during this period,

some of them carrying VIPs to meetings in France and to the French colonies in Africa.

Among them were Lord Gort, Commander in Chief of the British Field Force and Duff Cooper, Minister of Information, who were taken to Rabat in French Morocco for talks. The pilot of the Sunderland, Flt Lt Cohen, had to make a very difficult landing and takeoff on the narrow river, and the effort was marred by local officials making life as difficult as possible for everyone, even going as far as preventing Cohen going ashore to deliver an urgent message to Lord Gort.

Pistols were drawn at one stage and the scene remained ugly until the Sunderland escaped very early the next morning, right under the nose of a boat crewed by armed personnel which had spent the night circling the Sunderland. Using guile, Cohen had managed to get the message to Gort, but in true French bureaucratic splendour, the local police had made it extremely difficult for the party to get back to the aircraft. More than half a century later, some would say nothing's changed ...

Diplomatic Doings

These flights to France and its colonies were designed to persuade the French government to fight on from Africa. It was generally a lost cause, as described by one 10 Squadron pilot who later wrote of a trip to France with a VIP on board. Flt W H Garing was the Sunderland's first pilot.

"Churchill ... sent Lord Lloyd, leader of the House of Lords, to urge chaotic France to continue the battle. An Australian Sunderland crew took Lord Lloyd to Lake Biscarosse, near Bordeaux, for the historic conference. 'They will not fight', he said sadly as the Sunderland rose on her return to England.

"Just before noon on June 19, 1940 we were told to prepare for the trip to Biscarosse. It was a secret mission. We knew we were to have an important passenger. That was all. That it would be exciting, perhaps dangerous, no-one doubted, for France was on the edge of the precipice and things were about as bad as they could be.

"Even at that stage, I do not think many people in England realised how rotten at the core France was and they still cherished the hope that France would fight on. They were soon to be disillusioned and, as the rapidly moving events in the next few days unfolded, the scales fell from their bewildered eyes, and they saw that England was alone and in her greatest peril.

"We were introduced to Lord Lloyd when he came aboard and I remember very distinctly his thick-set athletic figure and powerful personality. The captain took his seat, tested the engines and was about to take off when a power boat signalled us, came alongside and passed aboard a crate. We took a dim view of that crate, for it contained champagne and in the drama of

Sunderland II W3986 of 10 Squadron is hauled up the slipway for maintenance. This aircraft was lost in May 1943. (via Neil Mackenzie)

As mentioned in a previous caption, working as ground crew on a flying boat squadron involved a lot of pushing and pulling! These shots were taken at Mount Batten in March 1940. (RAAF Historical)

The night of 27/28 November 1940 saw an air raid on Mount Batten which caused considerable damage. The smoke is from the burning oil tanks which caused 10 Squadron to fly its aircraft to Pembroke Dock.

are going to Bordeaux', he said, 'since you are all taking the same risk'. We appreciated that, because all too often we were regarded as taxi drivers by our passengers – particularly by the less senior ones. 'My job', Lord Lloyd continued, 'is to try to persuade the French government to fight on from Africa'.

"We were profoundly impressed by the importance of the task, and I for one felt a good deal of pride that I was seeing history in the making. Lord Lloyd spoke freely of his experiences in France – of the last days in Paris, of sleeping on a park bench with Tommies, and of other hardships. He spoke bitterly and I suspected that none knew better than he that the heart of France was beating weakly, and that his mission was hopeless.

"Biscarosse lay stagnant and inert except for the animation of the Sunderland's wake. It was typical of the torpor of France and the spirit of pugnacious England. We tied up to a buoy that would have held the Queen Mary and a boat took Lord Lloyd ashore. We then began a period of

the hour there seemed to be a Nero touch about it. Later, we were to think even less of it ...

"The weather was perfect. From the [Plymouth] Sound we could see the Lizard, and in about 45 minutes we were over the Scillies and setting a southward course to take a wide berth of Brest. The Germans had been quick to grasp the strategic value of Brest, and with an excellent radio location system and a few squadrons of long range fighters – usually Ju 88s – they were making this corner a not very happy hunting ground for our slow and vulnerable Sunderlands.

"While we kept our eyes skinned for some of these unwelcome visitors, the wireless began to crackle and grunt. It seemed to be inordinately garrulous, and eventually the operator passed a longish code message to the captain. I remember wondering what urgent, epoch-making event had happened which necessitated such a long message.

"The captain took the slip and instructed the operator to acknowledge receipt by the single letter 'R', the universal signal for 'message received'. The usual procedure was to repeat back the whole message, but the captain feared that such a procedure would disclose our position to the Ju 88s and bring them shooting about our ears. This, however, did not meet the approval of the zealous bloke on the other key, and he called again and again, demanding a repeat back.

"When decoded the message said: 'The champagne is for Lord Lloyd'... subsequent revelations by the intelligence people confirmed the enemy had picked up our signals and had obtained an exact fix of our position.

"I was at the controls and the second dickie was alongside me when Lord Lloyd stood between us and told us of the object of the trip. 'You have a right to know why we

10 Squadron Sunderlands at Mount Batten later in the war, the aircraft displaying the underwing radomes housing ASV Mk.VIc radar. (Ray Winston via Keith Western)

tense, nerve jangling waiting. It was macabre, depressing, and now and again sent the flesh creeping up one's spine. Not far away, somewhere, some Germans were moving towards us.

"First we suffered the perils of having our hull holed by the clumsy French refueling methods, and we indulged in a frenzied pandemonium of yelling and screaming to ward them off. The French screamed back. In between we ordered 600 gallons, tried to convert it to litres, and tried to make ourselves understood in extremely bad French ...

"That evening we dined in the local French officers' mess and our hearts sank. The mess was very bright and noisy. I was astonished that the place was not blacked out, with the Huns only 30 miles or so away. The French officers answered my fears with a shrug of the shoulders and went on with the merrymaking.

"Out on the lake were 18 or 20 French seaplanes. Why was no one attempting to fly them to England? Again the shrug. The radio was blaring out the news. I watched the Frenchmen's faces. One of them turned to me and said: 'It is no use ... finish'. And that was that.

"In that mess there was not one Frenchman who cared, not one who would even try to prevent the catastrophe, not one who would try to recover the fortunes and honour of France. It was appalling. How Hitler must have laughed at Churchill's offer of union with the British Empire. He knew

that France was rotten. As I looked around, I felt depressed, afraid. It is not pleasant to see a nation in its death throes ...

"... after breakfast we stood about waiting for the return of Lord Lloyd ... a car pulled up in a cloud of dust soon after noon and three figures leapt out. One was an RAF Air Commodore, and he began to wave frantically to us to start our engines. He was apparently a landplane bloke and didn't know the engines of a seaplane or flying boat are not started until you are in a position to slip the moorings. So he kept waving, and I suppose swearing, all the way out.

"He must have been tired by the time he arrived alongside with Lord Lloyd. In thirty seconds we were away. Lord Lloyd looked terrible. He was haggard from a lack of sleep, and he had a heavy black growth of beard, a very fearsome sight.

"My look must have conveyed the question which was on all our minds, for he said: 'No, they won't fight'.

"Before Lord Lloyd left the boat, he thanked the crew and made them a present of the crate of champagne. They were sent ashore to drink it and have the day off. They drank it, and by all reports, they needed the day off.

"About that champagne, the garrulous code message, the radio location and the Junkers. Our intelligence officers told us a story a few days later that our signals had been received by the Hun, and that a force of fighters was brought to the standby in an attempt to intercept us. But, the IOs said,

some German, apparently unwilling to admit he had not broken the code, pretended to be able to do so, and said that the message stated that we had a cover of fighters. This caused the enemy to abandon his attempt, as he still had relatively few aircraft at Brest".

First Contact, First Kill

10 Squadron's first direct contact with a U-boat came on 17 June when Sqdn Ldr Pearce and his crew spotted a submarine on the surface some six miles (10km) distant. The decision was quickly made to attack before the submarine could fully submerge, the Sunderland arriving over its quarry just as it reached periscope depth. A salvo of six 250lb bombs was dropped just in front of the submarine's track and bubbles and a large patch of oil soon appeared on the water's surface.

Bubbles and oil continued to appear over the next 20 minutes, indicating the submarine was at least slightly damaged rather than just 'foxing' by blowing out air and oil, but despite remaining over the scene for more than three hours, Pearce and his crew saw no further signs emerge from under the water.

The squadron scored its first U-boat 'kill' on 1 July, sharing the prize with HMS *Gladiolus*, a 'Flower' class Corvette. On the morning of that date, Flt Lt W N Gibson (nicknamed 'Hoot' like just about everyone whose surname is Gibson!) departed Mount Batten in Sunderland I P9603 on an anti

The sinking of U-26 in July 1940 by 10 Squadron's Flt Lt W N Gibson in Sunderland I P9603. This was the first submarine sunk by the Australians and the kill was shared with the Royal Navy. The photograph shows the submarine after being forced to the surface by the Sunderland's attack. (RAAF Historical)

submarine patrol which would include escorting a ship from a convoy which had been attacked by a U-boat the previous night. The ship was situated about 250 miles (400km) west of the Scilly Isles.

The submarine responsible for the attack was the U-26, but it had been damaged by depth charges from the escorting *Gladiolus*. Surfacing in the early morning, U-26 intended running from the area but just after 6am it was spotted by the Sunderland and the nearby HMS *Rochester*. Gibson attacked with four 250lb anti submarine bombs, forcing the submarine to attempt to dive, but it came back to the surface. Gibson attacked again, and *Rochester* opened fire.

By now, U-26's captain had already given the order to abandon ship and scuttle the submarine and Gibson was able to send the signal "Have attacked enemy U-boat. Estimate five hits. Surfaced-sunk-survivors".

The Sunderland and HMS *Gladiolus* were jointly credited with the destruction of U-26, something which caused great jubilation in the squadron and in Coastal Command.

Pearce and Gibson were both awarded the Distinguished Flying Cross for these early actions against U-boats, the first of 26 awarded to squadron members along with nine Distinguished Flying Medals and numerous Mentions in Despatches.

That day, July 1, was a particularly busy one for 10 Squadron as it not only sunk U-26 but also endured the first of 41 minor air raids mounted against Mount Batten during that month alone.

Out at sea, the same day saw several sightings of oil and debris from torpedoed Allied shipping, but no U-boats. It would in fact be nearly three more years before the squadron could claim another enemy submarine sunk, although several were damaged in 1942.

As far as U-boat kills were concerned the remainder of 1940 and all of 1941 was a lean period for all of Coastal Command's Sunderland squadrons with only three more sinkings and one damaging being recorded. 1942 wasn't much better (two kills) but in 1943 the rate increased markedly to 13, five of them due to the efforts of the Australian Sunderland squadrons.

Varied Duties

July 1940 proved to be a very busy month for No 10 Squadron with many and varied activities taking place as well as first encounters with enemy aircraft. The first of these was on the 13th when Sqdn Ldr Gibson's aircraft was attacked by a Messerschmitt Bf 110 whilst returning from convoy protection duties. After an exchange of gunfire the Messerschmitt turned away with a smoking engine, and despite some 25 hits, some of which punctured fuel tanks, the Sunderland returned safely without injury to the crew.

Two days later, Flt Lt Birch and his crew sighted the British ship *City of Limerick* being attacked by five Heinkels. The Sunderland flew in to assist and three of the Heinkels engaged the flying boat in a gun battle. One of them was seen diving away trailing smoke and the others gave up the fight after receiving perhaps more than they had bargained for.

Flt Lt Birch had a potentially more formidable enemy on his hands two weeks later when he ran into six Ju 88s, but perhaps fortunately without engagement. On that same day, Birch had performed the squadron's first open sea landing in an attempt to rescue castaways – a hazardous activity – when four lifeboats and wreckage from the SS *Auckland Star* was sighted. Birch knew that surface rescue was not far away but landed to see if any of the survivors needed urgent medical attention. If so, they could be flown out.

Birch's involvement with enemy aircraft continued the next day when a Dornier flying boat was attacked. It was seen to be damaged before escaping but so was the Sunderland, which was hit in the wardroom area and in the front turret, injuring the gunner.

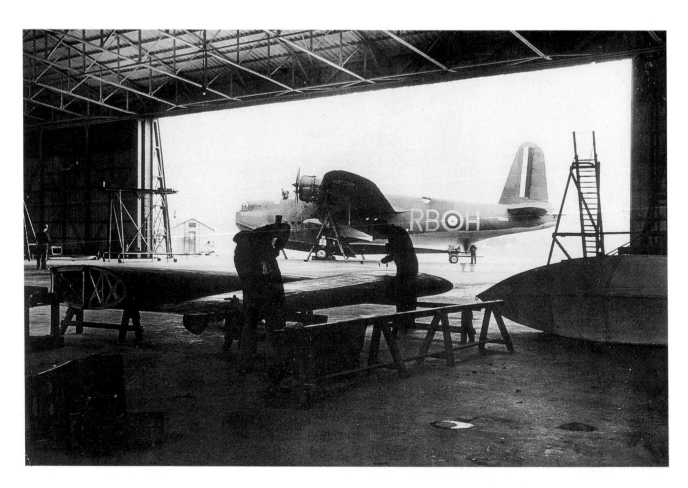

P9603/RB-H, the Sunderland in which Flt Lt Gibson sunk U-26 in July 1940. It survived until June 1941 when it crashed at Milford Haven. (via Neil Mackenzie)

The raid on Mount Batten on 27/28 November 1940 resulted in the loss of two 10 Squadron Sunderlands, N9048 in the hangar (above) and P9601 (below) burned and sunk at its moorings. (RAAF Historical)

General scenes of 10 Squadron Sunderlands undergoing or being prepared for maintenance. Operating over the sea has always been very tough on aeroplanes. (RAAF Historical)

10 Squadron's activities during the July-August 1940 period were typical of what would follow over the next few months. In July, Sqdn Ldr Garing had performed a photographic and visual reconnaissance of German emplacements along the occupied Biscay coast. This mission was successfully completed despite the close attention of German anti aircraft fire, some of which found its mark.

Miscellaneous duties in this period included the carrying of HRH the Duke of Kent from Pembroke Dock to Plymouth so he could inspect the squadron at Mount Batten, and a series of special duties and ferrying flights in the Mediterranean.

The fall of France had made direct communications with Malta impossible, so two Sunderlands were tasked with flying between Britain, Gibraltar and Malta, the small island which would later be awarded the George Cross for its heroic resistance. These flights often carried VIPs (including General Wavell), spare parts and personnel. The Sunderlands assisted in the delivery of Hurricane fighters to Malta, standing by to rescue pilots who may have been forced to ditch and they also carried out anti submarine patrols and photographic reconnaissance missions from Gibraltar.

Other detachments were also posted in an attempt to extend the squadron's patrol range into the Atlantic, these including Oban in Scotland and later on Loch Foyle and Loch Erne in Northern Ireland. The Oban detachment of four aircraft was established to protect convoys approaching Britain from the north-west and 22 convoy patrols, six anti submarine sweeps and one special reconnaissance flight were flown during August 1940.

Also in August, the squadron had a new commanding officer (Wng Cdr E G Knox-Knight RAAF), appointed and ASV Mk.I radar began appearing on some of the squadron's aircraft while MDS (Magnetic Detection of Submarines) equipment was tested in one aircraft. This was the forerunner of today's MAD – Magnetic Anomaly Detection – equipment.

The Battle of Britain and the threat of German invasion in August and September 1940 saw No 10 Squadron's prime activity of convoy protection temporarily change to that of security patrols off the Brest Peninsula. The object was to look out for any collections of ships, boats or barges in the occupied French ports which may be used in an invasion attempt. The squadron flew 30 such sorties in September.

German air raids made flying difficult in the last months of 1940 but one particular attack on Mount Batten during the night of 27/28 November caused the squadron damage and inconvenience. One of the squadron's hangars was burnt out with the loss of Sunderland N9048, and N9601 was sunk at its moorings. The setting on fire of nearby oil tanks caused the squadron to fly its aircraft to Pembroke Dock.

Back To Pembroke

They returned to Mount Batten in early December, but in the meantime most of the

Fitting the rear turret to a 10 Squadron Sunderland in 1944. (RAAF Historical)

squadron's patrols were being flown by the detachment at Oban during the northern hemisphere winter of 1940/41. Poor weather was a constant annoyance as was the frequency of air raids on Plymouth. Both conspired to limit flying and make life difficult for the maintenance crews. The raids caused damage to 10 Squadron's facilities on more than one occasion, and in May it was ordered back to the relative safety of Pembroke Dock, although it had also been subject to raids and was not immediately habitable when the squadron returned.

The Oban detachment had returned to the squadron's original base in Wales the month before where it carried out day and night patrols in the Brest area, keeping an eye on the German ships *Scharnhorst* and *Gneisenau*, which were assumed to attempt a breakout at some stage.

Administrative changes in early 1941 saw the establishment of No 19 Group, Coastal Command and the incorporation into it of No 10 Squadron. This changed the focus of the squadron's activities slightly to more of an emphasis on the Bay of Biscay area, over which most of its subsequent major actions would take place.

The May-June period of 1941 also saw No 10 Squadron achieve greater operational efficiency with the fitting of the first ASV Mk.II radars to its Sunderlands along with the replacement of the open dorsal gun positions in some Mk.I Sunderlands with turrets. Additionally, a few Mk.II Sunderlands began to appear on strength from the middle of the year.

No 10 Squadron remained at Pembroke Dock until early January 1942 when it returned to Mount Batten, by now suffering less from enemy raids. Wing Commander A X Richards replaced Wng Cdr Knox-Knight as commanding officer in December 1941, by which time most of the original air crews had been replaced by fresh faces.

Activities during 1941 resulted in numerous contacts with U-boats but with no sinkings. Despite this, the year was far from uneventful, as Sqdn Ldr Birch found out in early March. He and his crew were conducting a reconnaissance for two lifeboats which contained survivors from the torpedoed ship *Baltistan*.

During the patrol, two Ju 88s were sighted, these aircraft immediately attacking the Sunderland from the rear. Birch dived towards the sea and his gunners went to work, sending one of the Ju 88s into the sea and the other one scurrying to safety after receiving hits from the Sunderland. Patrols were often interrupted by the attentions of German aircraft, sometimes Ju 88s, sometimes other flying boats or seaplanes and the odd Focke-Wulf Fw 200 Condor four engined long range land based aircraft.

One of the latter, during June 1941, resulted in a remarkable action. The sight of a Sunderland and Fw 200 'dogfighting' must have been quite amazing, and in this case the Sunderland – flown by Flg Off A G H Wearne – came off second best but was saved by a member of the crew.

Both aircraft were hit before the Fw 200 broke off the engagement, but the Sunderland had damage below the waterline, in the port float and in the port outer oil tank which was badly leaking. Engine failure would have been the inevitable result were it not for the actions of mechanic LAC M T Griffin, who crawled into the wing on four occasions to inspect the damage, plug up the holes and then – using an empty peach tin – ladle the spilled oil back into the tank.

The Sunderland made it back to Mount Batten (to which it had been diverted) and LAC Griffin was awarded the Distinguished Flying Medal for his efforts. Also decorated at around the same time was Sqdn Ldr Birch, for his combat with the Ju 88s the previous March.

The remainder of 1941 provided the squadron with plenty of activity and in July it flew 664 operational hours, the highest number for a year and despite ongoing maintenance difficulties at Pembroke Dock. By contrast, only 385 hours were flown in August, the result of efforts to conserve long range aircraft and also because of several sorties which were abandoned due to problems with the Sunderlands' Pegasus engines.

It was in that same month – when no U-boats were sighted – that it was considered that perhaps the Germans had found a way of countering the Sunderlands' ASV radar. In order to test the theory, use of the radar was permitted only every second week for a period of five weeks.

Confidence was soon restored, but a counter had indeed been found as the U-boats had been fitted with responders which picked up the radar's emissions. It wasn't until ASV Mk.III centimetric radar came along in 1942 that the balance was fully restored, although there is a case which suggests the German counter-measures were not as effective as many thought.

Some aircraft also operated from Mount Batten, which was used as an advanced base. Patrols over the Bay of Biscay were occasionally interrupted by the need to cover other areas, notably in late July when the *Scharnhorst* slipped undetected out of Brest and back in again two days later. No 10 Squadron's Sunderlands joined in the search.

Earlier in the month Sunderland T9047 was lost during one of the many searches for survivors from sunk ships and downed aircraft. Flt Lt G R Thurston and his crew were diverted from their patrol to look for a dinghy containing survivors from a crashed RAF Hudson.

The dinghy was found and Thurston landed on the open sea to pick the four airmen up. Unfortunately, the landing resulted in No 1 engine being torn from its mountings and the port float broken. The Hudson crew was picked up and the Sunderland began an attempt to taxy towards the English coast. The Royal Navy destroyer

Sunderland II W4004 of 10 Squadron. (via Neil Mackenzie)

Two views of No 461 Squadron Sunderland III EK575 at Pembroke Dock in 1943. This Sunderland later served with No 10 Squadron. (via Neil Mackenzie)

Brocklesby was despatched to tow the stricken Sunderland in but on reaching the aircraft took everyone aboard but then sank the Sunderland by gunfire. The ship had been ordered to investigate a U-boat sighting and had no time to waste.

T9047 was the seventh 10 Squadron Sunderland which had been lost since operations began. N9048 and P9601 were destroyed in the raid on Mount Batten on 27 November 1940, N9049 was burnt out after being strafed by a Messerschmitt Bf 109 at Malta in May 1941, and P9602, P9603 and T9075 had all crashed. An eighth squadron Sunderland was lost in December when T9072 also crashed.

Despite the lack of submarine sightings a couple of indecisive attacks were made during the course of 1941, one of them, in September, resulting in certain damage when a bomb dropped from Wng Cdr A G H Wearne's Sunderland was seen to hit aft of the conning tower. The submarine apparently escaped.

461 Joins the Fray

No 10 Squadron's return to Mount Batten over the 1941/42 New Year period was its last move of the war, remaining there until disbanding in October 1945. In the meantime the squadron concentrated its efforts over the Bay of Biscay area, contacts with submarines increasing steadily in 1942-44, as did the number of anti shipping sorties flown. Many of these resulted in damage to enemy ships and one was sunk.

Commanding officers appointed to the squadron during that period were Wng Cdr J Alexander (September 1942), Wng Cdr G C Hartnell (March 1943), Wng Cdr R N Gillies (December 1943) and Wng Cdr H G Cooke (October 1944).

The second Australian Sunderland squadron at Mount Batten, No 461, was declared operational at the beginning of July 1942 after having been formed the previous April. No 461 remained at Mount Batten until September 1942 when it moved to Hamworthy Junction in Poole Harbour, on the south coast of England near Bournemouth. Night operations continued from Mount Batten. The squadron remained at Hamworthy only until April 1943 when it was transferred to Pembroke Dock, remaining there until disbanding in June 1945.

No 461 Squadron's first commanding officer was Sqdn Ldr R B Burrage. He was succeeded by Wng Cdr N A R Halliday in July 1942 but was killed in action just over a month later and replaced by Wng Cdr R C O Lovelock. Following commanding officers were Wng Cdrs D L G Douglas (January 1943), J McL Hampshire (February 1944) and R E Oldham (February 1945).

Wng Cdr Halliday and eight members of his crew were lost on 12 August during an air-sea rescue mission in the Bay of Biscay. The intention was to rescue the crew of a downed RAF Vickers Wellington. Flying Sunderland I T9090, Halliday somehow located the airmens' dinghy in a 25 knot wind and heavy swell. After jettisoning 500

Search and rescue was an important part of both Australian Sunderland squadrons' operations, although in this case W4004 of 10 Squadron (Flt Lt McKenzie) is assisting in the rescue of survivors from a U-boat. The lifeboat is from a British corvette and some Germans can clearly be seen in the water. The date is 11 May 1943. (RAAF Historical)

gallons of fuel an attempt was made to land, but this resulted in a long bounce and stall into the sea.

The result was the Sunderland's starboard wing being ripped off and the hull being subjected to cross waves which in combination with the broken wing, very quickly dragged the aircraft under.

Even though seven of the crew had got out of the Sunderland, only one survived. He was Flg Off J H Watson, the navigator, who had been knocked unconscious in the impact and had been saved by Flg Off D Laurenti, who returned to pull his comrade out. The dinghy to which the survivors were clinging burst as they attempted to climb in and Watson, by now conscious but still groggy, volunteered to swim to another dinghy which had been dropped to the Wellington crew by a previous searching aircraft but had not been reached.

Watson reached the other dinghy, lapsed into unconsciousness, and when he came to there was no sign of his fellow crew members, nor would there be. Watson and the surviving members of the Wellington crew were picked up five days later.

Halliday and his crew had made a successful open sea landing in the Bay of Biscay earlier in the previous month to rescue the crew of a downed Whitley. The sea was rough on that occasion also, but once

down it was impossible to get the Sunderland close enough to the dinghy for the men to climb aboard. The second pilot, Plt Off R D Baird, therefore crawled out onto the wing of the Sunderland and threw a rope to the dinghy which was then pulled in to the aircraft and those on board rescued.

461 Squadron's submarine patrols were largely uneventful over the next couple of months, with little contact, although the Sunderlands were frequently attacked by German aircraft – as were 10 Squadron's – mainly Ju 88s. Sunderland I T9113 fell victim to a pair of Ju 88s in September and other aircraft were damaged.

The squadron's first direct contact with an enemy submarine came in the same month when Plt Off H Cooke attacked a U-boat, causing some damage. This was not the first time 461 Squadron had attacked a submarine – that occurred in August when a British vessel was attacked by mistake. A problem had arisen with the identification of the limits of the safe area in which the submarine was operating, fortunately with no ill effects to the British boat or its crew. The same Sunderland found a German submarine a couple of hours later, but unfortunately had no bombs left with which to attack it!

461 Squadron's move to Hamworthy in September 1942 was not greeted with jubi-

They say any landing you walk away from is a good one, but this incident is probably pushing it a little. In May 1943 No 461 Squadron Sunderland T9114 captained by Flg Off Singleton picked up the crew of a downed RAF Whitley in the open sea. A Royal Navy destroyer took the survivors off T9114 but as the Sunderland was taking off it was hit by a huge wave which made a hole seven feet wide and four feet high in the lower hull. Singleton realised that to land on water would be not the best idea, so he gently put it down on Angle aerodrome instead, with little further damage to the Sunderland other than to the port float. The photo (above) shows the Sunderland on the aerodrome and (below) Singleton and two of his crew stand by the aircraft and the hole in its lower hull. (RAAF Historical)

lation because compared to the spacious and well equipped Mount Batten, this was a slum with no maintenance hangars, a general shortage of buildings and standing space for the Sunderlands, an unsatisfactory slipway and a poor standard of maintenance equipment. Additionally, the harbour was small with sand banks everywhere and narrow navigational channels. Operations after dark were difficult and dangerous, which is why the squadron's night flying continued to be performed from the previous base.

A further move to Pembroke Dock in April 1943 helped the situation, this date also marking the beginning of what may be termed the peak of the Battle of the Atlantic, with both Australian Sunderland squadrons participating in a hectic period of offensives against U-boats in the Bay of Biscay. This period brought results to both squadrons and proved to be the turning point of the battle.

10 Squadron 1942

Although they didn't sink any U-boats during 1942, 10 Squadron's Sunderlands damaged at least four in June and July and another in September. On 5 June Flt Lt S R Wood in W3986 sighted a surfaced submarine eight miles distant. The U-boat began to submerge but by diving fast at its quarry, the Sunderland reached the scene just 25 seconds later and dropped eight torpex depth charges about 120 metres ahead of the swirl left by the submarine.

The submarine (U-71) surfaced a minute later, at a steep angle and obviously damaged. The Sunderland's gunners poured 2,000 rounds into the submarine over the next ten minutes, but it finally

regained some sort of control and submerged. The adventure wasn't quite over, however, because as the Sunderland was leaving the scene it was attacked by an Fw 200. Both aircraft were hit but the Focke-Wulf came off second best and was listed as 'probably destroyed'.

Two days later, Plt Off T A Egerton in W3994 came across the Italian submarine *Luigi Torelli* on the surface with its stern awash, the result of damage inflicted by the RAF two days earlier. After exchanging gunfire, the Sunderland dropped depth charges and the submarine began to zig zag at reduced speed, at no time attempting to submerge. Another 10 Squadron Sunderland then joined the scene (Flt Lt E StC Yeoman) which also attacked with depth charges, two of which exploded under the submarine.

By now stationary but still afloat, the *Luigi Torelli* then appeared to eject a torpedo from its stern, and although crippled it wasn't finished off by the Sunderlands, both of which had sustained serious damage and were forced to break off the engagement. The submarine was subsequently beached at Santander in Spain with extensive damage.

Flt Lt Yeoman was involved in another action the following month, this time against U-162. Yeoman sighted the surfaced submarine at a distance of five miles and was able to get to within a half a mile before he was spotted and the submarine began a crash dive.

The submarine's stern was still visible as four depth charges were dropped, and although two of them appeared to explode directly on top of the target there was no evidence of damage.

Yeoman was killed in action shortly afterwards (on 9 August) as was Flt Lt E B Martin, the skipper of the Sunderland which damaged U-105 on 11 June. Martin and his crew died on 31 July, his aircraft presumed to have been shot down.

Martin's action against U-105 began when the submarine was spotted on the surface. It had insufficient time to dive as the Sunderland approached and for its trouble was straddled with six depth charges. It began to list, attempted to get underway and gradually turned and submerged. A minute later it was on the surface again, firing at the Sunderland with its deck gun. The Sunderland's guns replied and two anti shipping bombs were dropped, the second one exploding alongside and producing a substantial amount of oil. Although not sunk, this submarine was sufficiently damaged to ensure it would be of no threat to Allied shipping for the time being.

Another of 10 Squadron's 1942 actions which resulted in a damaged submarine was that which occurred on 1 September against Italy's *Reginaldo Guiliano*. Two Sunderlands were involved, Flt Lt Wood's W3986 and Flg Off H G Pockley in W3983.

On that morning, the two Sunderlands from No 10 Squadron and one from No 461 were despatched on an anti shipping strike, the aircraft loaded with armour piercing bombs.

En route to the designated area, Wood spotted a vessel which was making a large amount of smoke, so much it was thought to be a cargo ship. When the Sunderlands got closer to the vessel it was identified as an Italian submarine, and despite the fact that the bombs on board the aircraft were unsuitable for such an attack (they deto-

A gale at Mount Batten in February 1943 caused 10 Squadron to take emergency action in order to prevent damage to its Sunderlands. This involved running the outer engines to prevent them breaking away from their moorings. (RAAF Historical)

nated only with a direct hit), the assault was launched in the face of heavy anti aircraft fire.

Wood's bombs, although falling close to the submarine, had no effect. Pockley's bombs were similarly ineffective but he had first made two runs on the submarine, attacking with machine gun fire in an attempt to put the enemy guns out of action. All through this the *Guiliano* was belching large quantities of smoke from its diesel exhausts.

The Sunderlands withdrew to regroup for further attacks, by this time joined by the 461 Squadron aircraft. Before more passes could be made the aircraft were ordered to resume their original patrol although other Sunderlands looked for the submarine. It was found the next morning in a badly damaged state by an RAF Wellington. The submarine then made its way to Santander.

The Pockley Factor

Occasionally, operational flying produces a 'star' (for want of a better word) pilot or crew member, one whose activities somehow make him stand out and attract special attention. World War II produced numerous pilots who became household names – Bader, Tuck, Gibson, Gentile, Bong, Finucane, Caldwell, Atherton, Gibbes, Waddy, Truscott, Galland, Moelders, Cheshire and so on – mostly fighter pilots but one or two who flew bombers. Few from the less glamorous ranks of Coastal Command achieved such fame with the public, but some did with their contemporaries and to a lesser extent with the public.

One of those was H G (Grahame) Pockley DFC and Bar, who established a reputation within 10 Squadron and Coastal Command generally and who was described on his death in 1945 as an "anti submarine ace" after whom "Pockley's Corner in the Bay of Biscay was named as a tribute to Pockley's uncanny ability to nose out U-boats there".

Strangely, records of confirmed U-boat sinkings by the Australian Sunderland squadrons do not show his name on any of them, but he was involved in actions which resulted in the disabling of several, including that of the *Reginaldo Guiliano* as described above, and others which will follow. His actions against enemy shipping are also notable.

Something of a myth grew up around Pockley's activities but his worth to No 10 Squadron was unquestioned. The RAAF Official History summarised his career over the Atlantic thus:

"Pockley was overestimated by some of his contemporaries and underestimated by others. His engagements were magnified in popular accounts until he assumed the status of the 'U-boat magnet', while some of his fellows, perhaps influenced by his self conscious itch for action, dismissed him as being lucky.

"Although not in all respects a great pilot, he was an outstanding captain of aircraft. He studied, and made his crew study, every aspect of the existing tactical and technical situation, and had one of the best trained crews at the time serving in Coastal Command.

"He strove to master the difficulties of pilot bombing under all circumstances, and, although not one of his attacks was fully successful, he did show consistent judgement and accuracy. He represented a new tradition of single minded and well trained aircraft captain, who, by taking full advantage of the increasing scientific aids available to them, were to bring great changes in the war against U-boats".

After leaving 10 Squadron for the South West Pacific Area, Pockley flew Martin Mariners with No 41 Squadron and then Liberators with No 200 (Special Duties) Flight as its first commanding officer. No 200 Flight's jobs were covert operations in and around the Borneo area, inserting, retrieving and supplying people on the ground who collect intelligence behind enemy lines.

It was on one of these missions that Sqdn Ldr Pockley and his crew went missing in Liberator A72-191, in March 1945. He was 32 years old.

The following describe some of the sorties Pockley flew whilst with No 10 Squadron during the Battle of the Atlantic. If nothing else, they give some idea of the kind of activities in which the squadron's Sunderlands were generally involved ...

20 March 1942: Pockley and crew despatched to cover the Franco-Spanish iron ore coastal route. German motor launch sighted off Cape Breton. Two passes made out of sun but depth charges did not fall due to faulty release mechanism, launch strafed instead. Four depth charges finally released, exploding under launch and lifting it out of water on crest of the explosion.

Flt Lt Grahame Pockley (centre) and his crew in front of Sunderland W3983. From top, left to right: LAC E W Lee, Sgt J H Leach, LAC R K Scott DFM, Sgt J A MacDonald, LAC F Kerrison, Pockley, Sgt H D Gerke, Flg Off M K McKenzie, Flg Off H L Swan, Flg Off K G Fry, LAC J F Cureton. (via Neil Mackenzie)

U-boat in trouble as it attracts the attention of an Australian Sunderland. (Roy Winston via Keith Western)

8 May 1942: Pockley and Flt Lt Yeoman sighted a long oil streak which was apparently moving and attacked without apparent result. This was the first attack in the Bay of Biscay using new Torpex charges.

15 May 1942: While on an anti shipping transit flight to Gibraltar, Pockley sighted a vessel with U-boat nearby. U-boat submerged but surface vessel *Munsterland* attacked five times with one or two depth charges at a time. Several near misses reported and vessel strafed by machine gun fire.

Munsterland displayed British insignia as a ruse but this was ignored. Vessel shadowed until Pockley ordered to proceed on original duty but lack of fuel necessitated skillful forced landing in sea. Sunderland towed to Gibraltar.

28 May 1942: Surfaced Italian submarine making about 10 knots spotted in Western Mediterranean. Pockley dived to attack but forced to turn away due to heavy fire from submarine, which remained on surface.

Second attack also thwarted by anti aircraft fire but third pressed from very low level. Four depth charges released as submarine made emergency turn but stick overshot. All eight had been selected for dropping but faulty circuit in release mechanism prevented this. Remaining depth charges manhandled to operational bomb rack and dropped, causing visible damage. Anti aircraft fire continued before Sunderland withdrew upon arrival of RAF Hudson. Submarine damage assessed as 'probably Grade B'...

9 September 1942: Pockley (now a FLt Lt) homed in on radar indication 18 miles off port bow. U-boat discovered on surface but Pockley did not attack immediately as some crew were still on bridge. He assessed the submarine couldn't dive straight away so turned away and circled, waiting for it to dive so as to make best use of depth charges, which were of doubtful use against target on surface.

Pockley attacked when U-boat half submerged, straddling it with six depth charges. Large explosions brought enormous air and oil bubbles to surface, so serious damage assumed. Sunderland flown away briefly using baiting tactic (the idea was to drop only some of the aircraft's eight bombs, make the U-boat captain think the aircraft had left and then return to finish it off when it resurfaced) but it never reappeared.

3 October 1942: Three 10 Squadron Sunderlands (Pockley, Flt Lt Egerton, Plt Off Beeton) on combined anti shipping and U-boat patrol off north Spanish coast sighted a large vessel, later identified as the MV *Belgrano* (6,095 tons). Pockley recognised it as a blockade runner and dropped mixed load of anti submarine bombs and depth charges with near misses or possibly hits. Heavy anti aircraft fire experienced from multiple gun positions. Egerton and Beeton attacked in turn and *Belgrano* put into a Spanish port with surprisingly minor damage.

The U-boat Kills

As far as the Australian Sunderland squadrons were concerned, it was a fairly long time between 'drinks' when it came to confirmed U-boat kills since Flt Lt Gibson's successful action against U-26 in July 1940.

The squadrons had nevertheless achieved considerable results since then against enemy shipping, in the air-sea rescue and transport roles and against submarines, several of the latter having been most certainly seriously damaged and others at least temporarily put out of action.

As has been noted before, the tide began to turn firmly in favour of the Allied forces operating in and over the Atlantic in 1943. The first part of the year was relatively quiet with the U-boats becoming rather more circumspect in their activities as they sensed changing fortunes and many were in fact withdrawn from the area. Despite this, Allied shipping losses reached some 620,000 tons in March 1943 after a seven month period during which some 3.5 million tons of shipping had been lost. Peaks of 700,000 tons had been reached in June and October 1942.

By comparison, only 522,000 tons were lost in the 12 month period from May 1943. The period known as 'The U-boat Paradise' was well and truly over.

The Australian Sunderlands claimed 11 confirmed U-boat kills between May 1943 and August 1944, starting with U-332 on 2 May 1943 by 461 Squadron's Flt Lt E C Smith in DV968. Smith and that particular Sunderland had damaged U-415 the previous day.

To bag 461's first U-boat, Smith approached to within four miles at the rear of the submarine and then dived to attack, attracting anti aircraft fire as he did. Four depth charges were dropped, while gunfire from the Sunderland kept the enemy gunners' heads down. The blast from the charges put them out of action by blowing them overboard as well as causing the U-boat to circle tightly, then stop and list to port.

It then began to burn, Smith finishing it off with a second volley of depth charges which caused U-332 to settle, then rear upwards bow first before sliding under to the accompaniment of a bubbling pool of air, oil and wreckage.

Five days later, No 10 Squadron scored its second U-boat kill of the war when Flt Lt G G Rossiter and W3993 sank U-109. Shortly after spotting two submarines but not being able to attack, Rossiter sighted a third, some 17 miles away.

Flying blind through cloud he got to within four miles before breaking out, and encountering no opposing gunfire, dropped four depth charges from very low level. Two of them exploded close to the conning tower. Another attack forced the U-boat to stop before it gradually submerged, an oil patch marking the spot. The sinking of the submarine was later confirmed.

May 1943 was already proving to be a profitable month for the Australian Sunderlands, another 10 Squadron aircraft claiming a share in the destruction of U-563 on the 31st.

This time it was Flt Lt M S Mainprize in DV969 who was involved, his attack mortally wounding the submarine which was already damaged following attacks by an RAF Liberator and Halifax and was finished off by an RAF Sunderland.

May 1943 was a significant month in the Battle of the Atlantic and the successes by now being achieved were recognised by the Under Secretary of State for Air, Captain the Rt Hon Harold Balfour, whose remarks applied not just to that particular month but to Coastal Command in general:

"Hats off to Coastal Command, who, day and night, whatever the weather, fly the oceans on their allotted duties. Theirs is not the sharp glory of fighter combat, not the satisfaction of the concentrated destruction of Germany's war machine by the bomber offensive. Theirs is a physically arduous and equally hazardous job of flying far out to the west in the front line of the Battle of the Atlantic ...

"In May, the Germans made their biggest effort to date to halt our shipping with its vital supplies of food, munitions and manpower ... it was a major offensive mounted on a grand scale with great forces. Yet our shipping losses during the month of May were lower than at any time since the US entered the war.

"Coastal command, in co-operation with the Navy, can take a large measure of credit for the success of the month. Air cover, to the extreme limit of aircraft range, was given to our ships. More U-boats were attacked

The attack on U-71 by 10 Squadron's Flt Lt S R Wood on 5 June 1942. Wood's depth charge attack damaged the submarine and forced it to the surface, but with no more bombs on board, the Sunderland strafed its quarry. U-71 limped away to safety, but it was badly damaged. (RAAF Historical)

Date	Sqn	S/No	Aircraft Captain	Remarks
01/07/40	10	P9603	F/L W N Gibson	U-26 shared with HMS Gladiolus
02/05/43	461	DV968	F/L E C Smith	U-332
07/05/43	10	W3993	F/L G G Rossiter	U-109
31/05/43	10	DV969	F/L M S Mainprize	U-563, shared with RAF
30/07/43	461	W6077	F/L D Marrows	U-461
01/08/43	10	W4020	F/L K G Fry	U-454 W4020 shot down
02/08/43	461	DV968	F/O I A Clarke	U-106, shared with RAF
08/01/44	10	EK586	F/O J P Roberts	U-426
28/01/44	461	EK577	F/L R D Lucas	U-571
08/07/44	10	W4030	F/L W B Tilley	U-243
11/08/44	461	ML741	P/O I F Southall	U-385 shared with HMS Starling
12/08/44	461	ML735	F/L D A Little	U-270

by Coastal Command than have ever been attacked in any month before. The sighting of the U-boats reached a peak figure far above that ever previously attained ...

"Air cover does not mean Coastal Command just keeping aircraft hovering above a convoy. It means that the sea, for scores, sometimes hundreds of miles behind, on each side and in front of our ships, is swept night and day. The U-boat packs were often broken up miles away from their target and sent crash diving to temporary and problematical safety".

Sinkings Continue

The late July/early August 1943 period was also profitable for the Australian Sunderland squadrons, Nos 10 and 461 each sinking two U-boats. The first of this batch (on 30 July) contained a remarkable coincidence as the U-461 was sunk by Sunderland U/461! The latter designation was the standard way of identifying individual aircraft in reports, signifying aircraft 'U' of 461 Squadron. The pilot was Flt Lt D Marrows and the Sunderland's serial W6077.

This attack actually involved a group of three submarines along with two RAF Halifaxes, an American Liberator and a Catalina, although Marrows' attack on U-461 was the only one successfully pressed home, his seven depth charges causing the submarine to simply disappear in an enormous eruption of foam.

Two days later, on 1 August, Flt Lt K G Fry of 10 Squadron in W4020 claimed U-454 but with the loss of the Sunderland. Fry's U-boat was discovered near a convoy and as he swung in to attack, his aircraft was subjected to intense and accurate anti aircraft fire. Number three engine was hit and then the starboard main fuel tank, resulting in the bridge being flooded with fuel. It is assumed that those in the cockpit were seriously wounded at this stage, but still the attack was pressed, six depth charges being released, three falling on each side of the conning tower.

U-454 sank almost immediately, but the Sunderland was also in serious trouble, and staggered on for six miles in the general direction of the convoy before coming down heavily in the sea and breaking up within

seconds. Fry and some members of his crew died, but six survived, five of them by clinging to the still floating starboard wing. They were picked up by a Royal Navy vessel which had been escorting the convoy, HMS Wren.

Coincidentally, on board Wren was Flt Lt J B Jewell DFC, No 10 Squadron's navigation leader. He was there under the auspices of a scheme for closer co-operation between the Royal Navy and Royal Air Force, where officers of each service were posted to the other for short periods. Jewell had just witnessed one of his squadron's most gallant actions.

Another U-boat was sunk the next day by Flg Off I A Clarke of 10 Squadron in Sunderland DV968, the same aircraft in which Flt Lt Smith had sunk U-332 exactly three months earlier.

Clarke's victory over U-106 was the last recorded by the Australians in 1943 and

was shared with a Sunderland from No 228 Squadron RAF, which delivered the first wounds. Each Sunderland attacked twice before the submarine exploded and sank.

The Australian Sunderlands sank five more U-boats in 1944, the last of them on 12 August. By then, the liberation of Europe was underway and the war against Germany had only eight more months to run. U-boat activity was substantially reduced as was their success rate, although the number of them sunk was greater than in any other year of the war. Coastal Command's Sunderlands accounted for 16, compared with 13 in 1943, two in 1942, one in 1941 and six in 1940.

The following is an official report of the Australian Sunderlands' penultimate U-boat sinking, that of U-385 by 461 Squadron's Plt Off I F Southall on 11 August 1944. The victory was shared with the Royal Navy.

The sinking of U-106 by 461 Squadron's Flt Lt I A Clarke in August 1943. This victory was scored in conjunction with an RAF Sunderland.

(right) Battered and worn, 461 Squadron's Sunderland II DV960 patrols the Atlantic.

Flying Officers M S Mainprize (third from left) and T A Egerton in front of 10 Squadron's DV969 in December 1942. Five months later, in May 1943, Mainprize sunk U-563 in this aircraft (in conjunction with the RAF) while Egerton damaged the Italian submarine 'Luigi Torello' the following month in a different Sunderland. The remainder of the crew pictured here is (from left to right): Sgt A E Couldrey DFM (tail gunner), Cpl E G Luck (rigger), Mainprize (first pilot), Flg Off B C W Fogg (navigator), Egerton (captain), LAC F H Clarke (second fitter), Sgt C C Clarke (second pilot), Sgt S W Reeves (first fitter), Sgt M R Delaney (first radio operator), Sgt G M Walker (second radio operator), LAC L J Lang (armourer). (via Neil Mackenzie)

OPERATIONS No. 461 SQUADRON, R.A.A.F.

AUGUST, 1944.   U - 385

Coastal Command Intelligence Summary No. 267.

> Sunderland P/461
> P/O. Southall
> 0235 - 11th August, 1944
> 46.09 N - 03.10 W.
> West of La Rochelle.

Aircraft on A/U patrol obtained radar contact eight miles, homed and sighted a fully surfaced U-Boat. 'P' attacked dropping six 250 lb. depth charges, setting 25 feet, spacing 55 feet, from 100 feet. Depth charges straddled U-Boat. Contact disappeared five minutes later, nothing further was seen other than an oil patch. Light erratic flak was experienced just as aircraft passed over U-Boat. 'P' homed an Escort Group to the position and the vessels reported finding an empty U-Boat dinghy. The U-Boat was later seen by the escort group which completed its destruction.

Coastal Command Review - August, 1944 - Vol. III, No. 8.

At 0235 hours on August 11 Sunderland P/461 (R.A.A.F.) was flying at 1,000 feet in calm weather and bright moonlight when the Radar operator picked up a contact at 10 miles, fine on the port bow. The captain held his course until he sighted a fully surfaced U-Boat in the moon-path 5 miles away bearing Red 70°. Her position was 46°09'N., 03°10'W., and she was proceeding south-westwards at eight knots. She appeared to be a normal 500-tonner mounting a big gun forward of the conning tower. The Sunderland captain turned away until the range had opened to eight miles and then turned back towards the target, which had been held all the time by Radar. He made a series of 'S' turns to get the U-Boat in the moonpath, eventually sighting her again at a range of six miles. At four miles he lost height to 500 feet and at two miles he dived to attack, releasing from 100 feet six depth charges spaced at 55 feet. He used no illuminant, as he could see the target up moon in perfect visibility. The depth charges were dropped across the U-Boat's beam, and stated to have straddled her amidships, four entering the water to starboard and two to port. The explosion plumes completely obliterated the target. Immediately before the attack the U-boat fired a few shots and what may have been a red recognition cartridge. At the moment of the depth charge explosions a bluish-white flash was seen on the U-Boat. After the plumes had subsides she was still on the surface, but was stationary. The Sunderland turned to port after the attack and flew past the enemy's stern at a range of 1,000 yds. The German gunners opened up with about six guns, but their fire, though fairly heavy, was most inaccurate. At two miles range the U-Boat disappeared from view, and two minutes later the blip also disappeared. The Sunderland flew off to make contact with an Escort Group, which was then nine miles south-east of the position of the attack, and led the ships back to the area. On returning to the marker the crew found a patch of oil 100 feet wide. Later they picked up a Radar contact at three miles on the U-Boat's original track about two miles ahead of her last position. After three attempts this was illuminated with flares and identified as a Radar decoy balloon. The Sunderland reported the position to the ships and continued to stand by. About two and a half hours after the attack the Radar operator picked up another contact, but it disappeared when the aircraft was a mile away. This was also reported to the ships, which began to sweep towards the new contact. After about an hour they reported having found an empty dinghy. After having stayed in the area for three and a half hours the Sunderland reached P.L.E. and set course for base.

At 0636 hours on August 12 the U-Boat surfaced 3,000 yards ahead of H.M.S. Starling, and was heavily engaged and hit by gunfire. She sank five minutes later.

Comments. An exceedingly well executed stalk, aided by good Radar work which enabled a surprise attack to be delivered. On the evidence the attack was very accurate and the U-Boat was mortally wounded. The co-operation with the Escort Group was excellent. The whole operation demonstrated efficiency and good crew drill.

Prisoners of War Evidence. This U-boat, U 385, left St. Nazaire on August 9 to try to make La Pallice. On the 11th, after proceeding submerged for about 20 hours the Commanding Officer decided to use ths schnorkel. According to the prisoners it had never worked, and on this occasion, as usual, the boat began to fill with exhaust fumes. The ship's company stuck it as long as they could, but after the Commanding Officer had passed out the boat surfaced to ventilate. While she was doing this, Sunderland P/461 attacked. Most of the depth charges overshot

Sunderland III EK573 of 10 Squadron being towed from the Scilly Islands by an air-sea rescue launch in November 1943. (RAAF Historical)

on the starboard quarter, but two did a great deal of damage.
The starboard after hydroplane and the rudder were torn
off and the starboard screw was put out of action. In
addition, the outer cap of No. 5 torpedo tube was blown in and
the washer on the inside of the cap was blown off; this
caused a serious leak.   The boat dived, but the air was by
no means pure. It was necessary to pump a great deal, and
the batteries were very low as it had not been possible to put
in a charge during the time the schnorkel was being used.

By 0600 hours on the 12th the air in the boat was so
foul that something had to be done. The Commanding Officer
wished to make a run for port, but steering had become
almost impossible. Her therefore had to surface, although
he knew that there were two ships hunting him. To his
surprise there were five.   These ships opened fire and scored
hits forward and aft of the conning tower, which caused a further
entry of water and a short on the armature of the only
serviceable motor.   The order was therefore given to abandon
ship.

For names and numbers of crew see Squadrons Operations Records Book
for this date.
See Air Ministry Bulletin No. 16037. Copy attached.

x-x-x-x-x-x-x-x-x

Coastal Command Intelligence Summary No. 268

Sunderland A/461
F/O. Little
0014 - 13th August, 1944
46.19 N - 02.58 W.
West of La Rochelle.

Aircraft on A/U patrol obtained a radar contact at $6\frac{1}{2}$
miles, homed and dropped flares, sighting a fully surfaced
U-boat at $\frac{3}{4}$ mile range, course 100 degrees, at 15 knots.
Aircraft attacked from 300 feet, dropping six Torped depth
charges, set at 25 feet, spaced 55 feet.   Depth charges are
estimated to have straddled the target. No results were seen
by the aircraft, but at 0150 a message was received from an
Escort Group saying that the U-Boat had sunk and that survivors
had been rescued.   After the attack numerous lights, including
two flashing S.O.S., were seen.

Coastal Command Review - August, 1944 - Vol.III, No. 8.

Soon after midnight on August 13 Sunderland A/461

(R.A.A.F.) was patrolling at 1,150 feet in hazy conditions when the Radar operator picked up a contact $6\frac{1}{2}$ miles away bearing Red 72°. The aircraft continued on course and after one minute the contact bore Red 120° at seven miles. The Sunderland captain then turned to investigate. At four miles range he was still at 800 feet, but he then lost height as quickly as possible, ran out the bomb racks and ordered the crew to action stations. At three quarters of a mile he released flares which illuminated a surfaced U-Boat dead ahead in position 46°19'N., 02°56'W. The U-Boat, which was steering 110° at 15 knots, looked very big and had a high conning tower with two bandstands aft. About ten men were seen in the conning tower or manning the guns aft of it. These gunners promptly opened fire with light and medium tracer which came up in four streams from points abaft the conning tower. The Sunderland replied with 120 rounds from the nose gun and 380 from the fixed guns. This fire discouraged the U-Boat's gunners so effectively that the last 400 yards of the Sunderland's approach was unopposed. The aircraft attacked from abaft the U-Boat's starboard beam and from 300 feet released six depth charges spaced at 55 feet. The low level bomb sight was used. The aircrew did not see the points of entry of the depth charges and saw only two of the explosions, the nearer being about 15 feet from the port side of the conning tower. As the aircraft passed over the target the midships and rear gunners got in bursts of about 100 rounds each. At two miles range the contact disappeared and when the Sunderland returned to the position ten minutes later, intending to attack again, the crew neither saw the U-Boat nor picked up any contact. However, about an hour after the attack, they saw many small lights in the water, two of which were flashing S.O.S. About 0130 hours some escort vessels arrived in response to the Sunderland's homing signals and twenty minutes later the S.N.O. reported by R/T that the U-boat had been sunk and survivors rescued.

<u>Comments.</u> The crew is congratulated on their excellent drill which resulted in the certain destruction of the U-Boat.

<u>Prisoners of War Evidence.</u> U 270 had been lying in dock temporarily out of commission when it was decided that she was to try to soil to safely in the south. The boat was not fitted with schnorkel. A scratch crew was formed, which included even Admin. people who thought that the U-Boat was a means of escape.

The boat slipped at about 2100 hours on August 10. She was escorted by three 'm' class minesweepers until 2315 hours when they were suddenly recalled. Several aircraft warnings were received and the boat dived at 2345 hours.

On the 11th at 1400 hours it was decided to bottom as the batteries, which were old and in bad condition, were only partially charged. At 2300 hours U 270 surfaced again but once more there were many aircraft alarms. The Commanding Officer tried to keep these G.S.R. contacts astern of the boat, but there were so many that it proved too difficult and he submerged again after 20 minutes.

At 0200 hours on the 12th he surfaced once more and proceeded at 15 knots, again getting many contacts. He carried on until 0330 hours when he once again gave up the struggle and submerged, running on one motor. At 0700 hours the boat again had to bottom to save the batteries. At 1230 hours she went up to periscope depth but a warning was received to the effect that there were enemy surface craft between her and La Pallice and she therefore bottomed again. The batteries and available high pressure air were then very low. At 1700 hours a number of surface craft were heard and between then and 2200 hours they seemed to be hunting. Distant depth charge explosions were also heard. U 270 waited until 2300 hours before attempting to surface and then did so very gradually. At 2340 hours she was on the surface and about two hours out from La Pallice. Once again there were many G.S.R. contacts and the U-Boat steered a zigzag course. The contacts seemed to be all round.

At 0010 hours on the 13th the Sunderland approached from Green 80°. The U-Boat opened up with her full armament at 2,000 yards range. The aircraft returned the fire and dropped depth charges. None of these hit but all fell very close and the pressure hull was damaged right forward near No. 5 diving tank. The U-Boat attempted to dive but it was impossible to open the vents for No. 5 tank so the other tanks had to be blown to avoid stern heaviness. She then continued at 17 knots on the surface but water was entering and she seemed liable to sink. The diesels were stopped and all hands mustered on deck ready to abandon ship if necessary.

The commanding Officer and the Engineer Officer went below and managed to blow No. 5 tank and they reconsidered the possibilities of making port after all. Some of the engine room ratings were ordered below and U 270 set off again at top speed. At this stage one man, who was standing right aft, was caught on the wrong leg and swept overboard complete with his one-man dinghy. He was picked up by Allied ships off the Gironde some days later.

Later on the boat again became bow heavy and the Commanding Officer ordered the diesels to be stopped and the bow hatch

to be opened to accelerate the sinking in case he was attacked
again.   An aircraft again flew over but it did not open fire.
The effect of its presence was enough, however, and most of the
men on the upper deck jumped overboatd.   The aircraft, which
was Wellington W/179, had not opened fire because the Captain
saw that the U-Boat was being abandoned.

In the boat the lights had gone out and chlorine was
developing from the batteries.   The Commanding Officer gave the
order to abandon ship.   At 0145 hours the boat sank and 10
minutes later the survivors were picked up by a destroyer.

For names and numbers of crew see Squadron's Operations Records Book
for this date.

x-x-x-x-x-x-x-x

Coastal Command Intelligence Summary No. 268

Sunderland T/461
F/O. Alexander
0540 - 14th August, 1944
46.27 N - 03.25 W.
Bay of Biscay.

Aircraft on A/U patrol obtained radar contact 11 miles,
homed and sighted by the light of flares, at $\frac{3}{4}$ mile, a fully
surfaced U-Boat.   Aircraft attacked, dropping six 250 lb.
Torpex depth charges set at 25 feet, spaced 55 feet, from
300 feet, at an angle of 130 degrees red to U-Boat's track.
Explosions appeared to envelope U-boat and silence flak.
Rear gunner saw conning tower between two plumes.   Contact
disappeared after explosions.   At 0700 hours a large
spreading oil patch was observed at 46.30 N - 03.43 W.

For names and numbers of crew see Squadron's Operations Records
Book for this date.

War In The Air

The Sunderlands attracted considerable attention from enemy fighters during the course of operations in the Battle of the Atlantic. They were often attacked by heavily armed Junkers Ju 88s, and many stories came out of these actions.

Perhaps one of the most amazing occurred on 2 June 1943 when a 461 Squadron Sunderland captained by Flt Lt C B Walker was attacked by no fewer than eight Ju 88s. It turned into an epic of major proportions and resulted in the destruction of three, possibly five Ju 88s.

The first attack by the Ju 88s caused the Sunderland's No 1 (port outer) engine to burst into flames while incendiary bullets hit the cockpit, one of them causing the compass to explode and spray Walker with blazing alcohol, all of this going on while the aircraft was taking violent evasive action.

Over the next three quarters of an hour the Junkers made more than 20 separate attacks on the Sunderland which simply refused to die. As one Ju 88 came into attack, the midships gunner, Flt Sgt A E Fuller, with bullets crashing all around him, poured hundreds of rounds into the fighter which broke away, turned over, dived vertically into the sea and disintegrated.

The battle continued and yet another Junkers hit by the Sunderland's guns burst into flames and crashed into the sea. The rear gunner was thrown against the turret during the violent evasive action being taken and was knocked unconscious.

Suddenly, the bridge filled with smoke and shrapnel as a cannon shell burst against the radio bulkhead, shattering petrol gauges and wrecking the wireless. The first pilot, navigator and wireless operator were injured. So badly battered was the Sunderland by this time that it required the combined strength of Walker and the first pilot (Plt Off W J Dowling) to keep it in the air.

The intercommunication system had been shot away (the crew passed notes by hand!), the control wires were damaged and the airframe twisted. The port outer propeller and its reduction gear fell off and crashed into the sea.

The second pilot then discovered the flight engineer, Sgt Miles, collapsed across the starboard galley gun, mortally wounded. He died 20 minutes later. On the bridge, the pilots and navigator struggled on in conditions of unbelievable chaos, Walker suffering from his burns, and Plt Off Simpson the navigator bleeding profusely from a wound in the leg.

The six surviving Junkers reformed for the third time and returned to the attack. The rear gunner (Flt Sgt Goode) had regained consciousness by this time and he and Flt Sgt Fuller poured rounds into one of the fighters which screamed away in a blazing arc and hit the sea at high speed. The Sunderland's gunnery was phenomenal; every attacking aircraft was hit.

A Ju 88 closing in across the starboard bow had ammunition poured into its port wing by Sgt Watson, the nose gunner, and disappeared with an engine on fire and smoke pouring from the cockpit. Eventually, the remaining attackers realised that further combat was useless and broke away. The 45 minute action was over.

The next problem was to get the Sunderland back to base. Although in great pain, the navigator insisted on making a sun sighting from the astrodome and gave Walker a correction of course. Walker estimated there were about 500 holes in the fuselage and mainplane, and realised that when a landing was made the Sunderland could not possibly stay afloat.

The return journey saw all spare hands plugging the countless holes below the waterline with odd pieces of clothing, while an axe was used to remove every item of heavy equipment which was no longer considered necessary for the aircraft's survival – the wrecked radios, radar equipment, personal kit, pyrotechnics, the anchor and mooring chain.

Eventually, the English coast came into sight but Walker realised he was not going to make Pembroke before dark so elected to ditch on the leeward side of the coast off Cornwall. All the while, a makeshift radio had been transmitting SOS signals but to no avail.

Many hazards faced the skipper in this landing – the aircraft was badly holed and strained, one engine was out, there was no way of knowing the Sunderland's airspeed and the trimmers were out of action.

The vigilance of the gunners was a major factor in the ability of the Sunderlands to protect themselves from enemy fighters. This 10 Squadron gunner keeps his eyes peeled. (RAAF Historical)

Sunderland III ML822 of 10 Squadron. It was delivered in October 1944 and scrapped nine months later. (Ray Wilkie via Mike Kerr)

Walker edged close to the shore and point was selected. He throttled back and the starboard inner backfired and stopped dead. Close to the seven feet swell he flattened out, the Sunderland dropping and hitting the water near the crest of a wave. It slid into a trough and stopped, about 300 yards from the beach.

The order was given to get out and climb onto the wing in preparation for boarding the dinghy, but the aircraft was not sinking as quickly as expected and the decision made to beach it. As it charged towards the sand with its two good engines at full throttle, it began to go down, water quickly flooding the lower deck.

Then there was a crunch as the Sunderland hit bottom within walking depth of the shore. A group of locals was quickly on the scene offering tea (or perhaps something stronger), food and assistance.

Wrapping It Up

No 10 Squadron flew its final wartime sortie on 7 May 1945, ceased operations on 1 June and was disbanded on 26 October.

Its remaining personnel returned to Australia at the end of the year.

Before that, in early May, a 10 Squadron Sunderland skippered by Flt Lt R C Allardyce had accepted the first surrender of a U-boat. The submarine was spotted on the surface and the Sunderland prepared to attack, but on approach it could be seen the submarine's guns were not manned and it was flying the black flag of unconditional surrender. On the foredeck, 20 German sailors were sanding rigidly to attention.

Allardyce said, "...it was a great moment, although it seemed strange that we should be circling an enemy sub without attacking it. This was the first U-boat I had seen, after more than a year of operations.

"The enemy flashed to us with a signalling lamp and we hurriedly transmitted our message to base. The U-boat then steamed towards England ..."

No 10 Squadron's service in Britain had seen it chalk up some impressive statistics: 3,239 wartime sorties; 42,956 flying hours (of which 34,111 were operational); six submarines sunk and eight damaged; six enemy aircraft destroyed, four probably destroyed and 28 damaged; one enemy ship destroyed and eight damaged. On the debit side there was the loss of 151 personnel and 19 Sunderlands, nine by enemy action in the air, three by enemy action on the ground and seven due to operational accidents.

No 461 Squadron flew its last operational sortie on 18 June 1945 and was disbanded two days later. One of its last tasks had been to assist in the location of surrendering U-boats after the German capitulation and help escort them to British ports.

Sunderland III EK594 of No 10 Squadron on the slipway at Mount Batten in 1944. (Roy Winston via Keith Western)

A formation of seven 10 Squadron Sunderlands flies over Plymouth Sound in April 1944. (RAAF Historical)

A plaque at Plymouth commemorating 10 Squadron's efforts during World War II: "To the people of Plymouth with affection and admiration from the members of 10 Squadron Royal Australian Air Force who operated from Mount Batten 1939-1945". (R J Wilson)

The squadron flew 18,649 operational hours, was involved in the destruction of six U-boats and flew a total of 4,742,773 nautical miles (8.785 million kilometres) between 1942 and 1945. It lost 86 aircrew and 14 Sunderlands during the course of its service.

40 Squadron Activities

By comparison with their brothers in the United Kingdom, the six Sunderlands operated by No 40 Squadron in the Pacific had a much quieter time, operating in the transport role, although there were several incidents and one aircraft written off.

In late July 1944 the squadron moved from Townsville to Port Moresby, but a fortnight before that Sqdn Ldr Egerton in A26-1 completed a flight from Townsville to Rathmines NSW on three engines. The nuts having sheared off one cylinder of the starboard inner engine, it was decided to remove the propeller before departure and the journey was completed without incident.

On 18 August, A26-5 was damaged at Townsville when it was involved in a collision with a freighter. Eleven days later, the same Sunderland collided with the moored A26-1 while taxying at Port Moresby. A26-5 lost three feet of its starboard wing tip and A26-1 had its starboard outer engine, nacelle and propeller damaged.

In September 1944, A26-2 was involved in an incident of a rather different ilk. Scheduled to fly from Cooktown to Port Moresby with prisoners, including US prisoners under escort, the Sunderland found itself in the middle of an armed insurrection.

The departure of 10 Squadron crews to Australia in 1944 to ferry Sunderlands to Australia and establish No 40 Squadron was celebrated in the Officers' Mess. With the squadron's spotted pigs mascots are (standing, from left to right): Flt Lt G C Strath, Sqdn Ldr T A Egerton DFC, Flt Lt G G Rossiter, Wng Cdr G C Hartnell (former CO), Sqdn Ldr A C H Patherick, Sqdn Ldr R N Gillies (present CO), Flt Lt C M Austin, AVM B E Baker CB DSO MC AFC (Group AOC), AVM H N Wrigley CBE DFC AFC (AOC RAAF Overseas HQ), Flt Lt C Brigstock (Adjutant), AVM A Durston CB AFC (SASO Coastal Command), Flt Lt E H Farmer, Wng Cdr R S Rice (Acting Station Commander). In front: Flg Off W L Woodland, Flg Off V H Dyason, Flg Off L W Wilson. (RAAF Historical)

A 40 Squadron Sunderland at Rathmines, on Lake Macquarie NSW. (via Neil Mackenzie)

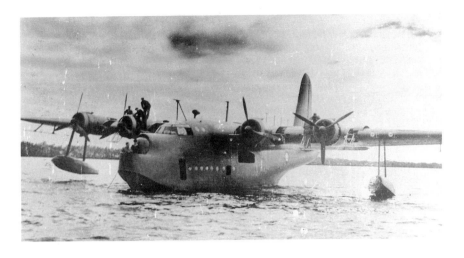

Sunderland IIIs of 40 Squadron: A26-1 in Lake Boga (top) and A26-4 at Port Moresby (bottom). 40 Squadron provided a valuable transport service between New Guinea and Australia in 1944-46. (via Bob Livingstone)

On landing, the Sunderland overshot by about 500 yards and at the completion of the landing run attempted to turn into the harbour. It got into difficulties and collided with a post, damaging its nose.

Water was rapidly entering the aircraft as it was taken under tow and that combined with the swell made it impossible for the towing launches to continue. The engines were restarted and an attempt made to taxy the Sunderland onto a sandbank, but once again the swell caused problems and the aircraft sank nose first in 18 feet (5.5m) of water. A26-6 was converted to components.

In February 1945 the squadron's 'bread and butter' service between Port Moresby, Cairns, Milne Bay, Madang and Townsville was curtailed and replaced with one from Port Moresby to Cairns via Darwin and Kurumba. The 'airline' style operation of the squadron was emphasised over the next few days when daily (except Sunday) direct flights to Cairns began, as did one to Treasury Island.

Other activities the squadron was sometimes called upon to perform included search and rescue, a successful mission being performed on 20 March 1945 when the survivors from a ditched Douglas C-47 were located. The sea was too rough to land on but the Sunderland (A26-5, Flt Lt Hugall) circled the dinghy until relieved by a Liberator. Contact was lost during the night but Hugall and A26-5 returned the following morning and found them again. They were picked up by a naval trawler.

Hugall was involved in another incident the following month whilst flying A26-3 to Rose Bay NSW, where maintenance was performed by QANTAS. Thirty-seven passengers were on board the Sunderland which suffered engine problems near Bundaberg Qld and was forced down on the Burnett River. The aircraft was flown out on three engines after attempts to fix the problem failed and continued to Rose Bay.

A launch had delivered its passengers to the aircraft, but a second launch (which had the Sunderland's captain and navigator on board) found itself under siege when one of the prisoners grabbed a guard's revolver, disarmed the other guards and handed the weapons to the other prisoners.

Upon arrival at the Sunderland, the armed prisoners tried to persuade those already aboard the aircraft to join in, but without success. The ringleader in the second launch then ordered the boat's coxswain towards some jetties on the other side of the harbour, although drawing alongside a corvette proved to be a mistake as an officer on board was able to talk one and eventually all of the mutineers into throwing their weapons overboard and surrendering.

The squadron suffered its only loss on 28 November when A26-6, flown by Flt Lt B A Williams, had a landing accident at Townsville after a flight from Port Moresby. Twenty-nine people and freight were on board.

VH-AKO, the former RAAF A26-4 in postwar service with Trans Oceanic Airways.

An unusual activity for one of the squadron's aircraft was performed in April 1945 when A26-1 was requisitioned by the Air Board for War Loans duties. This involved a publicity tour lasting a month and the aircraft was flown by Flt Lt M S Mainprize, one of several Battle of the Atlantic veterans who were now with 40 Squadron.

Despite its unspectacular role, 40 Squadron and its Sunderlands performed important duties between 1944 and disbandment in June 1946. In the period between late August 1944 and March 1946 it carried nearly 13 million pounds (5.9 million kg) of freight and passengers in the course of 1,613 flights and 7,097 hours in the air.

The five surviving Sunderlands were sold in 1947 and all eventually appeared on the Australian civil register, joining other Sunderlands and Sandringhams. But that is another story ...

One of many Sandringhams which flew in Australia after the war, VH-BRC 'Beachcomber' of Ansett Airways started life as Sunderland III JM715 in 1943 and after service with the RAF was converted to a Sunderland V and then Sandringham V. It served with TEAL, Barrier Reef Airways and then Ansett from 1953-74 before moving on to Antilles Air Boats and subsequently the Science Museum in Britain. It is pictured here at Rose Bay, Sydney.

Abbreviations: w/o – written off; cvtd to compnts – converted to components; deliv – delivery; sqn – squadron; ops – operations; ftr – failed to return; dbr – damaged beyond repair; e/a – enemy action; t/o – takeoff; RCAF – Royal Canadian Air Force; RAF – Royal Air Force; avn – aviation; n/a – not available; wfu – withdrawn from use; ff – first flight; TOA – Trans Oceanic Airways.

10 and 461 Squadron Sunderlands

Notes: the 'Sqn' column refers to the RAAF Squadron (10 or 461) to which the Sunderland was first delivered. Subsequent movements are noted in the 'Disposal/Remarks' column. Many of these Sunderlands served with RAF squadrons before being transferred to the Australian units.

RAF No	Mark	Deliv	Sqn	Disposal/Remarks
L2163	I	06/41	461	to RAF 1941
L5802	I	07/42	461	to RAF 11/42
N9047	I	10/39	10	to RAF 11/39
N9048	I	09/39	10	w/o air raid Mount Batten 11/40
N9049	I	09/39	10	strafed by Bf109 and burned Malta 05/41
N9050	I	11/39	10	to RAF 03/41
P9600	I	10/39	10	to RAF 11/41
P9601	I	10/39	10	w/o air raid Mount Batten 11/40
P9602	I	11/39	10	crashed Lismore (Scotland) 09/40
P9603	I	11/39	10	crashed Milford Haven 06/41
P9604	I	12/39	10	to RAF 10/41
P9605	I	12/39	10	to RAF 03/42
P9606	I	01/40	10	to RAF 04/40
T9047	I	10/40	10	deliberately sunk by Royal Navy 07/41
T9071	I	12/40	10	to RAF 12/41
T9072	I	09/41	10	crashed near Skerries 12/41
T9073	I	1941	10	to RAF 01/44
T9075	I	04/41	10	crash landed 04/41
T9084	I	01/42	10	to RAF 02/42
T9085	I	04/42	461	crashed Western Approaches 01/43
T9086	I	03/42	10	to RAF 08/42
T9088	I	05/42	10	to RAF 05/42 (6 days only with 10 Sqn)
T9090	I	04/42	461	crashed Biscay 08/42
T9109	I	04/42	461	to RAF 09/43
T9110	I	06/42	10	crash landing Plymouth 01/44
T9111	I	05/42	461	crashed on t/o Hamworthy 03/43
T9113	I	06/42	461	shot down Biscay 09/42
T9114	I	07/42	461	crash landed Angle airfield 05/43
T9115	I	07/42	461	to RAF 04/43
W3979	II	06/41	10	sunk by Royal Navy 03/42
W3980	II	06/41	10	to RAF 06/41 (2 weeks with 10 Sqn)
W3983	II	07/41	10	to RAF 01/42, to 10 Sqn 07/42, to RAF 03/44
W3984	II	08/41	10	to manufacturer 12/43
W3985	II	08/41	10	lost to e/a Biscay 08/43
W3986	II	08/41	10	to RAF 02/42, to 10 Sqn 06/42, crashed on fire near Eddystone Light 05/43
W3993	II	11/41	10	collided with W4024 at moorings Mount Batten 10/43, returned to manufacturer
W3994	II	10/41	10	to RAF 06/42, to 10 Sqn 07/42, lost Biscay 07/42
W3997	II	02/42	10	tc RAF 07/42
W3999	III	01/42	10	shot down by Ar196 Biscay 06/42
W4001	III	01/42	10	to RAF 01/42
W4003	III	01/42	10	to RAF 02/42
W4004	III	02/42	10	to RAF 05/42, to 10 Sqn 12/42, lost Biscay 05/43
W4019	III	02/42	10	to RAF 05/42, to 10 Sqn 04/42, lost Biscay 08/42
W4020	III	03/42	10	lost Biscay 01/43 while sinking U-454
W4024	III	04/43	10	to manufacturer 07/44
W4030	III	04/43	10	to RAF 11/44
W6050	II	08/42	461	to RAF, date n/a
W6054	II	08/42	10	to RAF 12/42
W6077	III	05/43	461	to RAF 03/44

RAF No	Mark	Deliv	Sqn	Disposal/Remarks
DD852	III	05/43	10	wrecked 09/44
DD853	III	03/45	461	scrapped 06/45
DD865	III	08/43	10	to Scottish Aviation 01/45
DD866	III	08/43	461	to RAF 08/44
DD867	III	08/43	10	to RCAF 08/43, to 461 Sqn 1945
DP177	III	11/42	10	missing in action Biscay 08/43
DP179	III	08/43	10	lost Biscay 10/43
DP192	III	11/43	10	to Australia as RAAF A26-6 03/44
DP196	III	02/44	461	to RAF 09/44
DP199	III	03/44	461	to manufacturer 06/45
DP200	III	03/44	461	to RCAF 06/45
DV958	II	07/44	10	to Scottish Aviation 12/44
DV960	II	07/42	461	to RAF 08/44
DV961	II	07/42	461	to RAF 11/41
DV962	II	04/43	461	damaged by fire 06/43, dbr
DV968	II	09/42	461	lost Biscay 08/43
DV969	II	09/42	10	missing in action Biscay 09/43
DV985	III	05/43	461	to RAF 06/43
DV986	III	05/43	461	to RAF 06/43
DV989	III	09/43	461	to RAF 10/44
DV993	III	09/43	10	lost to e/a Biscay 11/43
DW113	III	12/43	10	to Scottish Aviation 11/44
EJ132	III	10/42	461	to RAF 11/42
EJ133	III	04/43	461	to RAF 04/44, to 461 Sqn, wrecked on landing Pembroke Dock 12/44
EJ134	III	12/42	461	damaged in action 06/43 and w/o
EJ138	III	07/44	461	to RAF 04/45
EJ141	III	04/43	461	to RAF 1945
EJ142	III	04/43	461	to RAF 05/44
EJ153	III	1944	461	to manufacturer 04/45
EJ154	III	07/44	461	sunk Pembroke Dock 12/44
EK573	III	08/43	10	to RAF 05/45
EK574	III	08/43	10	sunk Mount Batten 06/44
EK575	III	08/43	461	to RAF 03/44, to 10 Sqn 09/44, to Scottish Aviation 11/44
EK577	III	08/43	461	to RAF 04/44
EK578	III	08/43	461	lost Biscay 09/43
EK579	III	1945	461	to RAF 1945
EK586	III	08/43	10	to Scottish Aviation 12/44
EK590	III	05/44	461	to RAF 07/44
EK594	III	06/44	10	to Scottish Aviation 12/44
JM675	III	03/43	461	lost Biscay 05/43
JM676	III	04/43	461	lost Biscay 11/43
JM678	III	09/43	461	to RAF 02/44, to 10 Sqn 05/44, burnt at moorings 06/44
JM683	III	06/43	461	to RAF 04/43
JM684	III	05/43	10	to RAF 06/45
JM685	III	06/43	461	to RAF 11/43, to 10 Sqn 05/44, wfu 12/44
JM686	III	06/43	461	to RCAF 04/44
JM707	III	06/43	461	shot down by Ju 88s Biscay 08/43
JM721	III	08/43	10	to RAF 04/44
ML735	III	04/44	461	lost Bergen 10/44
ML739	III	11/44	461	to manufacturer 04/45
ML740	III	02/44	461	lost Biscay 05/44, combat with Ju 88s
ML741	III	10/44	461	to RAF 02/45
ML743	III	03/44	461	to RAF 05/44
ML744	III	04/44	461	to RCAF 03/45
ML746	III	03/44	461	to RCAF 12/44
ML747	III	02/44	461	to manufacturer 03/45
ML748	III	04/44	461	landing accident St Mary's 06/44, sunk by Royal Navy
ML757	III	04/44	461	to manufacturer 03/45
ML758	III	04/44	461	to RAF 05/45
ML771	III	05/44	461	to RAF 06/46
ML774	III	11/44	461	sunk in gale 01/45
ML778	III	12/44	461	to manufacturer 03/45

RAF No	Mark	Deliv	Sqn	Disposal/Remarks
ML781	III	01/45	461	to manufacturer 04/45
ML816	III	04/45	461	to RAF 06/45
ML822	III	10/44	10	scrapped 07/45
ML826	III	10/44	461	to RAF 03/45
ML827	III	10/44	461	to RAF 04/45
ML828	III	10/44	10	to RAF 06/45, later VH-EBZ
ML829	III	10/44	10	crashed on t/o Plymouth Sound 02/45
ML830	III	10/44	10	to RAF 06/45
ML839	III	12/43	10	cvtd to prototype Mk.V by 10 Sqn ff 05/44, sunk during gale 10/44
ML848	III	02/44	10	to Scottish Aviation 01/45
ML856	III	03/44	10	to Scottish Aviation 11/44
ML879	III	11/44	461	to RCAF 02/45
NJ193	III	03/45	461	to 10 Sqn 06/45, to RAF 10/45
NJ253	III	10/44	10	to RAF 06/45
NJ254	III	10/44	10	to RAF 06/45
NJ255	III	10/44	10	to RAF 06/45, later VH-EBX/BRE
NJ256	III	10/44	10	to RAF 06/45
NJ264	V	03/45	461	to 10 Sqn 06/45, to RAF 03/46
NJ267	V	03/45	461	to 10 Sqn 06/45, to RAF 10/45
NJ268	V	04/45	461	to 10 Sqn 06/45, to RAF 11/45
PP113	V	02/45	461	to 10 Sqn 06/45, to RAF 10/45
PP114	V	02/45	461	to 10 Sqn 06/45, to RAF 10/45
PP115	V	03/45	461	to 10 Sqn 06/45, to RAF 11/45
PP116	V	02/45	461	crashed Pembroke Dock 05/45
PP119	V	03/45	461	to 10 Sqn 06/45, to RAF 10/45
PP122	V	04/45	461	to 10 Sqn 06/45, to RAF 10/45
PP135	III	11/44	10	to RAF 06/45
PP138	III	09/44	10	to RAF 06/45
PP139	III	11/44	10	to RAF 06/45
PP142	III	12/44	10	to RAF 07/45
PP162	V	02/45	461	to 10 Sqn 06/45, to RAF 10/45
RN279	V	02/45	461	to RAF 03/45
RN280	V	02/45	461	to RAF 03/45
RN282	V	03/45	461	to 10 Sqn 06/45, to RAF 10/45
RN300	V	03/45	461	to 10 Sqn 06/45, to RAF 10/45

40 Squadron Sunderlands

RAAF No	RAF No	Mark	Deliv	Disposal/Remarks
A26-1	ML730	III	03/44	sold B W Monkton for TOA 07/47 (VH-BKO)
A26-2	ML731	III	03/44	sold B W Monkton for TOA 04/47 (VH-BKQ)
A26-3	ML732	III	03/44	sold B W Monkton for TOA 04/47 (VH-BFX)
A26-4	ML733	III	04/44	sold B W Monkton for TOA 04/47 (VH-AKO)
A26-5	ML734	III	04/44	sold B W Monkton for TOA 04/47 (VH-AKP)
A26-6	DP192	III	03/44	collision on water Townsville Qld 11/44, converted to components.

Sunderland MkI P9605/RB-K of No 10 Sqn, England, 1940
Extra dark sea grey and dark slate grey upper surface with sky undersurface. Medium grey codes and white serial.

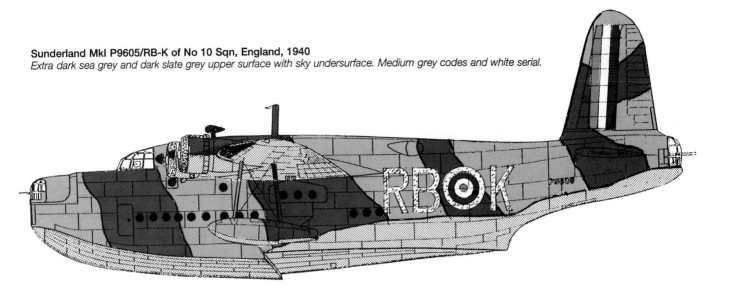

Sunderland MkI N9048/RB-B of No 10 Sqn, England, 1940
Dark sea grey and dark slate grey upper surface with sky undersurface. Medium grey codes and white serial.

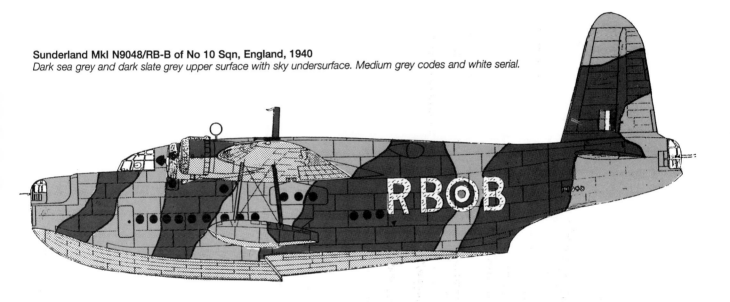

Sunderland MkI T9072/RB-V of No 10 Sqn, England, 1941
Extra dark sea grey and dark slate grey upper surface with sky undersurface. Medium grey codes and white serial.

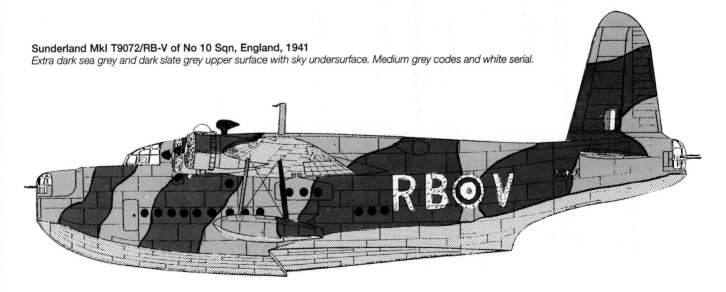

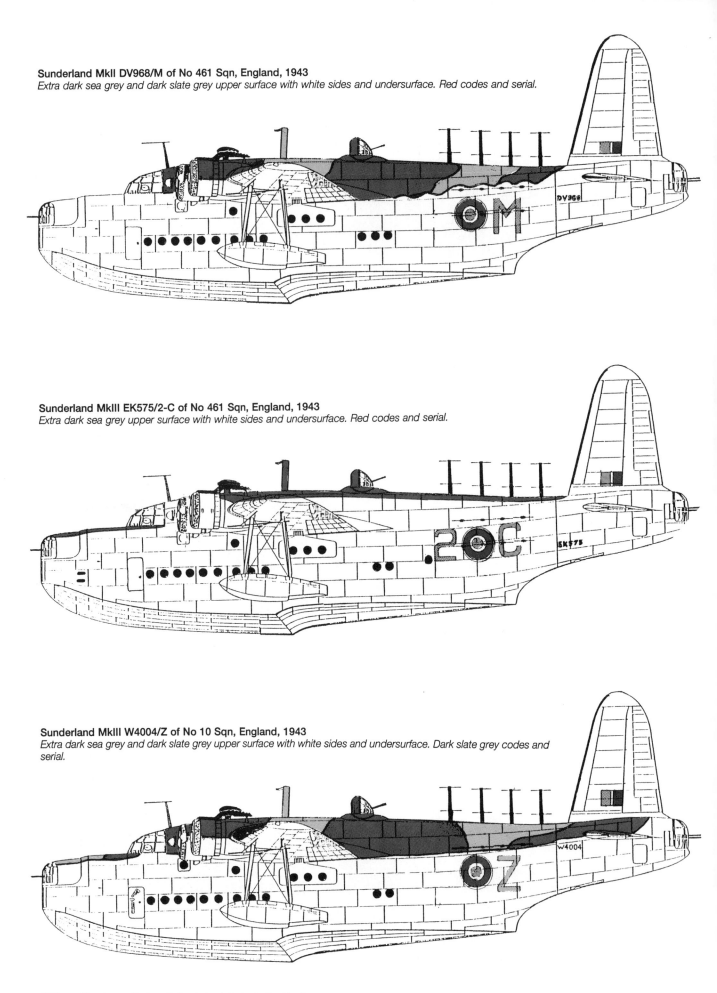

Sunderland MkII DV968/M of No 461 Sqn, England, 1943
Extra dark sea grey and dark slate grey upper surface with white sides and undersurface. Red codes and serial.

Sunderland MkIII EK575/2-C of No 461 Sqn, England, 1943
Extra dark sea grey upper surface with white sides and undersurface. Red codes and serial.

Sunderland MkIII W4004/Z of No 10 Sqn, England, 1943
Extra dark sea grey and dark slate grey upper surface with white sides and undersurface. Dark slate grey codes and serial.

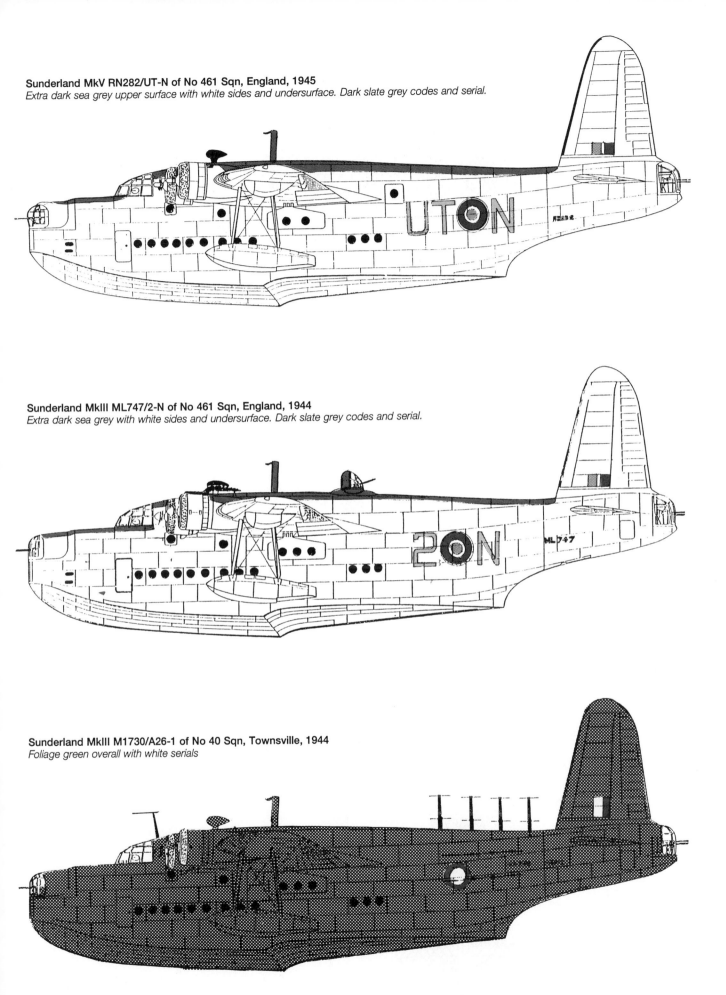

Sunderland MkV RN282/UT-N of No 461 Sqn, England, 1945
Extra dark sea grey upper surface with white sides and undersurface. Dark slate grey codes and serial.

Sunderland MkIII ML747/2-N of No 461 Sqn, England, 1944
Extra dark sea grey with white sides and undersurface. Dark slate grey codes and serial.

Sunderland MkIII M1730/A26-1 of No 40 Sqn, Townsville, 1944
Foliage green overall with white serials

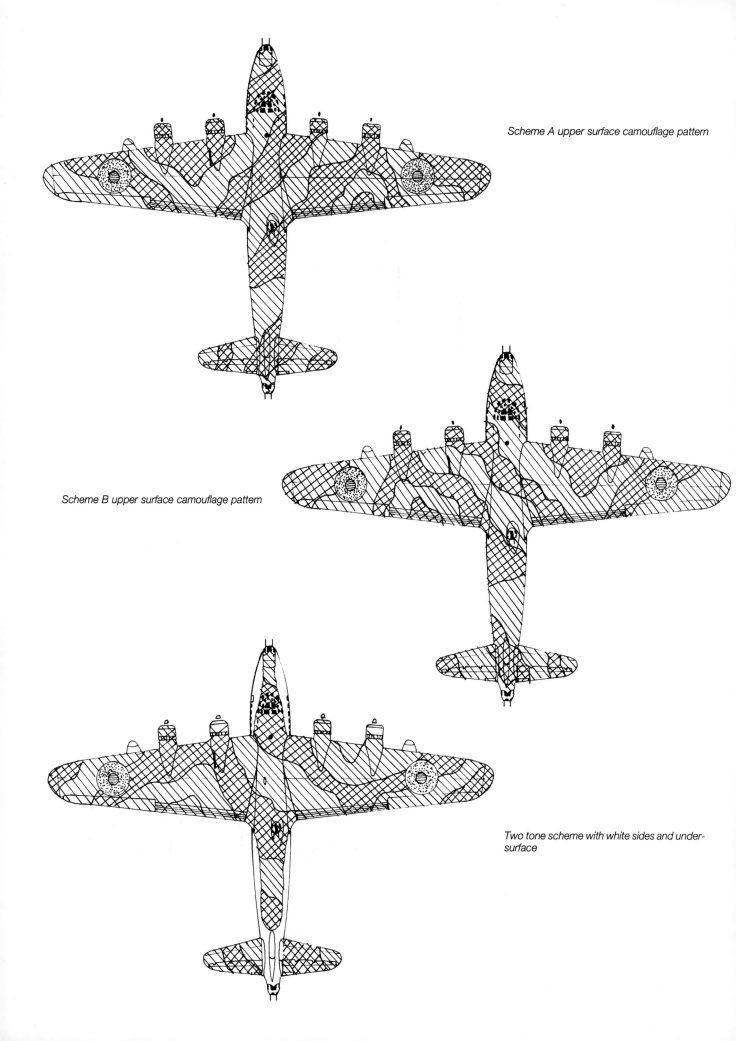

Scheme A upper surface camouflage pattern

Scheme B upper surface camouflage pattern

Two tone scheme with white sides and under-surface

Late war scheme of extra dark sea grey with white sides and undersurface

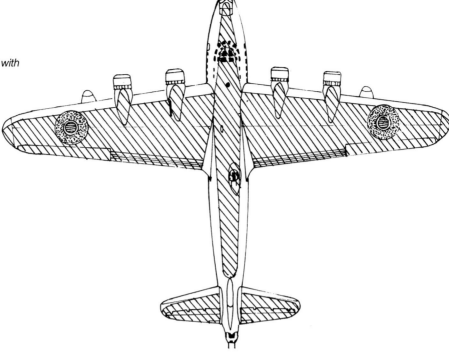

Extra Dark
Sea Grey

Dark Slate
Grey

Sky

Yellow

Insignia
Blue

Insignia
Red

Foliage
Green

Medium
Grey

IS
AVIATION
IMPORTANT
TO
YOU?

If so, then Australia's largest selling aviation journal can be your private consultant. Established in 1977, Australian Aviation is the largest selling aerospace journal in the southern hemisphere with a 96% paid circulation. That type of performance in a fiercely competitive and professional market does not come from being second best. If you need to know exactly what is happening in the fast paced world of aviation then Australian Aviation is YOUR answer.

One year (10 issues) mail subscriptions are available for $39.00 domestic. Overseas sea mail subs are $57 whilst overseas economy air mail rates are $60 for NZ and New Guinea and $80 elsewhere. All rates in Australian dollars. Or otherwise write requesting a free sample copy.

POST TO: AEROSPACE PUBLICATIONS PTY LTD
PO BOX 3105, WESTON CREEK ACT 2611
PHONE: (06) 288 1677, FAX (06) 288 2021

This is a: ☐ **New Subscription**   ☐ **Renewal**

☐ **I enclose my cheque/MO for $ .... payable to Aerospace Publications P/L or please charge to:**

☐ **Bankcard**   ☐ **MasterCard**   ☐ **American Express**   ☐ **Visa**   **Expiry Date ....**

Card No: .... **Signature** ....

NAME ....

ADDRESS ....

.... **POSTCODE** .... **PHONE** ....

☐ *ONE YEAR RATE: $39.00 (10 issues) – YOU SAVE $10.00*

☐ *TWO YEAR RATE: $69.00 (20 issues) – YOU SAVE $38.95**

Overseas SEA MAIL rates are $57 (one year) and $105 (two years).
Overseas ECONOMY AIR MAIL rates are: NZ and New Guinea – $60 per year. Elsewhere – $80 per year.
All rates are expressed in Australian dollars.

YOUR SUBSCRIPTION WILL COMMENCE WITH THE NEXT AVAILABLE ISSUE. BACK COPIES ARE AVAILABLE AT $5 PER COPY POSTAGE PAID (O/SEAS RATES ON APPLICATION).

* $29.00 on actual subscription plus $9.95 by receiving *Say Again* free.

THANK YOU FOR YOUR PATRONAGE